Praxis II Elementary Education Multiple Subjects (5001)

STUDY GUIDE WITH PRACTICE TEST QUESTIONS

Table of Contents

Introduction

Congratulations on choosing to take the Praxis Elementary Education: Multiple Subjects (5001) exam! By purchasing this book, you've taken the first step toward becoming an elementary educator.

This guide will provide you with a detailed overview of the Praxis Elementary Education exam, so you know exactly what to expect on test day. We'll take you through all the concepts covered on the test and give you the opportunity to test your knowledge with practice questions. Even if it's been a while since you last took a major test, don't worry; we'll make sure you're more than ready!

WHAT IS THE PRAXIS?

Praxis Series tests are a part of teaching licensure in approximately forty states. Each state uses the tests and scores in different ways, so be sure to check the certification requirements in your state by going to www.ets.org/praxis/states. There, you will find information detailing the role of the Praxis tests in determining teaching certification in your state, what scores are required, and how to transfer Praxis scores from one state to another.

WHAT'S ON THE PRAXIS?

The content in this guide will prepare you for the Praxis Elementary Education: Multiple Subjects (5001) exam. This test uses multiple-choice and numeric-entry questions to assess whether you possess the knowledge and skills necessary to become an elementary educator. The exam consists of four subtests that each assess your subject knowledge in a different area. Each subtest has a different time limit and number of questions; the approximate number of questions for each subtopic is given below. Altogether, the exam is four hours and fifteen minutes long.

Praxis 5001 Elementary Education

Section	Questions per Section	Concepts	Percentage	Number of Questions
Reading/ Language Arts	80	Reading	47%	38
		Writing, Speaking, and Listening	52%	42
Mathematics	50	Number and Operations	40%	20
		Algebraic Thinking	30%	15
		Geometry and Measurement, Data, Statistics, and Probability	30%	15
Social Studies	55	United States History, Government, and Citizenship	45%	25
		Geography, Anthropology, and Sociology	30%	16
		World History and Economics	25%	14
Science	50	Earth Science	32%	16
		Life Science	34%	17
		Physical Science	34%	17
Total			4.25 hours	235

You will answer approximately eighty multiple-choice questions on reading and language arts. Questions in this section will assess your own reading comprehension and vocabulary usage as well as your understanding of teaching strategies that reinforce vocabulary and language development. The foundations of reading and the use of language in writing will be assessed. You'll need to know the purposes and characteristics of effective listening and communication; likewise, you should understand the barriers that hinder interpersonal exchange.

You will answer approximately fifty multiple-choice questions on mathematics. The test will cover mathematical processes, number sense and numeration, algebraic concepts, informal geometry and measurement, and data organization and interpretation. A scientific calculator will be provided for you on this portion of the test.

You will answer approximately fifty-five multiple-choice questions on social studies. The social studies section is interdisciplinary; it will test your ability to understand relationships among fields in social studies. These fields include geography, anthropology, sociology, world and US history, government/civics/ democracy, economics, and social studies as inquiry. You'll need knowledge of all of these subjects in order to answer the questions correctly.

You will answer approximately fifty multiple-choice questions on science. This section assesses your knowledge of scientific fundamentals in a wide spectrum of the sciences, including earth, life, and physical sciences, science in personal and social perspectives, and science as inquiry. Questions will explore the structure of systems, such as matter, living systems, and earth systems. Be sure to familiarize yourself with the unifying processes of science and science as a process and human endeavor.

How Is the Praxis Scored?

The questions are equally weighted. Keep in mind that some multiple-choice questions are experimental questions for the purpose of the Praxis test writers and will not count toward your overall score. However, since those questions are not indicated on the test, you must respond to every question. There is no penalty for guessing on Praxis tests, so be sure to eliminate answer choices and answer every question. If you still do not know the answer, guess; you may get it right!

Your score report will be available on your Praxis account for one year, but you can also opt for a paper report. The score report includes your score and the passing score for the states you identified as score recipients. Your score will be available immediately after the test.

How Is the Praxis Administered?

The Praxis Series tests are available at testing centers across the nation. To find a testing center near you, go to http://www.ets.org/praxis/register. At this site, you can create a Praxis account, check testing dates, register for a test, or find instructions for registering via mail or phone. The Praxis Elementary Education: Multiple Subjects (5001) exam is administered as a computerized test. The Praxis website allows you to take a practice test to acclimate yourself to the computerized format.

On the day of your test, be sure to bring your admission ticket (which is provided when you register) and photo ID. The testing facility will provide pencils and erasers and an area outside of the testing room to store your personal belongings. You are allowed no personal effects in the testing area. Cell phones and other electronic, photographic, recording, or listening devices are not permitted in the testing center at all, and bringing those items may be cause for dismissal, forfeiture of your testing fees, and cancellation of your scores. For details on what is and is not permitted at your testing center, refer to http://www.ets.org/praxis/test_day/bring.

ABOUT CIRRUS TEST PREP

Cirrus Test Prep study guides are designed by current and former educators and are tailored to meet your needs as an incoming educator. Our guides offer all of the resources necessary to help you pass teacher certification tests across the nation.

Cirrus clouds are graceful, wispy clouds characterized by their high altitude. Just like cirrus clouds, Cirrus Test Prep's goal is to help educators "aim high" when it comes to obtaining their teacher certification and entering the classroom.

ABOUT THIS GUIDE

This guide will help you master the most important test topics and also develop critical test-taking skills. We have built features into our books to prepare you for your tests and increase your score. Along with a detailed summary of the test's format, content, and scoring, we offer an in-depth overview of the content knowledge required to pass the test. Our sidebars provide interesting information, highlight key concepts, and review content so that you can solidify your understanding of the exam's concepts. Test your knowledge with sample questions and detailed answer explanations in the text that help you think through the problems on the exam as well as practice tests that reflect the content and format of the Praxis. We're pleased you've chosen Cirrus to be a part of your professional journey!

Part I: Review

Reading and Language Arts

Reading, writing, speaking, and listening are the four cornerstones of a language arts curriculum in elementary education. Teacher content knowledge is demonstrated in the following areas: reading foundational skills, student comprehension of literature and informational texts, the stages and characteristics of the writing process and effective writing, and techniques for oral communication and collaboration.

READING: FOUNDATIONAL SKILLS

PHONOLOGICAL AWARENESS

Phonological Awareness is an understanding of how sounds, syllables, words, and word parts can be orally manipulated to break apart words, make new words, and create rhymes. It is an important foundational skill for learning to read and literacy development. **Phonemic awareness** is a type of phonological awareness that focuses on the sounds in a language. It is an understanding of how each small unit of sound, or **phoneme**, forms the language by creating differences in the meanings of words. For example, the phonemes /m/ and /s/ determine the difference in meaning between the words *mat* and *sat*. There are forty-four different phonemes in the English language. These includes letter combinations such as consonant diagraphs like /sh/ and vowel dipthongs like /oi/ where the letters work together to produce one sound. Teachers build phonemic awareness in their students using a variety of techniques such as phoneme blending, phoneme segmentation, phoneme substitution, and phoneme deletion.

Table 1.1. Phoneme Chart

s sun	t tan	p paint	n now	m mark	a apple	e edge	i innertube	o obvious
g girl	d dark	c k cat, kite	r ring	h heat	u under	ai pain	ee flee	igh night
b buy	f find	l lamb	j joy	v vehicle	oa float	oo foot	oo scoot	ar far
w wipe	x exit	y yellow	z zip	qu quiet	or port	ur turn	ow brow	oi foil
ch sandwich	sh sharp	th thick	th them	ng ring	ear fear	air flair	ure lure	er driver

Phoneme blending is combining phonemes to make a word; for example, /m/ /a/ /t/ combines to form *mat*. In contrast, **phoneme substitution** is the replacement of phonemes in words to make new words; removing the /m/ from the beginning of the word *mat* and replacing it with /s/ creates the word *sat*. **Phoneme segmentation** is separating phonemes in words; separating the sounds in the word *mat* isolates the phonemes /m/ /a/ /t/. Finally, in **phoneme deletion**, phonemes are removed from words to make new words. Removing /m/ from *mat* leaves the word *at*.

DID YOU KNOW?

The Reading Teacher's Book of Lists by Edward Fry and Jacqueline Kress is an excellent resource for becoming familiar with the range of phonemes formed by two letters in addition to recommended teaching tactics.

Building phonemic awareness in students is the latter part of a developmental sequence that contributes to a strong foundation in phonological awareness. Prior to focusing on phonemic awareness, teachers build phonological awareness with exercises that task students with orally manipulating the phonological units of spoken **syllables**. These phonological units are defined as onsets and rimes and can be blended, substituted, segmented, and deleted just like phonemes. The **onset** of a syllable is the beginning consonant or consonant blend. The **rime** includes the syllable's vowel and its remaining consonants. For example, in the word *block*, the consonant blend /bl/ is the onset, and the remainder of the word –*ock* is the rime.

STUDY TIP

Remember that phonological and phonemic awareness are auditory skills that do not involve printed letter or word recognition.

Once students have a solid foundation in phonological awareness, they are ready to begin phonics instruction. **Phonics** is the study of the relationship between the spoken sounds in words and the printed letters that correspond to those sounds, or **letter-sound correspondence**. In explicit phonics instruction, letters and their corresponding sounds are first taught in isolation, then blended into words, and finally applied to decodable text. Initially, the most common sounds for each letter and **high frequency** letter-sound correspondences, or those that occur most often in the English language, are introduced. In order to assist students beginning to read simple VC (vowel-consonant), VCC (vowel-consonant-consonant), CVCC (consonant-vowel-consonant-consonant), and CVC (consonant-vowel-consonant) words early on, a few short vowel sounds are introduced as well. Letters with names that bear a strong relationship to their sounds are introduced before letters that do not. For example, the sound of the letter *s* can be heard at the end of its name.

> **DID YOU KNOW?**
>
> A majority of words used to build phonological awareness are one-syllable words, or words made up of only one onset and one rime.

Phonics instruction progresses from simple to more complex letter-sound correspondences and sound/spellings (or the spelling of words based on letter-sound correspondences). Short-vowel sound spellings are introduced before long-vowel sound/spellings, and letters that are similar in appearance (e.g., *b* and *d*) or sound (e.g., /m/ and /n/) are taught separately along the instructional continuum. As students move through kindergarten and the primary grades, they progress from decoding two- or three-phoneme words with letters representing their most common sounds to longer words and more complex sound/spelling patterns.

Sight words, words that are repeated most often in text, are taught in conjunction with phonics. These are words that students need to learn to recognize by sight, such as *a*, *in*, *the*, *at*, and *I*, in order to read sentences with optimal fluency. As with letter-sound correspondences and sound/spellings, sight word instruction begins with the most common words, or highest frequency words. Teachers develop sight word lists for students using either the *Dolch List of Basic Sight Words* or *Fry's Numerical List of Instant Words*. These lists change and evolve across grade levels so that students build a large repertoire of instantly recognizable words as they move through the primary grades.

ROOTS AND AFFIXES

Beginning in second grade, language arts students also receive instruction in identifying and understanding roots and affixes in order to determine the meanings of unfamiliar words. **Roots** are typically derived from Latin or Greek and establish the basis of new words. *Cent* is a Latin root meaning "one hundred." **Affixes** are added to words or roots to change their meanings. They consist of prefixes, added to the beginning of a word or root, and suffixes, added to the end of a word or root. For example, the prefix *per-* can be added to *cent* to make the word *percent*, effectively changing the meaning to "one part in a hundred." Likewise, the suffix *-ury* can be added to *cent* to make the word *century*, effectively changing the meaning to "a period of one hundred years." By understanding how roots and affixes work together to form words and change the meanings of words, students can steadily add new words to their automatic memory banks of known words and decode unfamiliar words with greater ease and precision. As with instruction in phonics and sight words, elementary language arts teachers begin with the most common prefixes and suffixes and progress from simple to complex combinations of roots and affixes.

Table 1.2. Common Roots and Affixes

Root	Definition	Example
ast(er)	star	asteroid, astronomy
audi	hear	audience, audible
auto	self	automatic, autograph
bene	good	beneficent, benign
bio	life	biology, biorhythm
cap	take	capture
ced	yield	secede
chrono	time	chronometer, chronic
corp	body	corporeal
crac or crat	rule	autocrat
demo	people	democracy
dict	say	dictionary, dictation
duc	lead or make	ductile, produce
gen	give birth	generation, genetics
geo	earth	geography, geometry
grad	step	graduate
graph	write	graphical, autograph
ject	throw	eject
jur or jus	law	justice, jurisdiction
log or logue	thought	logic, logarithm
luc	light	lucidity
man	hand	manual
mand	order	remand
mis	send	transmission
mono	one	monotone
omni	all	omnivore
path	feel	pathology
phil	love	philanthropy

phon	sound	phonograph
port	carry	export
qui	rest	quiet
scrib or script	write	scribe, transcript
sense or sent	feel	sentiment
tele	far away	telephone
terr	earth	terrace
uni	single	unicode
vac	empty	vacant
vid	see	video
vis	see	vision

Table 1.3. Common Prefixes

Prefix	Definition	Example
a- (also an-)	not, without; to, toward; of, completely	atheist, anemic, aside, aback, anew, abashed
ante-	before, preceding	antecedent, anteroom
anti-	opposing, against	antibiotic, anticlimax
com- (also co-, col-, con-, cor-)	with, jointly, completely	combat, codriver, collude, confide
dis- (also di-)	negation, removal	disadvantage, disbar
en- (also em-)	put into or on; bring into the condition of; intensify	engulf, entomb
hypo-	under	hypoglycemic, hypothermia
in- (also il-, im-, ir-)	not, without; in, into, toward, inside	infertile, impossible, influence, include
intra-	inside, within	intravenous, intrapersonal
out-	surpassing, exceeding; external, away from	outperform, outdoor
over-	excessively, completely; upper, outer, over, above	overconfident, overcast
pre-	before	precondition, preadolescent, prelude
re-	again	reapply, remake
semi-	half, partly	semicircle, semiconscious
syn- (also sym-)	in union, acting together	synthesis, symbiotic
trans-	across, beyond	transatlantic
trans-	into a different state	translate
under-	beneath, below	underarm, undersecretary
under-	not enough	underdeveloped

READING FLUENCY

Language arts teachers apply strategic phonics, sight word, and word analysis strategies to help students become fluent readers who can use their reading skills as a means of accessing literature and deriving information from printed text. In other words, reading to learn is the end-all goal of learning to read and **fluency**, or the ability to read with ease and automaticity, is the key. Reading fluency is composed of three factors: rate, accuracy, and prosody.

Reading **rate** is the speed and fluidity with which a student can read. It is determined by the number of words read correctly per minute or the length of time it takes for a student to read a selected passage. A steady, fluid reading rate is important because it allows the reader to focus on constructing meaning from text without being distracted by the effort it takes to slowly plod through word pronunciations.

Reading **accuracy** refers to a student's ability to recognize or decode words correctly. Meaningful comprehension of reading material is dependent on reading accuracy, which in turn depends upon the reader having a significant inventory of known sight words and an ability to decode words effortlessly. Without accuracy, a student is unlikely to understand what an author or text is communicating. By examining patterns in word-identification errors, the elementary language arts teacher can identify decoding strategies that a student is not using and provide appropriate instruction.

Prosody encompasses the range of vocal expressions a reader uses when reading aloud. It includes rhythm, intonation, and stress patterns. Being able to read text orally while conveying the meaning of what is being read with appropriate vocal cues is evidence of reading prosody. In other words, when a student reads out loud, the spoken words should reflect natural speech patterns. Typically, when prosody is lacking, a student will read in a stilted, monotone voice, which often means the student does not understand the words.

TEACHING ENGLISH TO SPEAKERS OF OTHER LANGUAGES

Many elementary language arts classrooms include both students whose first language is English and students who are learning English as a second language. Five **stages of language acquisition** have been identified for students learning a second language. These stages are defined as preproduction, early production, speech emergence, intermediate fluency, and advanced fluency. These stages correlate to five **levels of language proficiency**, L1 through L5, which are L1) Entering, L2) Beginning, L3) Developing, L4) Expanding, and L5) Bridging.

Table 1.4. Stages of Second-Language Acquisition

Stage	Characteristics
Preproduction	Preproduction is also known as the silent period. Though these learners may have close to 500 words in their receptive vocabulary, they refrain from speaking but will listen and may copy words down. They can respond to visual cues such as pictures and gestures, and they will communicate their comprehension. However, sometimes students will repeat back what they have heard in a process referred to as parroting. This can aid them in adding to their receptive vocabulary, but it should not be mistaken for producing language.
Early Production	In this stage learners have achieved a 1000-word receptive and active vocabulary. They now produce single-word and two- to three-word phrases and can respond to questions and statements. Many learners in this stage enjoy engaging in musical games or word plays that help them to memorize language chunks that they can use later.
Speech Emergence	English language learners have a vocabulary of about 3000 words by the time they reach this stage of second-language acquisition. They are able to chunk simple words and phrases into sentences that may or may not be grammatically correct. They respond to modeling of correct responses better than direct correction. At this stage, learners also are more likely to participate in conversations with native English speakers, as they are gaining confidence in their language skills. These learners can understand simple readings when reinforced by graphics or pictures and can complete some content work with support.
Intermediate Fluency	By the intermediate fluency stage, English language learners have acquired a vocabulary of about 6000 words. They are able to speak in more complex sentences and catch and correct many of their errors. They are also willing to ask questions to clarify what they do not understand. Learners at this stage may sound fluent, but they have large gaps in their vocabulary as well as in their grammatical and syntactical understanding of the language. They are often comfortable speaking in group conversation that avoids heavy academic language.
Advanced Fluency	Second-language learners who reach advanced fluency have achieved cognitive language proficiency in their learned language. They demonstrate near-native ability and use complex, multi phrase and clause sentences to convey their ideas. Though accents are still detectable and idiomatic expressions are sometimes used incorrectly, the language learner has become essentially fluent.

The **preproduction stage** of language acquisition is defined as the silent stage during which a student is primarily absorbing new input. At this proficiency level—L1 Entering—a student rarely uses English to communicate and responds nonverbally to instruction, constructing meaning primarily from illustrations, graphs, and charts. This is followed by the early production stage in which a student begins to speak a few words and simple phrases. At this proficiency level—L2 Beginning—a student can communicate basic information in a limited manner but exhibits a number of predictable errors.

During the **emergence of speech stage**, the student begins to speak more clearly and accurately and increases his or her spoken vocabulary. It is during this stage that the student takes steps toward reading and writing in the second language. At this proficiency level—L3 Developing—a student understands more complex speech and can communicate spontaneously in simple sentences. However, the student's vocabulary and comprehension of language structure remains limited.

During the **intermediate fluency stage**, the student gains competency speaking in more complex sentences and demonstrates a larger vocabulary. This is the stage at which a student can begin to think in the second language as well as speak it. At this proficiency level—L4 Expanding—a student can read in the second language with demonstrated fluency, but may still struggle with comprehending text that describes complex or abstract concepts.

Finally, the student enters the **advanced fluency stage** in which he or she can converse fluently and think clearly in the second language. At this proficiency level—L5 Bridging—a student requires only minimal language support and can function at the same level as peers with a first language of English. Progression through these five stages of language acquisition typically takes around two years. It is important for language arts teachers to recognize these stages and proficiency levels in order to best facilitate and recognize student understanding and internalization of both the new language and new content.

SAMPLE QUESTIONS

1) **A teacher says *hat* and instructs students to produce the sounds they hear in the word. Which strategy is the teacher using to build phoneme awareness?**

   A. phoneme blending

   B. phoneme deletion

   C. phoneme segmentation

   D. phoneme substitution

   Answers:

   A. Incorrect. The strategy of phoneme blending requires students to combine phonemes to make a word.

B.   Incorrect. The strategy of phoneme deletion requires students to remove phonemes in words to make new words.

C.   **Correct.** The strategy of phoneme segmentation requires students to separate the phonemes in a word.

D.   Incorrect. The strategy of phoneme substitution requires students to replace phonemes in words to make new words.

2)   **Which of the following is an example of prosody?**

A.   using appropriate vocal cues when reading aloud

B.   decoding words correctly when reading aloud

C.   reading at an appropriate speed when reading aloud

D.   reading smoothly and steadily when reading aloud

Answers:

A.   **Correct.** Prosody is a reader's ability to use appropriate vocal expressions when reading aloud.

B.   Incorrect. Decoding words correctly while reading aloud is an example of reading accuracy.

C.   Incorrect. Reading aloud at an appropriate speed is an example of reading rate.

D.   Incorrect. Reading smoothly and steadily when reading aloud is an example of reading rate.

READING LITERATURE AND INFORMATIONAL TEXT

In order to effectively teach students to comprehend the literature and informational text they are tasked with reading, the elementary language arts teacher needs to demonstrate an understanding of comprehension strategies, point of view, comparing information from a variety of texts and multimedia sources, and the role of text complexity in reading development.

COMPREHENSION STRATEGIES

Expertise in language arts requires an ability to use key ideas and details from literary or informational text to determine the moral, theme, or central idea; make inferences; and summarize information. Readers must also be able to analyze characters, setting, plot, and relationships among ideas, events, and concepts. The **theme** of a literary text is the basic idea that the author wants to convey. It weaves in and out of the text as the story, play, or poem unfolds. It expresses an underlying opinion related to the text's subject. On the other hand, the **moral** of a literary text is the lesson the author wants to teach the reader. It is more direct than a theme. The basic underlying idea of informational text is referred to as the **central idea**. This is the major focus of the information provided in the text.

The key purpose of reading text is to obtain information or experience a story. In order to do this, readers must have the ability to comprehend what is being read. Without comprehension, reading is simply an exercise in making sounds that have no meaning. Being able to comprehend what is being read is what connects the words an author writes to the reader's experience of the world; it is what gives text meaning and makes it relatable. Elementary language arts teachers help students to comprehend what is being read by teaching students a variety of comprehension strategies. One of these strategies is the ability to make **inferences**, or determine what an author is suggesting by using clues in text. It is the ability to understand what is not directly stated by an author.

Summarization is the distillation and condensation of a text into its main idea and key details. It is a short encapsulation of what the text is about to clarify the general message. However, to properly summarize, it is important to **identify story elements**. More specifically, this is identifying the characters (e.g., main, minor, protagonist, antagonist, dynamic, static), **setting** (where the story takes place), and **plot** development (e.g., exposition, rising action, problem/climax, falling action, resolution) in a text. Understanding the role of a character in a story via the character's actions, traits, relationship, and personality is **character analysis**. Analyzing how a character thinks and behaves allows a reader to understand his or her motivations and beliefs.

Recognizing genre is the ability to name the genre of a text (e.g., poetry, drama, picture book, graphic novel, folktale, myth, fairy tale, tall tale, historical fiction, science fiction) and the features of that genre. Readers who understand and recognize the characteristics of a variety of genres can gain additional insights into an author's purpose or message. For example, a reader is able to comprehend a text with a greater depth and breadth if he or she knows how the **rhyme scheme** (e.g., abab, aabb, aabba) and **meter** (basic rhythmic structure of the lines or verses in poetry) of a poem affect its tone or how **stage directions** develop the rising action in a play.

An author uses a specific point of view to tell a story. When **identifying point of view**, readers use genre and pronoun clues to identify who is telling a story to best form accurate conclusions about the events of the story. Typically, authors use one of five points of view: first-person, second-person, third-person objective, third-person limited omniscient, and third-person omniscient. In **first-person** point of view, one character tells the story from his or her direct experience using pronouns such as *I, my, mine,* and *we.* In **second-person** point of view, the perspective of the text is from an external "you," whether that be the reader or unknown other. In **third-person objective** point of view, a detached narrator relates the actions and dialogue of the story, but not the thoughts or feelings of any characters. In **third-person limited omniscient** point of view, a detached narrator tells the story from one character's point of view including that character's internal thoughts and feelings. In **third-person omniscient** point of view, a detached and all-knowing narrator tells the story from the point of view of all of the characters, including all of their thoughts and feelings. Any text told from a third-person point of view includes pronouns such as *he, she, it,* and *they.*

Some texts offer supplemental information outside of the main text. These **text features** include imagery like photographs, drawings, maps, charts, graphs. They also include organizational features like chapter **headings**, titles, **sidebars** (boxes of explanatory or additional information set aside from main text), and **hyperlinks** (highlighted sections or words in digital text that take a reader to another digital location or document for additional information). Readers should be able to **analyze text features** to better comprehend an author's message.

Finally, **analyzing text organization** is the ability to analyze the way a text is organized in order to better comprehend an author's purpose for writing. Different forms of textual organization facilitate an author's message. Some of the more common organizational structures are cause and effect, problem and solution, sequence of events or steps-in-a-process, compare and contrast, and description. Each **text structure** can be identified by the use of particular signal words (words that provide clues to how the author has organized information) and features.

TEXT COMPLEXITY

The teaching of reading comprehension strategies is best facilitated when students are reading text that is at developmentally appropriate reading levels. Students improve their reading skills best when the text provided is neither too easy nor too difficult. **Text leveling**, or complexity, is determined by three factors: quantitative measures, qualitative measures, and reader and task considerations. **Quantitative measures** include readability scores determined by computer algorithms that evaluate text elements such as word frequency and sentence length. **Qualitative measures** include analysis of text elements such as structure (i.e., low or high complexity), language clarity (i.e., literal vs. figurative or familiar vs. unfamiliar), and knowledge demands (i.e., assumptions about what a reader already knows). **Reader and task considerations** are determined by the professional judgment of educators who match texts to particular students, classes, and/or tasks based on their inherent needs.

SAMPLE QUESTIONS

3) **Which of the following is true of quantitative measures of text complexity?**

A. They are task considerations determined by professional judgment.

B. They are analytical measurements determined by knowledge demands.

C. They are statistical measurements determined by computer algorithms.

D. They are leveling measurements determined by text structure.

Answers:

A. Incorrect. Quantitative measures of text complexity are free of human judgment.

B. Incorrect. The analysis of knowledge demands is a qualitative measure of text complexity.

C. Correct. Quantitative measures are objective and based on statistics.

D. Incorrect. Leveling measurements based on text structure are qualitative measures.

4) **Read the excerpt from *Treasure Island* by Robert Louis Stevenson.**

I remember him as if it were yesterday, as he came plodding to the inn door, his sea-chest following behind him in a hand-barrow—a tall, strong, heavy, nut-brown man, his tarry pigtail falling over the shoulder of his soiled blue coat, his hands ragged and scarred, with black, broken nails, and the sabre cut across one cheek, a dirty, livid white.

This text is written from which point of view?

A. second-person

B. first-person

C. third-person objective

D. third-person omniscient

Answers:

A. Incorrect. Second person point of view is written from the perspective of an external "you."

B. Correct. First person point of view is written directly from the perspective of one character.

C. Incorrect. Third-person objective point of view is written from the perspective of a detached narrator.

D. Incorrect. Third-person omniscient point of view is written from the perspective of an all-knowing, detached narrator.

WRITING

Elementary school is where students establish a solid foundation of writing skills that lead to a lifelong ability to communicate ideas, opinions, experiences, and beliefs. Language arts teachers across the grades are tasked with building student understanding of writing styles, purposes, and practices.

Table 1.5. Developmental Stages of Writing

Stage	Age	Students in this stage...
Preconventional	3 – 5	▶ are aware that print conveys meaning, but rely on pictures to communicate visually. ▶ include recognizable shapes and letters on drawings. ▶ can describe the significance of the objects in their drawings.
Emerging	4 – 6	▶ use pictures when drawing, but may also label objects. ▶ can match some letters to sounds. ▶ copy print they see in their environment.
Developing	5 – 7	▶ write sentences and no longer rely mainly on pictures. ▶ attempt to use punctuation and capitalization. ▶ spell words based on sound.
Beginning	6 – 8	▶ write several related sentences on a topic. ▶ use word spacing, punctuation, and capitalization correctly. ▶ create writing that others can read.
Expanding	7 – 9	▶ organize sentences logically and use more complex sentence structures. ▶ spell high frequency words correctly. ▶ respond to guidance and criticism from others.
Bridging	8 – 10	▶ write about a particular topic with a clear beginning, middle, and end. ▶ begin to use paragraphs. ▶ consult outside resources (e.g., dictionaries).
Fluent	9 – 11	▶ write both fiction and nonfiction with guidance. ▶ experiment with sentence length and complexity. ▶ edit for punctuation, spelling, and grammar.

Stage	Age	Students in this stage...
Proficient	10 – 13	▶ write well-developed fiction and nonfiction. ▶ use transitional sentences and descriptive language. ▶ edit for organization and style.
Connecting	11 – 14	▶ write in a number of different genres. ▶ develop a personal voice when writing. ▶ use complex punctuation.
Independent	13 and older	▶ explore topics in depth in fiction and nonfiction. ▶ incorporate literary devices in their writing. ▶ revise writing through multiple drafts.

In order to best facilitate student progress, elementary language arts teachers must have a firm understanding of the characteristics and stages of common types of writing, strategies for producing effective writing, digital tools for writing, and the research process.

TYPES OF WRITING

There are four main writing **styles** that students learn in elementary school. Each style is selected based on an author's **purpose** for writing—to explain, to entertain, to describe, or to persuade—and the needs of the **audience**, the people reading the material. Different audiences have different needs. For example, people reading a humor blog will most likely prefer an informal style, while the audience for a magazine article explaining environmental problems caused by deforestation will appreciate writing with a well-organized structure and paragraphs that expand on key issues. The four main styles of writing are as follows:

▶ **Expository Writing**: This style of writing is primarily used to explain an idea or concept or inform the reader about a topic. It is most often used in formal essays that include a main idea and supporting details based on fact.

▶ **Narrative Writing**: This style of writing is primarily used to tell a personal or fictional story that entertains the reader. The author includes descriptive details and figurative language in order to maintain the reader's attention with dynamic characters, interesting settings, and captivating plots. Poems that tell stories, or **narrative poems**, also use this writing style.

▶ **Descriptive Writing**: This style of writing emphasizes the production of imagery using words and figurative language that appeal to the reader's five senses. It is a writing style that produces vivid pictures in the reader's imagination and is often used to write poetry or detailed descriptions of experiences or events.

> ▶ **Persuasive Writing:** This style of writing is used to convince, or persuade, a reader to subscribe to the author's opinion or point of view. It follows a formal progression that aims to sway the reader into accepting the author's stance and often plays on the reader's emotions to achieve its goal. Persuasive writing is often used for **speeches** and **advertisements**.

THE WRITING PROCESS

Elementary students also need to learn that writing is a process that begins with an idea and ends with a final draft. The writing process is made up of five key stages: prewriting, drafting, **revising/editing**, rewriting, and publishing. This process allows students to experience writing as it takes place in the profession. It is a process that enables students to capture the inspiration of the initial idea and then carefully shape and polish that idea until it can best capture a reader's interest. During the prewriting phase of the writing process, authors brainstorm ideas for writing by organizing them in charts, lists, or by other means. This **organization** of ideas is used to write the first draft of a writing piece. During the next stage of the process, a writer reviews the first draft for **coherence** by identifying sections that need elaboration, correction, and/or reorganization. The original draft is revised based on these observations and those of peer editors. Once the **revisions** have been determined, the first draft is rewritten with corrections and changes made. It is only after the first draft has been carefully examined and rewritten that it is ready for an audience during the publishing phase of the writing process.

USING SOURCES

As students grow as writers, they begin to learn how to cite sources to support their ideas in research papers. The research paper is an expository essay that contains references to outside materials that legitimize claims made in the essay. Students learn to **paraphrase** supporting information, or briefly restate it in their own words, in order to avoid **plagiarism**, the intentional copying and credit-taking of another person's work. They also learn to include **citations** that name original sources of new information and are taught how to differentiate between primary sources, secondary sources, reliable sources, and unreliable sources.

Primary sources are original materials representative of an event, experience, place, or time period. They are direct or firsthand accounts in the form of text, image, record, sound, or item. **Secondary sources** inform about events, experiences, places, or time periods, but the information is provided by someone who was not directly involved and who used primary sources to discuss the material.

Reliable sources are trustworthy materials that come from experts in the field of study. These sources have **credibility** because they include extensive bibliographies listing the sources used to support the information provided. Some examples of reliable sources are published books, articles in credible magazines, and research studies provided by educational institutions. **Unreliable sources** are untrustworthy materials from a person or institution that does not have the educational background, expertise, or evidence of legitimate sources to support a claim. Some examples of unreliable sources are self-published materials, studies done to sell products, and opinion pieces.

SAMPLE QUESTIONS

5) **Which of the following can be classified as persuasive writing?**

   A.   an advertisement for a new product

   B.   a research paper on the effects of climate on ecosystems

   C.   a poem about the ocean on a foggy day

   D.   a short story with a suspenseful plot

Answers:

   A.   **Correct.** Persuasive writing aims to influence the reader to agree with what is stated and to act accordingly.

   B.   Incorrect. A research paper is an example of expository writing and is often neutral in tone.

   C.   Incorrect. A poem using sensory imagery is an example of descriptive writing.

   D.   Incorrect. A short story with a plot arc is an example of narrative writing.

6) **Which of the following is considered a reliable source for research about California?**

   A.   a personal blog about living in California

   B.   a research paper published by the State of California

   C.   an advertisement for California real estate

   D.   a letter to the editor about California roadways

Answers:

   A.   Incorrect. A personal blog is an unreliable source for research on a broad topic.

   B.   **Correct.** A published study by a government institution is a reliable research source.

   C.   Incorrect. Advertisements present biased information and are therefore unreliable sources of information.

   D.   Incorrect. Letters to the editors of newspapers typically include opinions, which are unreliable sources of information.

LANGUAGE

Throughout elementary school, students are introduced to the conventions of Standard English grammar, usage, mechanics, and spelling as tools to facilitate communication and comprehension when writing, speaking, reading, and listening. They learn how to utilize the English language in both formal and informal contexts through exposure to conversational, academic, and content area language. In addition, they build vocabulary by learning how to use context and word structure to determine the meanings of unknown words and phrases. Elementary language arts teachers are responsible for implementing a curriculum and providing feedback that best help students develop and strengthen these language skills.

GRAMMAR

Grammar refers to how parts of speech work together in sentences and how words are grouped to make meaning such as in phrases or clauses. Students learn the functions of nouns, verbs, adjectives, adverbs, prepositions, pronouns, and articles. They also learn about subject-verb agreement, verb tense, and how to identify, construct, and use simple sentences, compound sentences, complex sentences, and compound-complex sentences. Knowing how to order words, select appropriate verbs, and vary sentence structure are significant factors in learning how to write proficiently in elementary school.

▶ **Simple sentence**: A simple sentence is the most basic type of sentence. It is short and contains a subject, a verb, and a completed thought. Simple sentences can also act as independent clauses in compound or complex sentences.

▶ **Compound sentence**: A compound sentence is made up of two independent clauses (or simple sentences) joined by a coordinating conjunction such as *for, and, nor, but, or, yet,* and *so.* A comma is used before the coordinating conjunction to separate the two clauses.

▶ **Complex sentence**: A complex sentence is made up of an independent clause and one or more dependent clauses, which cannot stand alone as simple sentences. Dependent clauses can be subordinate or relative. Subordinate clauses are preceded by subordinating conjunctions such as *because, if,* and *after.* Relative clauses are preceded by relative pronouns such as *who, which,* and *that.* If the dependent clause comes first in the sentence, it is separated from the independent clause by a comma. However, if the dependent clause comes *within* the independent clause, it may need to be set off with commas on either side if the information it contains is not essential to comprehension of the independent clause. If the information in the dependent clause is essential to understanding the independent clause, no commas are used.

▶ **Compound-complex sentence**: A compound-complex sentence has two or more independent clauses joined by coordinating conjunctions and one or more dependent clauses that begin with subordinating conjunctions.

Modifiers are words or phrases that change the meanings of or add details to other words or phrases in a sentence. They can cause problems when a reader is unable to understand a sentence's meaning because the modifier has not been used correctly. A **misplaced modifier** is one that causes confusion because it does not modify its intended word or phrase. This happens when the modifier is placed in the wrong part of a sentence. For example, in the sentence, "I rose from my seat after the sad movie I saw slowly," the modifier *slowly* is misplaced. Instead of modifying "rose," it modifies "saw," which makes it seem as though the writer watched the movie slowly instead of rising slowly after watching it. A **dangling modifier** is one that has no clear connection to any other part of a sentence. It can cause a sentence to mean something other than intended. For example, in the sentence, "After putting on my socks, the doorbell rang," the phrase "after putting on my socks" dangles because the subject it is supposed to modify (*I*) is missing. It ends up modifying "the doorbell" instead, which is nonsensical because a doorbell doesn't put on socks.

> **STUDY TIP**
>
> The word *FANBOYS* is a mnemonic device for remembering the following coordinating conjunctions: **F**or, **A**nd, **N**or, **B**ut, **O**r, **Y**et, **S**o.

MECHANICS

Mechanics are the conventions of print that are not necessary in spoken language, such as punctuation, capitalization, and indentation. These conventions allow a reader to easily follow and understand what a writer is communicating. For example, the correct **punctuation** in a sentence (e.g., period, comma, question mark, exclamation mark) helps a reader know when to change pace or read with inflection. **Spelling** is a component of mechanics but is treated as a separate category in elementary school. In the earlier grades, it begins with the use of phonics to "invent" spellings in writing assignments and becomes more formalized as students move up through the grades.

> **DID YOU KNOW?**
>
> Emergent writers "invent" spellings by listening for the sounds they hear in a word and transferring those sounds to paper using written letters. The focus is more on creating writing than on using conventional spellings.

An understanding of **syntax**, or the grammatical formations and patterns of sentences, not only is a necessary concept for elementary students to master with respect to writing clearly and effectively but also is one that aids in reading comprehension. It can be utilized to determine the **literal** meanings, or most basic or exact meanings, of unknown words encountered while reading. It is a source of knowledge taught in elementary school that empowers students to decipher word meanings in **context**—to use the construction of sentences immediately surrounding a difficult word or phrase to determine its meaning. Another method elementary students learn for decoding unknown words in text is **structural analysis**, or an analysis of the roots and affixes of words.

Roots are the most basic forms of words and therefore form the basis of many new words. Affixes, in the form of prefixes or suffixes, are additions to a root word that change its meaning. Many roots and affixes derived from Greek and Latin are used fairly consistently throughout the English language and are responsible for a large percentage of its vocabulary. By learning a repertoire of roots, prefixes, and suffixes, students can analyze words they come across by deconstructing the parts in order to uncover meaning. For example, if a student knows that the Latin root *-port-* means "carry," he or she will know that words containing that root are related to "carry" in some way. By knowing that the prefix *trans-* means "across," the word *transport* can be determined to mean "carry across." By knowing that the prefix *ex-* means "out" and the suffix *-ation* means "process," the word *exportation* can be determined to mean "a carry out process." Roots and affixes are examples of *morphemes*, or the smallest units of language that contain meaning.

FOR REFERENCE

See page 6 for a list of common roots and affixes.

USAGE

Usage refers to the agreed-upon rules for how language is used under certain conditions or within particular styles. It concerns itself with how English varies depending upon regional, historical, societal, and contextual factors. Such things as dialect, register, academic language, and conversational language fall under this category as does the study of how an author's **word choice** contributes to the **tone**, or attitude, of a text. Writers use and manipulate words to engender reactions in their readers that cross a whole range of human feeling: surprise, calm, joy, fear, anger, etc. As elementary students become familiar with concepts such as figurative language and connotation, they can comprehend not only the words used but also the unstated impressions writers include in text, or that which is "between the lines."

DID YOU KNOW?

The register for the field of medicine includes medical terms and particular ways of communicating information, such as "The hospital board has decided to explore an ambulatory model that supports outpatients and attendances at A&E."

Dialect is language that is particular to a geographical location or consolidated social group. Characters in novels may speak in dialect to give a story authenticity.

Nonregional, **register** refers to particular styles of language determined by purpose, audience, and social context. Registers include specialized vocabulary and specific language structures depending on the lexicon of a particular subset of people. Register can also be used to reference formal and informal language.

DID YOU KNOW?

Academic language is the language of school that students must internalize in order to achieve success in educational and professional institutions.

Academic language is language used in formal settings and academic writing. It includes professional standards, discipline-specific vocabulary, conventions of etiquette, and proper formats for specific types of presentations. In contrast, **conversational language** is familiar and informal, the language used with friends, to convey humor, and to communicate in nonacademic contexts.

Language also conveys general impression and meaning. **Figurative language** is constructed to convey images and ideas separate from the actual meanings of the words used. It includes several types of literary devices that add expression, sensory appeal, impact, and insight to text. A few of these devices are simile, metaphor, personification, onomatopoeia, hyperbole, and alliteration. On the other hand, **connotation** is the intended meaning of a word beyond its literal meaning, or detonation. It is a suggested response attached to a particular word selected by a writer. The connotations of words hold emotional or cultural associations that can contribute positive or negative tones to writing. For example, to cast an immature character in a positive light, a writer may describe the character as *childlike*, invoking a sensation of protectiveness or compassion in the reader. However, to cast that same character in a negative light, the writer may describe the character as *childish*, invoking a feeling of distaste or contempt in the reader.

SAMPLE QUESTIONS

7) **Andre will study in the school library, while his brother auditions for the school play.**

   What error has been made in the sentence above?

   A. The sentence is a run-on sentence.

   B. No comma is necessary.

   C. The dependent clause always comes first.

   D. The adverb phrases belong before the verbs.

   Answers:

   A. Incorrect. The sentence is a complex sentence with incorrect punctuation between the independent clause and the dependent clause.

B. **Correct.** When a dependent clause follows an independent clause in a complex sentence, a comma is not used before the subordinating conjunction.

C. Incorrect. A dependent clause can come before or after an independent clause in a complex sentence.

D. Incorrect. In this sentence, the adverb phrases work best by following the verbs they modify.

8) **Read the sentence from *The Wonderful Wizard of Oz* by Frank Baum.**

There now came a sharp whistling in the air from the south, and as they turned their eyes that way they saw ripples in the grass coming from that direction also.

How would the tone of the sentence change if *sharp* were replaced by *gentle*?

A. The tone of the sentence would remain about the same.

B. The tone of the sentence would become more negative.

C. The tone of the sentence would be indistinguishable.

D. The tone of the sentence would become more positive.

Answers:

A. Incorrect. The word *gentle* has a more positive connotation than *sharp*, so the tone of the sentence would change to one that is positive instead of negative.

B. Incorrect. The word *gentle* has a more positive connotation than *sharp*, so the tone of the sentence changes to suggest that the storm is more playful than sinister.

C. Incorrect. A writer's word choice always gives text a recognizable tone.

D. **Correct.** The use of *gentle* instead of *sharp* would change the tone of the sentence by making the storm seem less threatening and more playful.

LISTENING AND SPEAKING

Listening and speaking are a child's first pathway to literacy. Children typically enter elementary school with an ability to orally communicate ideas, experiences, and concepts. The role of the elementary language arts teacher is to help students hone this skill set for academic and social growth. Students learn how to use strategies for listening and speaking that contribute to their abilities to listen carefully, think critically, differentiate relevant from irrelevant information, articulate clearly, and use appropriate vocal cues and word choice. Students are tasked with communicating for a variety of purposes, audiences, and contexts and have opportunities to engage in active listening during discussions of text, topics, and community.

Active listening is listening that is focused and empathetic. It is listening to authentically "hear" a perspective, feeling, or point of view. The following characteristics make up active listening:

▶ **Focusing**: Students practice keeping their attention on the person who is speaking.

▶ **Using positive nonverbal cues**: Students demonstrate interest by looking at the speaker and by using appropriate facial expressions and body language.

▶ **Allowing speaker to finish uninterrupted**: Students wait for a speaker to finish and concentrate on the message before formulating a response.

▶ **Not judging**: Students listen and respond with respect for the speaker's views and feelings. They agree or disagree using methods that maintain respect within the whole group.

▶ **Paraphrasing**: Students verify understanding by restating the speaker's main points concisely and in different words.

Students in elementary school also learn how to prepare and engage in small group and individual oral presentations. They learn the steps necessary to organize the information they want to present and techniques for presenting the information in ways that capture and maintain the attention of the audience. The following oral presentation skills provide an overview of what elementary school students need to know in order to effectively communicate with their audience:

▶ **Logical structure**: Ideas follow a logical line of reasoning.

▶ **Supporting evidence**: Information is supported by relevant evidence.

▶ **Word choice**: Only necessary and relevant words and sentences are included.

▶ **Collaboration**: Group presentations are creative, cohesive, and logical.

▶ **Eye contact**: Eyes are directed at the audience to the extent possible.

▶ **Articulation**: Enunciation is clear.

▶ **Volume**: Intonation is natural and neither too soft nor too loud.

▶ **Audience**: The style of presentation matches the needs of the audience.

▶ **Displays**: Visuals, props, and/or sounds that enhance presentation are used.

SAMPLE QUESTIONS

9) **Which of the following quotes is a demonstration of active listening?**

    A. "If I understand correctly, you think the classroom needs a pet."

    B. "I think you meant to say that you wish you had a pet at home."

    C. "You didn't talk about the kind of pet our classroom should have."

    D. "There's no way the principal will let us have a classroom pet."

Answers:

A.   **Correct.** This quote demonstrates active listening because the listener is paraphrasing the message to clarify understanding.

B.   Incorrect. This quote does not demonstrate active listening because the message is changed to what the listener thinks instead of remaining as the speaker intended.

C.   Incorrect. This quote does not demonstrate active listening because the listener changes the topic; furthermore, the listener speaks in a critical manner.

D.   Incorrect. This quote does not demonstrate active listening because the listener dismisses the message.

10) **Students have been placed in small groups to prepare reader's theater presentations that they will perform for each other. How might each group best meet the needs of its audience?**

A.   by reciting their lines in quiet voices during the performance

B.   by passing around a script to read from during the performance

C.   by using classroom materials as props during the performance

D.   by skipping some parts of the story during the performance

Answers:

A.   Incorrect. Reciting lines in quiet voices makes it difficult for an audience to hear important details.

B.   Incorrect. Reading from a shared script interrupts the flow of a performance and causes the audience to become restless.

C.   **Correct.** Props add interesting visuals to a performance and reinforce comprehension.

D.   Incorrect. Skipping some parts of a story is confusing to an audience.

Go on

TERMS

academic language: language used in formal settings and academic writing

active listening: listening that is focused and empathetic

advanced fluency stage of language acquisition: learners demonstrate near-native ability and use complex, multiphrase and multiclause sentences to convey their ideas

affixes: added to words or roots to change their meanings; include prefixes (added to the beginning of a word or root) and suffixes (added to the end of a word or root)

analyzing text organization: analyzing how a text is organized in order to better comprehend an author's purpose for writing

audience: the reader/readers

central idea: the basic underlying idea of informational text

character analysis: understanding the role of a character in a story via the character's actions, traits, relationships, and personality

citations: identification of original sources of outside information

complex sentence: a sentence made up of an independent clause and one or more dependent clauses

compound sentence: a sentence made up of two independent clauses (or simple sentences)

compound-complex sentence: a sentence that has two or more independent clauses and one or more dependent clauses

connotation: the intended meaning of a word beyond its literal meaning

conversational language: familiar and informal language

credibility: proof of the reliability of a source

denotation: the literal meaning of a word

descriptive writing: a writing style that emphasizes the production of imagery using words and figurative language that appeal to the reader's five senses

dialect: language that is particular to a geographical location or consolidated social group

early production stage of language acquisition: learners produce single-word and two- to three-word phrases and can respond to questions and statements

expository writing: a writing style that explains an idea or concept or informs the reader about a topic

figurative language: language that conveys images and ideas separate from the actual meanings of the words used

first-person point of view: one character tells the story from his or her direct experience using pronouns such as *I*, *my*, *mine*, and *we*

fluency: the ability to read with ease and automaticity

genre: type of a text (e.g., poetry, drama, picture book, graphic novel, folktale, myth, fairy tale, tall tale, historical fiction, science fiction)

grammar: the way parts of speech work together in sentences and how words are grouped to make meaning such as in phrases or clauses

high frequency letter-sound correspondences: letter-sound correspondences that occur most often in the English language

identifying point of view: using genre and pronoun clues to identify who is telling a story to best form accurate conclusions about the events of the story

inferences: conclusions about what an author suggests in a text based on context clues

intermediate fluency stage of language acquisition: learners are able to speak in more complex sentences and catch and correct many of their errors

letter-sound correspondence: the relationship between the spoken sounds in words and the printed letters that correspond to those sounds

levels of language proficiency: L1) entering, L2) beginning, L3) developing, L4) expanding, and L5) bridging

literal: the most basic or exact meaning of a word

mechanics: the conventions of print that are not necessary in spoken language, such as punctuation, capitalization, and indentation (spelling is a component of mechanics but is treated as a separate category in elementary school)

meter: the basic rhythmic structure of the lines or verses in poetry

misplaced modifier: a modifier that causes confusion because it does not modify its intended word or phrase

modifiers: words or phrases that change the meanings of or add details to other words or phrases in a sentence

moral: the lesson the author intends to teach the reader in a literary text

morphemes: the smallest units of language that contain meaning

narrative poems: poems that tell stories

narrative writing: a writing style that tells a personal or fictional story that entertains the reader

onset: the beginning consonant or consonant blend of a syllable

paraphrasing: briefly restating information in one's own words

persuasive writing: a writing style that convinces, or persuades, a reader to subscribe to the author's opinion or point of view (often used for speeches and advertisements)

phoneme: each small unit of sound in a language

phoneme blending: combining phonemes to make a word

phoneme deletion: removing phonemes from words to make new words

phoneme segmentation: separating phonemes in words

phoneme substitution: replacing phonemes in words to make new words

Go on

phonemic awareness: a type of phonological awareness; an understanding of how phonemes form a language by creating differences in the meanings of words

phonics: the study of the relationship between the spoken sounds in words and the printed letters that correspond to those sounds

phonological awareness: an understanding of how sounds, syllables, words, and word parts can be orally manipulated to break apart words, make new words, and create rhymes

plagiarism: intentionally copying and taking credit for another person's work

plot development: the exposition, rising action, problem/climax, falling action, and resolution

preproduction stage of language acquisition: the silent period; learners refrain from speaking but will listen, may copy words down, and can respond to visual cues

primary sources: original materials representative of an event, experience, place, or time period

prosody: the range of vocal expressions a reader uses when reading aloud, including rhythm, intonation, and stress patterns

punctuation: periods, commas, question marks, exclamation marks, and other markings that divide text or help a reader know when to change pace or read with inflection

qualitative measures: contributors to text leveling that include analysis of text elements such as structure, language clarity, and knowledge demands

quantitative measures: contributors to text leveling that include readability scores determined by computer algorithms that evaluate text elements such as word frequency and sentence length

reader and task considerations: matching texts to particular students, classes, and/or tasks based on their inherent needs as determined by the professional judgment of educators

reading accuracy: the ability to recognize or decode words correctly

reading rate: the speed and fluidity with which a reader can read

register: particular styles of language determined by purpose, audience, and social context

reliable sources: trustworthy materials that come from experts in the field of study

rhyme scheme: rhyme pattern in a poem; may be represented as letters (e.g., *abab, aabb, aabba*)

rime: a syllable's vowel and its remaining consonants (not including the onset)

roots: the basis of many words in the English language, typically derived from Latin or Greek

second-person point of view: a narrative perspective from an external "you," whether that be the reader or unknown other

secondary sources: sources that inform about events, experiences, places, or time periods using primary sources but that were not directly involved in the event in any way

setting: where a story takes place

sight words: words that are repeated most often in text

silent period: the preproduction stage of language acquisition

simple sentence: a sentence that contains a subject, a verb, and a completed thought

speech emergence stage of language acquisition: learners can chunk simple words and phrases into sentences that may or may not be grammatically correct and can understand simple readings when reinforced by graphics or pictures

stages of language acquisition: preproduction, early production, speech emergence, intermediate fluency, and advanced fluency

structural analysis: an analysis of the roots and affixes of words

summarization: distilling and condensing a text into its main idea and key details by identifying story elements

syllables: phonological units composed of onsets and rimes that can be blended, substituted, segmented, and deleted like phonemes

syntax: the grammatical formations and patterns of sentences

text features: supplemental information outside of the main text such as chapter headings, titles, sidebars (boxes of explanatory or additional information set aside from main text) and hyperlinks

text leveling: complexity of text as determined by quantitative measures, qualitative measures, and reader and task considerations

text structure: organizational structures like cause and effect, problem and solution, sequence of events or steps-in-a-process, compare and contrast, and description

theme: the basic idea that the author wants to convey in a literary text

third-person limited omniscient point of view: a narrative perspective in which a detached narrator tells the story from one character's point of view, including that character's internal thoughts and feelings

third-person objective point of view: a narrative perspective in which a detached narrator relates the actions and dialogue of the story, but not the thoughts or feelings of any characters

third-person omniscient point of view: a narrative perspective in which a detached and all-knowing narrator tells the story from the point of view of all of the characters, including all of their thoughts and feelings

tone: the attitude of a text

Go on

unreliable sources: untrustworthy materials from a person or institution that does not have the educational background, expertise, or evidence of legitimate sources to support a claim

usage: common rules for how language is used under certain conditions or within particular styles

writing styles: specific types of writing that convey the author's purpose for writing—to explain, to entertain, to describe, or to persuade

2

Mathematics

NUMBERS AND OPERATIONS

PLACE VALUE

While historically some civilizations have used other numbering systems, today most of the world uses the base-10 system. In the **base-10** system, each **digit** (the numeric symbols 0 – 9) in a number is worth 10 times as much as the number to the right of it.

Table 2.1 Place Value Chart		
1,000,000	10^6	millions
100,000	10^5	hundred thousands
10,000	10^4	ten thousands
1,000	10^3	thousands
100	10^2	hundreds
10	10^1	tens
1	10^0	ones
.		decimal
$\frac{1}{10}$	10^{-1}	tenths
$\frac{1}{100}$	10^{-2}	hundredths

For example, in the number 321, each digit has a different value based on its location. This is called **place value**. Knowing the place value of each digit allows students to write a number in expanded form. **Expanded form** is breaking up a number by the value of each digit. For example, the expanded form of 321 is written as 300 + 20 + 1.

Figure 2.1. Expanded Form

Number Theory

A basic foundation in numeracy is vital for establishing the groundwork for understanding advanced mathematical concepts. Students begin working with **natural numbers**, which are used when counting (e.g., 1, 2, 3, etc.). Once a basic understanding of natural numbers is achieved, more advanced concepts, such as whole numbers and integers, can be introduced. **Whole numbers** are similar to natural numbers, except that whole numbers include 0. **Integers** are positive or negative whole numbers (not fractions or decimals).

Rational numbers are numbers that can be made by dividing two integers. Rational numbers must be expressed as a terminating or a repeating decimal, such as 0.125 or $0.\overline{66}$. Pi (π) is not a rational number because it does not terminate or repeat (π = 3.14159265...); instead, pi goes on forever with no repeating pattern. Integers are rational numbers because they can be written as a fraction with a denominator of 1.

Every whole number (except 1) is either a prime number or a composite number. A **prime number** is a natural number greater than 1 which can only be divided evenly by 1 and itself. For example 7 is a prime number because it can only be divided by the numbers 1 and 7.

On the other hand, a **composite number** is a natural number greater than 1 which can be evenly divided by at least one other number besides 1 and itself. For example, 6 is a composite number because it can be divided by 1, 2, 3, and 6.

Composite numbers can be broken down into prime numbers using factor trees. For example, the number 54 is 2 × 27, and 27 is 3 × 9, and 9 is 3 × 3, as shown in the figure on the right.

Once the number has been broken down into its simplest form, the composite number can be expressed using exponents. An **exponent** shows how many times a number should be multiplied by itself. In the factor tree, the number 54 can be written as 2 × 3 × 3 × 3 or 2 × 3³.

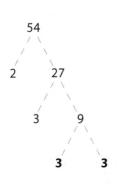

Figure 2.2. Factor Tree

OPERATIONS WITH WHOLE NUMBERS

Rational numbers can be used to perform mathematical operations. **Addition** is combining numbers, while **subtraction** requires finding the difference between numbers. **Multiplication** is the repeated addition of the same number to itself; in contrast, **division** is splitting a number into equal parts. Addition and subtraction are considered **inverse operations** because each operation cancels out the other operation. For example, 2 + 3 = 5 is true, and so is the inverse, 5 – 3 = 2. Multiplication and division are also inverse operations because 2 × 3 = 6, and the inverse, 6 ÷ 3 = 2, are both true. Knowing inverse operations allows students to check their answers.

In multiplication, the two numbers multiplied together are called **factors**. The answer is called the **product**. For example, in the operation 3 × 2 = 6 (3 added to itself 2 times), the numbers 3 and 2 are factors and the number 6 is the product.

Multiplication may be presented in a number of ways. One way to visually present a multiplication problem is with an **array**, such as the one shown below. In an array, each of the two factors is represented by the appropriate number of rows or columns, and the product will be the total number of boxes in the array.

4 × 3 = 12

Figure 2.3. Array

Another way to represent multiplication is by using **area models** (also called the box method). Although this is a nontraditional approach to multiplication, it promotes the understanding of place value.

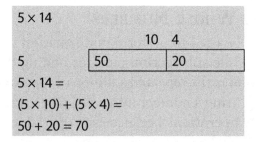

Figure 2.4. Area Models

In division, the number that is being divided into groups is called the **dividend**. The number by which the number is divided is the **divisor**. The answer is called the **quotient**. For example, in the operation $12 \div 3 = 4$, 12 is the dividend, 3 is the divisor, and 4 is the quotient.

Sometimes in a division problem, the dividend cannot be divided equally. The number that is left over when a number does not divide evenly into another number is called the **remainder**. For example, when twelve items are divided into five groups, each group will have two items in it, and there will be two items left over, meaning the remainder is 2.

In the figure below, 12 squares are divided into 5 different groups, each represented by a different color. There are 2 squares in each group (the quotient). Two squares are left, meaning there are not enough squares to put 3 squares in each group. Thus, the remainder is 2.

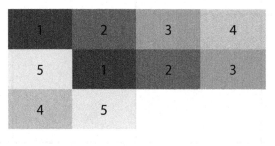

Figure 2.5. Remainder

An **algorithm** is a set of steps to follow when performing mathematical operations. Even the simplest of computations has an algorithm. As problems become more complicated, there are rules, or properties, that guide the problem solver.

Table 2.2. Mathematical Properties

Name	Description	Applies to	Example
commutative property	The order of the operation doesn't matter.	addition multiplication	$a + b = b + a$ $ab = ba$
associative property	Grouping of numbers doesn't matter.	addition multiplication	$(a + b) + c = a + (b + c)$ $(a \times b) \times c = a \times (b \times c)$
distributive property	Multiply a value by all the values inside brackets, then add.	multiplication	$a(b + c) = ab + ac$
identity property	Adding 0 or multiplying by 1 will not change the original value.	addition multiplication	$a + 0 = a$ $a \times 1 = a$
zero property	Multiplying any value by 0 yields a result of 0.	multiplication	$a \times 0 = 0$

When solving a multistep equation, the order of operations must be used to get the correct answer. Generally speaking, the problem should be worked in the following order: 1) parentheses and brackets; 2) exponents and square roots; 3) multiplication and division; 4) addition and subtraction. The acronym PEMDAS can be used to remember the order of operations.

<u>P</u>lease <u>E</u>xcuse (<u>M</u>y <u>D</u>ear) (<u>A</u>unt <u>S</u>ally)

P – Parentheses

E – Exponents

M – Multiply

D – Divide

A – Add

S – Subtract

> **STUDY TIP**
>
> To multiply binomials, use FOIL: First – Outer – Inner – Last. For example, $(a + b)(c + d) = ac + ad + bc + bd$.

The steps "Multiply-Divide" and "Add-Subtract" go in order from left to right. In other words, divide before multiplying if the division problem is on the left. For example, the expression $(3^2 - 2)^2 + (4)5^3$ is simplified using the following steps:

1. Parentheses: Because the parentheses in this problem contain two operations (exponents and subtraction) use the order of operations within the parentheses. Exponents come before subtraction.

    $(3^2 - 2)^2 + (4)5^3 = (9 - 2)^2 + (4)5^3 = (7)^2 + (4)5^3$

2. Exponents:

    $(7)^2 + (4)5^3 = 49 + (4)125$

3. Multiplication and division:

    $49 + (4)125 = 49 + 500$

4. Addition and subtraction:

    $49 + 500 = 549$

OPERATIONS WITH FRACTIONS AND DECIMALS

Fractions use two numbers separated by a horizontal bar to show as parts of a whole. Fractions include a **numerator**, the number on top of a fraction, and a **denominator**, the bottom number of a fraction. The denominator is the "whole," and the numerator is the "part." For example, if there are twelve students on the chess team, and five of students are selected to represent the school in a tournament, the fraction of the chess team going to the tournament is $\frac{5}{12}$.

If the numerator of a fraction is 1, it is called a **unit fraction**. In the chess team example, $\frac{1}{12}$ is the unit fraction. Five $\frac{1}{12}$ units represent the part of the team that is going to the tournament. As the "whole" gets larger, one "part" becomes smaller and smaller. Think of cutting a cake: cutting 8 slices creates smaller slices than cutting the same cake into 4 slices. So, as the denominator of unit fractions increases, the value of the fraction itself decreases.

The same basic operations that can be performed with whole numbers can also be performed on fractions, with a few modifications. When adding and subtracting fractions, each fraction must have a **common denominator**. The operation is performed in the numerator, and the denominator remains the same. For example, if $\frac{3}{12}$ of the chess team described above is eliminated in the second round of the tournament, the total fraction of the team remaining will be $\frac{5}{12} - \frac{3}{12} = \frac{5-3}{12} = \frac{2}{12}$.

In $\frac{2}{12}$, both the numerator and the denominator are divisible by 2, meaning the fraction is not in its simplest form. To simplify the fraction, reduce the numerator and denominator by dividing both by the same value: $\frac{2}{12} = \frac{2 \div 2}{12 \div 2} = \frac{1}{6}$.

If the fractions to be added or subtracted do not have a common denominator, the least common multiple of the denominators must be found. In the operation $\frac{2}{3} - \frac{1}{2}$, the common denominator will be a multiple of both 3 and 2. Multiples are found by multiplying the denominator by whole numbers until a common multiple is found:

▶ multiples of 3 are **3** (3×1), **6** (3×2), **9** (3×3) ...

▶ multiples of 2 are **2** (2×1), **4** (2×2), **6** (2×3) ...

Since 6 is the smallest multiple of both 3 and 2, it is the least common multiple and can be used as the common denominator. Both the numerator and denominator of each fraction should be multiplied by the appropriate whole number: $\frac{2}{3}\left(\frac{2}{2}\right) - \frac{1}{2}\left(\frac{3}{3}\right) = \frac{4}{6} - \frac{3}{6} = \frac{1}{6}$.

When multiplying fractions, simply multiply each numerator together and each denominator together. To divide two fractions, invert the second fraction (swap the numerator and denominator) then multiply normally. Note that multiplying fractions creates a value smaller than either original value.

STUDY TIP

SMURF is an acronym for dividing fractions. It stands for **S**ame – **M**ultiply – **U**pside down – **R**ename – **F**raction.

▶ $\frac{5}{6} \times \frac{2}{3} = \frac{10}{18} = \frac{5}{9}$

▶ $\frac{5}{6} \div \frac{2}{3} = \frac{5}{6} \times \frac{3}{2} = \frac{15}{12} = \frac{5}{4}$

Another way to represent parts of a whole is by using decimals. A **decimal** is any real number in the base-10 system, but it often refers to numbers with digits to the right of the decimal point.

5	4	.	3	2
$5 \times 10^1 =$ $5 \times 10 =$ 50	$4 \times 10^0 =$ $4 \times 1 =$ 4		$3 \times 10^{-1} =$ $3 \times \frac{1}{10} =$ 0.3	$2 \times 10^{-2} =$ $2 \times \frac{1}{100} =$ 0.02
tens	ones	decimal	tenths	hundredths
		$50 + 4 + 0.3 + 0.02 = 54.32$		

Figure 2.6. Decimals and Place Value

Fractions can be converted to decimals by simply dividing the denominator by the numerator. To convert a decimal to a fraction, place the numbers to the right of the decimal over the appropriate base-10 power and simplify the fraction.

▶ $\frac{1}{2} = 1 \div 2 = 0.5$

▶ $0.375 = \frac{375}{1000} = \frac{3}{8}$

Proportional Relationships

Ratios compare two things. For example, if Jaimie has 6 pairs of jeans and 8 t-shirts, then the ratio of jeans to t-shirts is 6:8. Like fractions, ratios can be reduced when both values are multiples of the same number. For example, the ratio 6:8 can be reduced by dividing both parts by 2: 6:8 = 3:4. The value of the ratio doesn't change because a ratio only describes a relationship. Whether Jaimie has 3 jeans and 4 shirts; 6 jeans and 8 shirts; or 12 jeans and 16 shirts, the ratio remains the same. In other words, for every 3 pairs of jeans Jaimie has, she has 4 t-shirts.

Problems involving ratios can often be solved by setting up a proportion, which is an equation stating that two ratios are equal. For example, if Jaimie wants to buy 9 pairs of jeans and maintain the ratio described above, a proportion can be used to find the number of shirts she'll need to purchase: $\frac{jeans}{t\text{-}shirts} = \frac{3}{4} = \frac{9}{x}$.

The two fractions can then be **cross-multiplied** to give the equation $3x = 36$, and the variable isolated: $x = 12$ shirts.

Unit rates are the ratio of two measurements in which the second term is 1. For example, if Patrick earns \$240 in 12 hours, he earns \$20 in 1 hour: $\frac{dollars}{hours} = \frac{240}{12} = \frac{x}{1}$, so $x = \$20$.

Percentages are another way to represent parts of a whole. In a percentage, the whole is always 100: $\frac{part}{whole} = \frac{percent}{100}$

In the example above, Jaimie bought 9 jeans and 12 shirts, for a total of 14 items of clothing. To find the percentage of her purchase representing shirts, a proportion can be set up where the shirts are the "part" and the total number of items are the "whole": $\frac{9}{12} = \frac{x}{100}$. By cross-multiplying, the equation can be solved to give a percentage: 0.75. Note that when using this equation, the percent is given as a decimal value. To find the percent, simply multiply by 100: $0.75 \times 100 = 75\%$.

> **STUDY TIP**
>
> cross-multiplication:
> $\frac{a}{b} = \frac{c}{d} \rightarrow ad = bc$

Reasonableness

Since minor mistakes can lead to major errors, mathematicians need quick and easy ways to assess the **reasonableness**, or common sense, of their answers. **Rounding**, or simplifying a number to any predetermined place value, enables a student to make an estimation. An **estimation** is a close prediction that involves minor calculations.

When rounding to a specific place value, the number in that place is rounded up if the digit immediately to the right is 5 or higher, and it remains the same if the number is less than 5. For example, the operation 22×8 is difficult to do quickly. However, rounding 22 to 20 and 8 to 10 allows for a quick and easy calculation: 20×10. This estimate will provide a product close enough to check for reasonableness of exact calculations. Math that can be done in the student's head without the use of tools is called mental math.

SAMPLE QUESTIONS:

1) **Which expression is equivalent to dividing 400 by 16?**

    A. $2(200 - 8)$

    B. $(400 \div 4) \div 12$

    C. $(216 \div 8) + (184 \div 8)$

    D. $(216 \div 16) + (184 \div 16)$

    Answers:

    A.   Incorrect. $400 \div 16 = 25$. Order of operations says to solve the parentheses first; $200 - 8 = 192$. Then, multiply by 2; $192 \times 2 = 384$.

    B.   Incorrect. $400 \div 16 = 25$. Order of operations says to solve the parentheses first; $(400 \div 4) = 100$. Then, $100 \div 12 = 8.333\ldots$

    C.   Incorrect. $400 \div 16 = 25$. Order of operations says to solve the parentheses first; $(216 \div 8) + (184 \div 8) = 27 + 23 = 50$.

    D.   Correct. $400 \div 16 = 25$. Order of operations says to solve the parentheses first; $(216 \div 16) + (184 \div 16) = 13.5 + 11.5 = 25$.

2) **What number is equal to $(5^2 + 1)^2 + 3^3$?**

    A.   703

    B.   694

    C.   30

    D.   53

    Answers:

    A.   Correct. $(5^2 + 1)^2 + 3^3 = (25 + 1)^2 + 3^3 = (26)^2 + 3^3 = 676 + 27 = 703$.

    B.   Incorrect. This answer is the result of incorrectly solving for the exponent 3^3. Remember that $3^3 = 3 \times 3 \times 3$.

    C.   Incorrect. Here, the exponents were solved incorrectly. $5^2 = 5 \times 5 = 25$, $3^3 = 3 \times 3 \times 3 = 27$.

    D.   Incorrect. This answer reflects failure to use order of operations; the parentheses must be solved first.

3) **A vending machine contains 12 types of snacks: some snacks are salty and some snacks are sweet. The ratio of sweet snacks to salty snacks is 1:3. How many types of sweet snacks are in the vending machine?**

    A.   1

    B.   3

    C.   4

    D.   12

Go on

Answers:

A.   Incorrect. There is only 1 sweet snack if there are only 4 snacks in total. Since there are 3 times as many snacks, both sides of the ratio must be multiplied by 3.

B.   **Correct.** If there are 12 snacks total, the numbers on both sides of the ratio = 12. If both sides of the ratio are multiplied by 3, the number of salty to sweet would be 3:9. 3 sweet snacks plus 9 salty snacks equals 12 snacks in all.

C.   Incorrect. If there are 4 sweet snacks, there would be 3 times as many, or 12, salty snacks. That would be 16 snacks in all. The problem states that there are only 12 snacks.

D.   Incorrect. There are 12 snacks in total.

ALGEBRAIC THINKING

ALGEBRAIC EXPRESSIONS AND EQUATIONS

Algebraic expressions contain numbers, variables, and at least one mathematical operation. Each group of numbers and variables in an expression is called a term (e.g., $3x$ or $16y$). A binomial is an algebraic expression with two terms (e.g., $3x + 16y$), a trinomial has three terms, and a polynomial has more than three terms. Algebraic expressions can be evaluated for a specific value by plugging that value into the expression and simplifying.

STUDY TIP

A formula is an equation that uses variables to represent patterns between numbers. For example, the formula for the distributive property is $a(b + c) = ab + ac$.

In an equation, two expressions are joined by an equal sign, which indicates that the two expressions are equal to each other. The two sides of an equation act like a balanced scale: operations can be performed on equations as long as the same operation is performed on both sides to maintain the balance.

This property can be used to solve the equation by performing operations that isolate the variable on one side. For example, the equation $4x + 12 = 2x + 48$ can be solved for x using the following steps:

1. Subtract 12 from both sides of the equation:

    $(4x + 12) - 12 = (2x + 48) - 12 \rightarrow 4x = 2x + 36$

2. Subtract $2x$ from both sides of the equation:

    $(4x) - 2x = (2x + 36) - 2x \rightarrow 2x = 36$

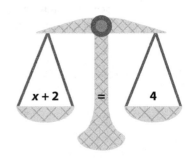

Figure 2.7. Equations

3. Divide both sides by 2:

$\frac{2x}{2} = \frac{36}{2} \rightarrow x = 18$

LINEAR EQUATIONS

Linear equations follow a specific pattern that results in a straight line when graphed. These equations have two variables, and the points on the graph can be determined using a function table. Functions demonstrate a relationship between input and output. The input is the independent variable, and the output is called the dependent variable because it depends on the input. Usually (but not always) x is the independent variable, and y is the dependent variable. The coordinates found in the function table can then be plotted on a set of axes to find the corresponding graph.

Table 2.3. Function Table		
x	y	$3x + y = 12$
1	9	$3(1) + y = 12$ $3 + y = 12$ $y = 9$
2	6	$3(2) + y = 12$ $6 + y = 12$ $y = 6$
3	3	$3(3) + y = 12$ $9 + y = 12$ $y = 3$

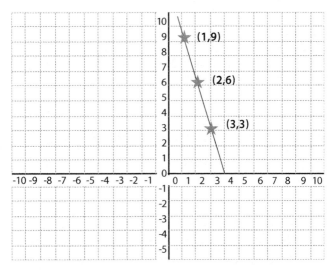

Figure 2.8. Dependent and Independent Variables

INEQUALITIES

Inequalities are similar to equations, but both sides of the problem are not equal ($\neq$). Inequalities may be represented as follows: greater than ($>$), greater than or equal to ($\geq$), less than ($<$), or less than or equal to ($\leq$).

Inequalities may be represented on a number line, as shown below. A circle is placed on the end point with a filled circle representing $\leq$ and $\geq$, and an empty circle representing $<$ and $>$. An arrow is then drawn to show either all the values greater than or less than.

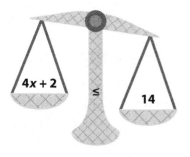

Figure 2.9 Inequality

Inequalities can be solved by manipulating them much like equations. However, the solution to an inequality is a set of numbers, not a single value. For example, simplifying $4x + 2 \leq 14$ gives the inequality $x \leq 3$, meaning every number less than 3 would also be included in the set of correct answers.

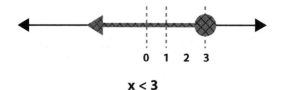

0   1   2   3

x < 3

Figure 2.10. Inequality Line Graph

SAMPLE QUESTIONS

4) **Using the table, which equation demonstrates the linear relationship between x and y?**

x	y
3	11
5	15
8	21

A. $y = 2x + 5$
B. $y = 5x + 5$
C. $y = 4x + 5$
D. $y = 3x + 5$

Answers:

A.   **Correct.** $y = 2x + 5$ is a linear relationship because $11 = 2(3) + 5$. Substitute the x and y values into the equation.

B.   Incorrect. $y = 5x + 5$ is not a linear equation because $11 \neq 5(3) + 5$.

C.   Incorrect. $y = 4x + 5$ is not a linear equation because $11 \neq 4(3) + 5$.

D.   Incorrect. $y = 3x + 5$ is not a linear equation because $11 \neq 3(3) + 5$.

5)   If $x = 5$, what is the value of the algebraic expression $2x - x$?

A.   5

B.   10

C.   15

D.   20

Answers:

A.   Correct. Substitute 5 for x; $2(5) - 5 = 10 - 5 = 5$.

B.   Incorrect. Substitute 5 for x; $2(5) - 5 \neq 10$.

C.   Incorrect. Substitute 5 for x; $2(5) - 5 \neq 15$.

D.   Incorrect. Substitute 5 for x; $2(5) - 5 \neq 20$.

GEOMETRY AND MEASUREMENT

CLASSIFYING GEOMETRIC FIGURES

Geometric figures are shapes composed of points, lines, or planes. A **point** is simply a location in space; it does not have any dimensional properties like length, area, or volume. A collection of points that extend infinitely in both directions is a **line**, and one that extends infinitely in only one direction is a **ray**. A section of a line with a beginning and end point is a **line segment**. Lines, rays, and line segments are examples of **one-dimensional** objects because they can only be measured in one dimension (length).

Figure 2.11. One-Dimensional Object

Lines, rays, and line segments can intersect to create **angles**, which are measured in degrees or radians. Angles between 0 and 90 degrees are **acute**, and angles between 90 and 180 degrees are **obtuse**. An angle of exactly 90 degrees is a **right angle**, and two lines which form right angles are **perpendicular**. Lines that do not intersect are described as **parallel**.

line   ray

Figure 2.12. Lines and Angles

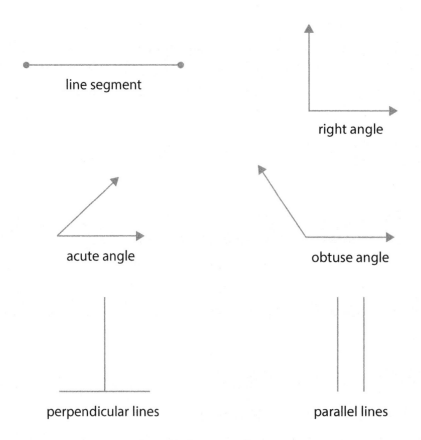

Figure 2.12. Lines and Angles (continued)

Two-dimensional objects can be measured in two dimensions (length and width). A **plane** is a two-dimensional object that extends infinitely in both dimensions. **Polygons** are two-dimensional shapes, such as triangles and squares, which have three or more straight sides. Regular polygons are polygons whose sides are all the same length.

Figure 2.13. Two-Dimensional Object

Figure 2.14. Polgygons

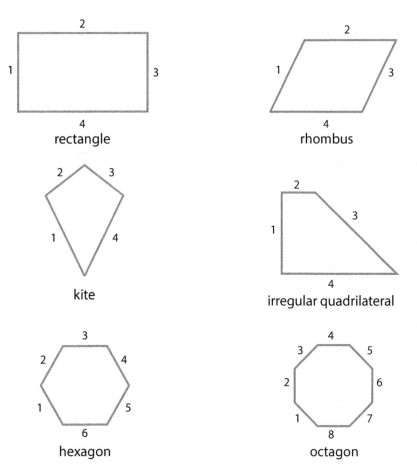

Figure 2.14. Polygons (continued)

Three-dimensional objects, such as cubes, can be measured in three dimensions (length, width, and height). Three-dimensional objects are also called **solids**, and the shape of a flattened solid is called a **net**.

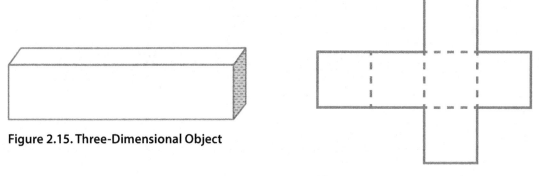

Figure 2.15. Three-Dimensional Object

Figure 2.16. Net

Go on

SOLVING MEASUREMENT PROBLEMS

The United States uses **customary units** of measure, such as inches or gallons. Metric units, like meters and grams, are the universal units of measure used in most of the world.

Table 2.4. Customary System

Length	Capacity and Weight
12 inches = 1 foot	2 tablespoons = 1 fluid ounce
36 inches = 1 yard	8 fluid ounces = 1 cup
3 feet = 1 yard	2 cups = 1 pint
5280 feet = 1 mile	2 pints = 1 quart
1760 yards = 1 mile	2 quarts = 1/2 gallon
	4 quarts = 1 gallon
	16 ounces = 1 pound
	2000 pounds = 1 ton
	4 cups = 1 quart
	16 cups = 1 gallon
	8 pints = 1 gallon

Table 2.5. Metric Units and Prefixes

Name	The Number	Prefix
billion	1,000,000,000	giga-
million	1,000,000	mega-
thousand	1000	kilo-
hundred	100	hecto-
ten	10	deca-
unit	1	
tenth	0.1	deci-
hundredth	0.01	centi-
thousandth	0.001	milli-
millionth	0.000 001	micro-
billionth	0.000 000 001	nano-

Prefixes affix to the following terms:

- meter (length); e.g., 10 centimeters would be 10 hundredths of a meter.
- gram (mass); e.g., 2 kilograms is 2000 grams of a substance.
- liter (volume); e.g., 1 deciliter is 1 tenth of a liter of a liquid.

The length, or distance from one point to another on an object, can be determined using a tape measure or a ruler. The size of the surface of a two-dimensional object is its area. The area of an object is its length times its width and is measured in square units. For example, if a cabinet is 3 feet long and 2 feet wide, its area would be 6 ft^2. The distance around a two-dimensional figure is its perimeter, which can be found by adding the lengths of all the sides.

Table 2.6. Area and Perimeter of Basic Shapes

Shape	Areas	Perimeter
Triangle	$A = \frac{1}{2}bh$	$A = s_1 + s_2 + s_3$
Square	$A = s^2$	$A = 4s$
Rectangle	$A = l \times w$	$A = 2l \times 2w$
Circle	$A = \pi r^2$	$A = 2\pi r$

For the rectangle below, the area would be 8 m^2 because 2 m $\times$ 4 m = 8 m^2. The perimeter of the rectangle would be 12 meters because the sum of the length of all sides is 2 m + 4 m + 2 m + 4 m = 12 m.

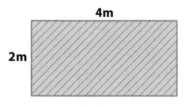

Figure 2.17. Fencing

The surface area of a three-dimensional object can be figured by adding the areas of all the sides. For example, the box below is 4 feet long, 3 feet wide, and 1 foot deep. The surface area is found by adding the areas of each face:

- top: 4 ft $\times$ 3 ft = 12 ft^2
- bottom: 4 ft $\times$ 3 ft = 12 ft^2
- front: 4 ft $\times$ 1 ft = 4 ft^2
- back: 4 ft $\times$ 1 ft = 4 ft^2
- right: 1 ft $\times$ 1 ft = 1 ft^2
- left: 1 ft $\times$ 1 ft = 1 ft^2

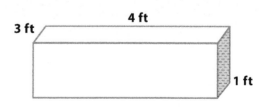

Figure 2.18. Surface Area

Volume is the amount of space that a three-dimensional object takes up. Volume is measured in cubic units (e.g., ft³ or mm³). The volume of a solid may be determined by multiplying length times width times height. In the rectangular prism below, the volume is $3 \text{ in} \times 1 \text{ in} \times 1 \text{ in} = 3 \text{ in}^3$.

The **mass** of an object is the amount of matter in the object. Mass is measured using a balance. Mass is different from weight because weight depends on the gravitational pull on the object, while mass stays the same whether on Earth, on the moon, or anywhere in the universe.

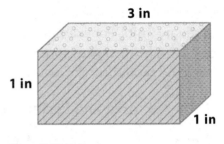

Figure 2.19. Volume

GRAPHING ON A COORDINATE PLANE

A coordinate plane is a plane containing the *x*- and *y*-axes. The *x*-axis is the horizontal line on a graph where $y = 0$. The *y*-axis is the vertical line on a graph where $x = 0$. The *x*- and *y*-axes intersect to create four quadrants. The first quadrant is in the upper right, and other quadrants are labeled counter-clockwise. Points, or locations, on the graph are written as ordered pairs, (*x,y*), with the point (0,0) called

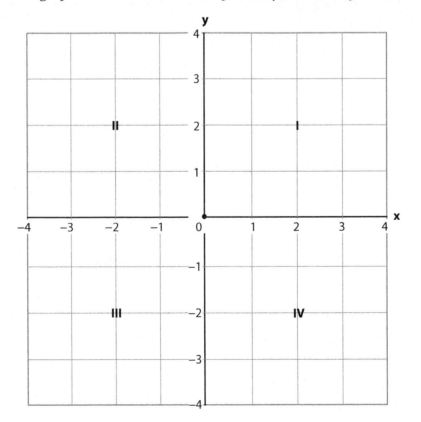

Figure 2.20. Four Quadrants

the origin. Points are plotted by counting over *x* places from the origin horizontally and *y* places from the origin vertically.

6) **What is the perimeter of the regular polygon?**

2 in

A.   4 in

B.   8 in

C.   10 in

D.   32 in

Answers:

A.   Incorrect. To find the perimeter, add the length of all sides.

B.   Incorrect. Add the length of all sides to find the perimeter.

C.   Correct. Adding the length of each side will determine the perimeter: 2 in + 2 in + 2 in + 2 in + 2 in = 10 in.

D.   Incorrect. This object only has 5 sides.

7) **In which quadrant is the point (−5, 2) located in Figure 2.20 on page 48?**

A.   I

B.   II

C.   III

D.   IV

Answers:

A.   Incorrect. The negative five (−5) means that the point will be to the left of the origin.

B.   Correct. Starting at the origin, move 5 units to the left, and then up 2 units.

C.   Incorrect. The positive two (2) means that the point will be above the origin.

D.   Incorrect. The negative five (–5) and positive two (2) means that the point will be above and to the left of the origin.

Data, Statistics, and Probability

Statistics

Statistics is the study of data. Analyzing data requires using **measures of center** (mean, median, and mode) to identify trends or patterns.

The **mean** is the average; it is determined by adding all outcomes and then dividing by the total number of outcomes. For example, the average of the data set {16, 19, 19, 25, 27, 29, 75} is equal to $\frac{17 + 19 + 19 + 25 + 27 + 29 + 75}{7} = \frac{210}{7} = 30$.

STUDY TIP
Mode is most common. Median is in the middle (like a median in the road). Mean is average.

The **median** is the number in the middle when the data set is arranged in order from least to greatest. For example, in the data set {16, 19, 19, 25, 27, 29, 75}, the median is 25. When a data set contains an even number of values, finding the median requires averaging the two middle values. In the data set {75, 80, 82, 100}, the two numbers in the middle are 80 and 82. Consequently, the median will be the average of these two values: $\frac{80 + 82}{2} = 81$.

Finally, the **mode** is the most frequent outcome in a data set. In the set {16, 19, 19, 25, 27, 29, 75}, the mode is 19 because it occurs twice, which is more than any of the other numbers. If several values appear an equal, and most frequent, number of times, both values are considered the mode.

Other useful indicators include range and outliers. The **range** is the difference between the highest and the lowest number in a data set. For example, the range of the set {16, 19, 19, 25, 27, 29, 75} is 75 – 16 = 59. **Outliers**, or data points that are significantly different from other data points, should be noted as they can skew the central tendency. In the data set {16, 19, 19, 25, 27, 29, 75}, the value 75 is far outside the other values and raises the value of the mean. Without the outlier, the mean is much closer to the other data points.

CONSIDER THIS
Why must teachers recognize the importance of outliers when looking at student data?

▶ $\frac{16 + 19 + 19 + 25 + 27 + 29 + 75}{7} = \frac{210}{7} = 30$

▶ $\frac{16 + 19 + 19 + 25 + 27 + 29}{6} = \frac{135}{6} = 22.5$

Generally, the median is a better indicator of a central tendency if outliers are present to skew the mean.

DATA PRESENTATION

Data can be presented in a variety of ways. The most appropriate depends on the data being displayed. **Box plots** (also called box and whisker plots) show data using the median, range, and outliers of a data set. They provide a helpful visual guide, showing how data is distributed around the median. In the example below, 81 is the median and the range is 100 – 0, or 100.

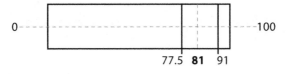

Figure 2.21. Box Plots

Bar graphs use bars of different lengths to compare data. The independent variable on a bar graph is grouped into categories such as months, flavors, or locations, and the dependent variable will be a quantity. Thus, comparing the length of bars provides a visual guide to the relative amounts in each category. **Double bar graphs** show more than one data set on the same set of axes.

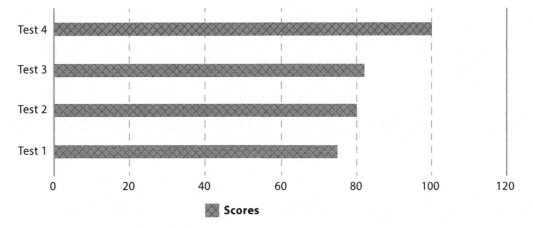

Figure 2.22. Bar Graph

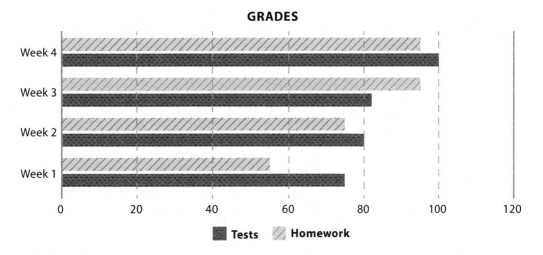

Figure 2.23. Double Bar Graph

Histograms similarly use bars to compare data, but the independent variable is a continuous variable that has been "binned" or divided into categories. For example, the time of day can be broken down into 8:00 a.m. to 12:00 p.m., 12:00 p.m. to 4:00 p.m., and so on. Usually (but not always), a gap is included between the bars of a bar graph but not a histogram.

Dot plots display the frequency of a value or event data graphically using dots, and thus can be used to observe the distribution of a data set. Typically, a value or category is listed on the *x*-axis, and the number of times that value appears in the data set is represented by a line of vertical dots. Dot plots make it easy to see which values occur most often.

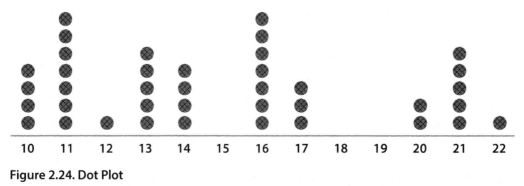

Figure 2.24. Dot Plot

Scatter plots use points to show relationships between two variables which can be plotted as coordinate points. One variable describes a position on the *x*-axis, and the other a point on the *y*-axis. Scatter plots can suggest relationships between variables. For example, both variables might increase, or one may increase when the other decreases.

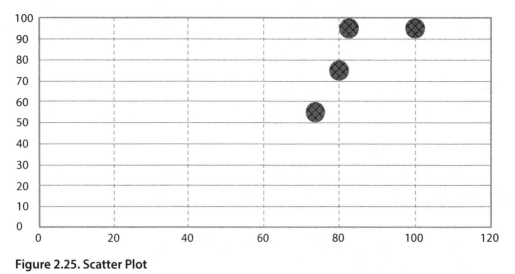

Figure 2.25. Scatter Plot

Line graphs show changes in data by connecting points on a scatter graph using a line. These graphs will often measure time on the *x*-axis and are used to show trends in the data, such as temperature changes over a day or school attendance throughout the year. Double line graphs present two sets of data on the same set of axes.

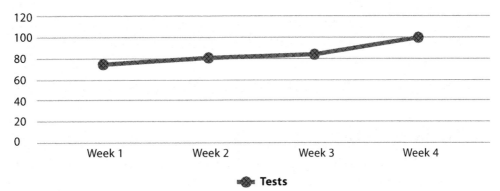

Figure 2.26. Line Graph

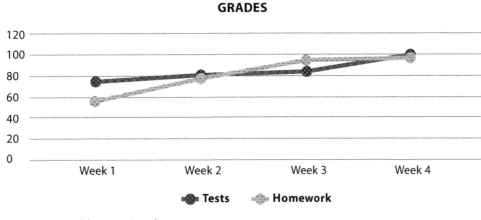

Figure 2.27. Double Line Graph

Circle graphs (also called pie charts) are used to show parts of a whole: the "pie" is the whole, and each "slice" represents a percentage or part of the whole.

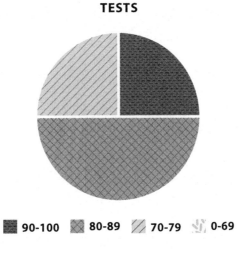

Figure 2.28. Circle Graph

PROBABILITY

Probability is the likelihood, or chance, that something will happen. Probability is expressed as a fraction with the numerator being the number of successful outcomes and the denominator being the total number of outcomes. For example, if there are 25 marbles in a bag and 4 marbles are red, the probability of randomly pulling a red marble out of the bag is $\frac{4}{25}$ (also written as 0.16 or 16%).

SAMPLE QUESTION

8) Ken has 6 grades in English class. Each grade is worth 100 points. Ken has a 92% average in English. If Ken's first 5 grades are 90, 100, 95, 83, and 87, what did Ken make for the 6th grade?

 A.   80
 B.   92
 C.   97
 D.   100

Answers:

 A.   Incorrect. If Ken made an 80 on the 6th test, his average score would be $90 + 100 + 95 + 83 + 87 + 80 = 535; 535 \div 6 \neq 92$.

 B.   Incorrect. If Ken made a 92 on the 6th test, his average score would be $90 + 100 + 95 + 83 + 87 + 92 = 547; 547 \div 6 \neq 92$.

 C.   **Correct.** If Ken has 6 scores that average 92%, his total number of points earned is found by multiplying $92 \times 6 = 552$. To find how many points he scored on the 6th test, subtract the sum of the other scores from 552. $90 + 100 + 95 + 83 + 87 = 455; 552 - 455 = 97$.

 D.   Incorrect. If Ken makes a 100 on the 6th test, his average score would be $90 + 100 + 95 + 83 + 87 + 100 = 555; 555 \div 6 \neq 92$.

TERMS

addition: the process of combining two or more numbers

algebraic expressions: contain numbers, variables, and a mathematical operation

algorithms: a set of steps to follow when solving a problem

angles: a shape formed by two rays that share a common point

area: the size of a surface measured in square units

area models (also called the box method): a nontraditional approach to multiplication that promotes understanding of place value

arrays: a pictorial representation of a multiplication problem

associative property: in multiplication and addition, the way numbers are grouped in parentheses does not matter, $(a + b) + c = a + (b + c)$

bar graphs: a graph that uses lengths of rectangles to show data

base-10: the numbering system where each digit is worth 10 times as much as the digit to the right of it

binomials: an algebraic expression with two different variables

box plots (also called box and whisker plots): data is shown using the median and range of a data set

circle graphs: a pie chart where each "piece" demonstrates a quantity

commutative property: in multiplication and addition, the order of the numbers on each side of the equation does not matter: $ab = ba$

composite numbers: a natural number greater than 1 that can be divided by at least one other number besides 1 and itself

coordinate plane: the plane containing the x-axis and y-axis

customary units: units of measure used in the United States

decimals: any real number in the base-10 system, but often refers to numbers with digits to the right of the decimal point

denominator: the number on the bottom of a fraction

dependent variables: variables whose value depends on other variables

digits: any number 0 – 9

distributive property: multiplication distributes over addition: $a(b + c) = ab + ac$

dividends: a number that is being divided by another number

division: splitting a number into equal parts

divisors: the number by which another number is divided

dot plots: a graphical display of data using dots

double bar graphs: bar graphs that present more than one type of data

double line graphs: a line graph that presents more than one type of data

equations: algebraic expressions that use an equal sign

estimation: a close prediction that involves minor calculations

expanded form: breaking up a number by the value of each digit

exponents: the number written to the upper right of another number that indicates how many times that number should be multiplied by itself

factors: numbers that are multiplied with each other

figures: geometric forms made up of points, lines, or planes

formulas: mathematical relationships expressed in symbols

fraction: a part of a whole

functions: a relationship between input and output

histograms: bar graph showing continuous data over time

inequalities: two mathematical quantities that are not equal to each other

independent variables: values that determine the value of other variables

integers: positive or negative whole numbers that are not fractions or decimals

inverse operations: an operation that reverses another operation

length: the measurement of something from end to end

linear equations: an equation that results in a straight line when graphed

line graphs: a graph that uses points connected by lines to show data

line segments: a part of a line that connects two points

lines: a one-dimensional geometric shape that is infinitely long

mass: the amount of matter in an object

mean: the average

measures of center: include mean, median, and mode

median: the number in the middle when the data set is arranged from least to greatest

mental math: math that can be done in the student's head without the use of tools

metric units: the universal units of measure

mode: the most frequent

models: a mathematical representation of the real world

multiples: the product of two whole numbers

multiplication: repeated addition of the same number to itself

natural numbers: numbers used when counting; do not include 0, fractions, or decimals

nets: the shape of a flattened three-dimensional object

numerator: the number on top of a fraction

one-dimensional: having only length

order of operations: work the problem in the order: 1) parentheses and brackets; 2) exponents and square roots; 3) multiplication and division; 4) addition and subtraction

ordered pairs: two numbers written to show the position of a point in a coordinate plane

origin: the point (0,0) on a graph

outlier: a data point that is vastly different from the other data points

parallel lines: lines that remain the same distance apart over their entire length and never cross

percentages: a part of a whole conveyed per 100

perimeter: distance around a two-dimensional shape

perpendicular lines: lines that cross at a 90 degree angle

place value: the value of the location of a digit within a number

points: location in a coordinate plane

polygons: two-dimensional shapes that have three or more straight sides

prime numbers: a natural number greater than 1 that can only be divided by 1 and itself

probability: the likelihood that something will happen

product: the result of multiplying two or more numbers

quadrants: the four areas created by the intersection of the x-axis and the y-axis

quotient: the result of dividing one number into another

range: the difference between the highest number and the lowest number in a data set

ratios: a comparison of two things

rational numbers: a number that can be made by dividing two integers; incudes fractions and terminating or repeating decimals

rays: a shape that starts at one point and goes infinitely in one direction

reasonableness: making common sense

remainder: the number that is left over when one number does not divide evenly into another

rounding: simplifying a number to any given place value

scatterplots: a graph of plotted points that compares two data sets

solids: three-dimensional objects

statistics: the study of data

subtraction: finding the difference between two numbers

surface area: the sum of the areas of all sides of a three-dimensional object

tessellations: creating patterns through the tiling of polygons

three-dimensional: having length, width, and height

trends: two sets of data that show a pattern

two-dimensional: having length and width

unit fractions: a fraction where the numerator is 1

unit rates: the ratio of two measurements in which the second term is 1

volume: the amount of space that an object occupies as measured in cubic units

whole numbers: counting numbers, including 0, that are not fractions or decimals

x-axis: horizontal position on a graph where $y = 0$

y-axis: vertical position on a graph where $x = 0$

Social Studies

The social studies portion of the elementary education test covers content aligned with state and national standards. Questions focus on concepts appropriate to elementary-level anthropology, sociology, economics, geography, world history, United States history, United States government, civics, and social studies skills and processes. Not only do teachers need to understand these subjects individually, but they also need to understand the relationships among these subjects and why they are taught at the elementary level.

GEOGRAPHY, ANTHROPOLOGY, AND SOCIOLOGY

GEOGRAPHY

The study of geography is the study of spatial distribution. It stresses analyzing information based on the distribution, location, and interactions of different human and physical features of the earth. Geography is divided into two main areas. **Physical geography** explores the natural process of the earth, whereas **human geography** explores the impact of people on the physical world, such as how humans alter their environments. It also looks at **social structures** as they relate to geography, such as how social events relate to places. An example of that would be how immigration affected urban populations in the US during the nineteenth century.

Geography uses maps to determine spatial distributions, such as ethnic demographics in various **regions**, languages in a particular country, or even the number of volcanoes in a determined area. The main reason for creating a map or developing a geographic information system is to assess the **spatial relationships** between features. An example of a spatial relationship is the distance between residential areas and transportation stops.

All maps use **cardinal directions**: north, south, east, and west. Some maps also feature **intermediate directions** between each point. All of these are featured on a compass rose, which is used to determine locations and directions.

Absolute location describes a location identifiable by specific geographic coordinates. For example, latitude and longitude delineate specific coordinates, so the absolute location of New York City is 40°70'58" N, 74°11'81" W. Addresses are also absolute locations: for instance, the absolute location of the White House is 1600 Pennsylvania Avenue NW, Washington, DC 20500. **Relative location** describes where a place is situated in relation to another place or places. For example, the state of Illinois is located in the Midwest region of the United States; it borders Wisconsin to the north, Indiana to the east, Iowa and Missouri to the west, and Kentucky to the south.

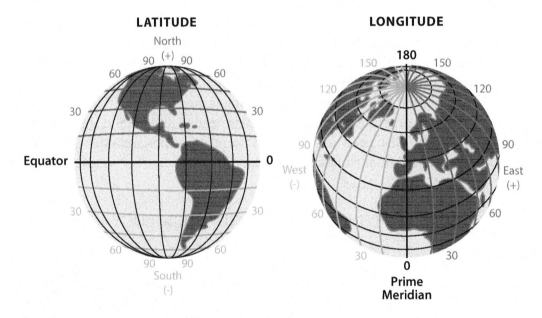

Figure 3.1. Latitude and Longitude

Maps display **geographic features**, physical features place like continents, bodies of water, plains, plateaus, mountains, and valleys. Raised elevations and bodies of water are indicated through shading or coloring; they are also labeled. In addition, maps show **political features** like towns and cities, and county, state, or national borders. They may also include significant bodies of water.

Despite their differences, physical and human geography are interconnected. For example, physical features can determine the feasibility of living in certain locations or practicing certain lifestyles. Physical features dictate the availability of **natural resources** such as fresh water, arable land, fuel, livestock, and game; they also affect climate patterns. Manmade resources also intersect with physical and human geography; for example, the Hoover Dam manages the Colorado River, a natural resource, in order to provide water and electricity to certain parts of the southwestern United States.

Physical regions of the world are broken down by distance from the equator. The **low latitudes**, from the equator to latitudes 23.5° north and south, have three distinct climates. **Tropical rainforests** can be found in the equatorial lowlands in Central Africa, Southeast Asia, and the Amazon basin. North and south of the rainforest is the **savannah**. The savannah is dry in the winter and wet in the summer, experiencing an average of 10 to 30 inches of rain. The **desert** lies beyond the savannah to the north and south. Deserts are the hottest and driest parts of the earth and receive less than 10 inches of rainfall a year. The best known deserts in the world are the Sahara Desert, the Australian Outback, and the Arabian Desert.

The **middle latitudes**, from latitudes 23.5° to 66.5° north and south, have a greater variety of climates, determined more by proximity to water than by the exact latitude. Three climates in the middle latitudes receive the most rain and therefore are the most fertile. The first is the **Mediterranean climate**, found in lands between latitudes 30° and 40° north and south that include land bordering the Mediterranean Sea, a small part of southwestern Africa, southern and southwestern Australia, a small part of the Ukraine near the Black Sea, central Chile, and southern California. The **humid subtropical climate** is located on coastal areas north and south of the tropics. This climate receives warm ocean currents and warm winds year round, leading to a climate that is warm and moist. This is also the climate that supports the greatest percentage of the world's population. Japan, southeastern China, northeastern India, southeastern South Africa, the southeastern United States, and parts of South America all have subtropical climates. Finally, several areas that are near or surrounded by water experience the **marine climate**. Marine climates are warm and rainy, resulting in part from the warm ocean winds. Western Europe, the British Isles, the US and Canadian Pacific Northwest, southern Chile, southern New Zealand, and southeastern Australia all have marine climates.

The climate best for farming is the **humid continental climate**, the true four-season climate. This climate can be found in the northern and central United States, south-central and southeastern Canada, northern China, and the western and southeastern parts of the former Soviet bloc. Those areas of continents far from the ocean are called **steppes**, or prairie. Flatlands with minimal rainfall, steppes can even become deserts if rainfall consistently dips below 10 inches per year.

The **high latitudes**, from latitudes 66.5° north and south to the poles, are home to two climates: **tundra** and **taiga**. The tundra features extremely cold and long winters; while the ground is frozen for most of the year, during the short summer the ground becomes mushy. With no arable land, it is home to few people. The taiga can be found south of the tundra in Northern Russia, Sweden, Norway, Finland, Canada, and Alaska. Home to the world's largest forestlands, the taiga also exhibits many swamps and marshes; importantly, it contains extreme mineral wealth. While there is a growing season, it is so short that meaningful agriculture is impossible; thus, the taiga is sparsely populated.

Students should understand that human activity, such as agriculture, ranching, logging, mining, and urban and suburban development impact the earth and the environment by interrupting ecosystems. Furthermore, they should also understand that **industrialization**, the process of manufacturing, creates byproducts that affect and can harm the environment. **Urbanization**, or the development of cities, became a feature of human development at the advent of the nineteenth-century Industrial Revolution, when unskilled jobs in factories offered higher wages for workers than an agricultural lifestyle did. Urbanization and **suburbanization** continue today as cities develop and as urban dwellers move to growing suburbs. Development necessarily results in the destruction of surrounding environment; however, new urban ecosystems result, and **urban planning** is itself a geographic specialty.

Another way to illustrate human and social behavior is by mapping **migration** patterns. This is the study of movement from one place to another, with the intention of settling permanently at the new location. As discussed above, urbanization is one type of migration. Some migration is internal—people moving from one place to another within the same region, like urbanization. Other migration involves people moving from one region of the world to another. Many immigrants have migrated to the United States from other countries. Push and pull factors cause people to migrate: economic, cultural, sociopolitical, or

DID YOU KNOW?

Migrants fleeing conflict or other dangers are called *refugees* if they cross an international border; if they flee to another part of their home country, they are called *internally displaced persons (IDPs)*.

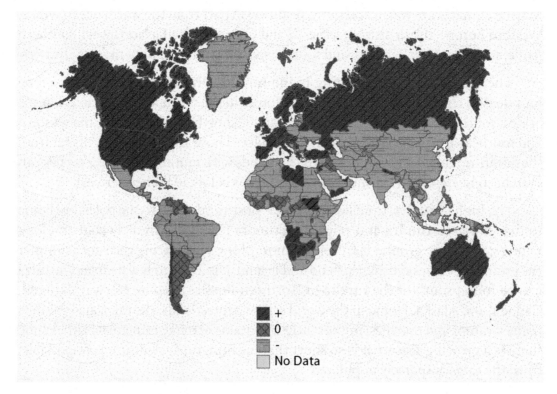

Figure 3.2. Human Migration Map

environmental reasons. Pull factors like job opportunities or better living standards attract people to new locations. Push factors like famine, drought, war, lack of economic opportunities, and political persecution drive people to leave their homes in search of relief.

ANTHROPOLOGY AND SOCIOLOGY

The elementary social studies curriculum also covers elements of **anthropology** and **sociology**. At the elementary level, these fields provide students insight into the behavior of individuals and groups relative to their location. Students should develop a knowledge of major world ethnic groups, organizations, and institutions, including understanding the major regions of the world and the general dominant cultures, religions, and languages therein. Students also begin developing their own personalities and learning the boundaries and limits of personal and social behavior.

Understanding personal identity in relation to peers, family, and institutions provides the tools for analyzing the reasons behind their behavior. Developing personal identity entails exploring and analyzing how individuals relate to others. **Socialization** is a process where individuals learn skills, beliefs, values, and behavior patterns of society and how these can influence their own norms and customs. For example, family roles differ depending on age and gender, and there are norms that dictate how certain family members should act.

Primary socialization occurs when children learn the values, actions, and attitudes that are appropriate for members of their particular culture. For example, if a family eats dinner together every night, that child will likely assume that he or she must regularly communicate with the closest and most important people in his or her life. **Secondary socialization** occurs when an individual learns the appropriate values, actions, attitudes, and behaviors as a member of a smaller group within a larger society. Secondary socialization generally occurs in adolescence or young adulthood, and influences will be teachers, employers, and other authority figures.

Examining **conflict**, **cooperation**, and **exchange** is a feature of social studies; students encounter these in history, economics, and geography. **Conflict** is the process of disagreement and is usually resolved when one of the two parties receives either the entirety or a satisfactory amount of their desired goal. **Cooperation**, on the other hand, is the process of working together to achieve similar goals; it often leads to positive outcomes. **Exchange** is the process of giving one thing and receiving another (usually with similar value) in return.

Students learn that **institutions** are extensions of core social values and are created in response to varying individual and group needs. Institutions are formally structured groups that comprise society. At the macro level they include government, private enterprise, religious institutions, and academic institutions. At the micro level, they include local communities and the family unit. They are composed of a usually formal, often top-down structure with a small governing body in charge (either the executives in a government or private company or the parents in the family unit). For example, labor unions fight for better conditions for workers; governments maintain social stability; businesses provide goods, services, and profit; and religious organizations fulfill social and personal needs.

The study of institutions also includes understanding how they are maintained and changed, as well as how they exert influence among individuals. Studying communities helps clarify how individuals, families, and institutions socialize and come together to form values, beliefs, and behavior patterns, and how they may differ from those of other communities.

More broadly, studying culture relates to understanding human and group behavior. Studying culture helps students understand that individuals develop culture and also adapt to it in changing circumstances (such as migration). Examining different belief systems and practices, such as celebrations, languages, and other norms, exposes students to multiple cultural perspectives on shared human experiences. Studies may also explore the similarities and differences among cultures and how they evolve in various regions.

The map above may be used as a general reference; however it is important for students to keep in mind that millions of people migrate temporarily or permanently throughout the world and that all regions have minority groups, so the map simply depicts dominant, not uniform, cultures.

SAMPLE QUESTIONS

1) **Which of the following are major physical regions in the continental United States?**

   A. humid continental, humid subtropical, Mediterranean, marine, desert

   B. humid continental, humid subtropical, taiga, tundra, Mediterranean

   C. humid continental, Mediterranean, marine, taiga, tropical rainforest

   D. the Sun Belt, the Bible Belt, and the Coasts

Answers:

   A. **Correct.** These are all major physical regions in North America.

   B. Incorrect. While Alaska has taiga and tundra, it is not considered part of the continental United States.

   C. Incorrect. While Hawaii and US territories in the Caribbean and Pacific Ocean have tropical rainforest, they are not considered part of the continental United States.

   D. Incorrect. These terms may be used in human geography, anthropology, or history but not in physical geography.

2)   **Which of the following is NOT an example of human geography?**

A.   studying the importance of trade among Central American countries

B.   examining regional differences in cuisine around the world

C.   studying the distribution of fauna and flora in North America

D.   deciding whether to build retail outlets based on local population

Answers:

A.   Incorrect. Studying international trade explores how the physical environment (differing countries) affects human behavior (trade agreements).

B.   Incorrect. Studying dishes from different regions relates to studying human behavior, consumption, and resource use in a geographical area.

C.   Correct. Studying only flora and fauna is physical geography; the geographer is not studying human interactions with or impact on the earth.

D.   Incorrect. Studying population and developing a commercial zone is an exercise in human geography and urban development.

WORLD HISTORY

ANCIENT (CLASSICAL) CIVILIZATIONS

Classical civilizations have had a lasting influence on human history. Elementary-level students should be aware of the ancient civilizations in the Fertile Crescent (including ancient Egypt), ancient Greece and Rome, and ancient China.

Around 2500 BCE (or possibly earlier) the **Sumerians** emerged in the Near East (eventually expanding into parts of Mesopotamia). Developing irrigation and advanced agriculture, they also developed **cuneiform**, the earliest known example of writing to use characters to form words. Sumer featured city-states, the potter's wheel, early astronomy and mathematics, early education, literary and artistic developments, and religious thought. Cuneiform also allowed advanced governance and administration.

Later, **Assyria** and **Babylonia** developed as important empires in the region. The Assyrians had based much of their culture on Sumer, contributing unique sculpture and jewelry, establishing military dominance, and playing an important role in regional trade. Babylonia also inherited elements of Sumerian civilization and developed them further. In the eighteenth century BCE, King Hammurabi in Babylonia had developed courts and an early codified rule of law—**the Code of Hammurabi**—which meted out justice on an equal basis: "an eye for an eye, a tooth for a tooth."

Meanwhile, development had been under way in the **Nile Valley** in ancient **Egypt**. The fertile land on the banks of the Nile River allowed the early Egyptians to develop settled communities thanks to agriculture and irrigation. Known for their pyramids, art, use of papyrus as paper, and pictorial writing (**hieroglyphs**), the ancient Egyptians emerged as early as 5000 BCE and were united under one monarch, or **pharaoh**.

Around 2500 BCE, Egypt's civilizational institutions, administrative structure, written language, art, and architecture were becoming well developed. In addition, the religious framework of ancient Egypt had become established, with a complex mythology of various gods. The ancient Egyptians also developed astronomy and the twenty-four-hour system of measuring time. It was during this period that the famous **pyramids** were erected at Giza; these structures were actually burial tombs for pharaohs. Major pharaohs included Hatshepsut, Thutmose III, Akhenaten, and Ramesses II.

Egyptian architecture also influenced many civilizations in the Western world. The use of columns in Pharaoh Hatshepsut's temple in Luxor is an example. It influenced Greek architectural design, which was copied by the Romans and many civilizations since.

Figure 3.3. Hatshepsut's Temple in Luxor

In **China**, the Shang Dynasty, the first known dynasty, emerged around the second millennium BCE and developed the earliest known Chinese writing, which helped unite Chinese-speaking people throughout the region. Like other early civilizations, the Shang Dynasty featured the use of bronze technology, horses, wheeled technology, walled cities, and other advances. Later, under the Zhou dynasty, China developed the concept of the **Mandate of Heaven**, in which the emperor had a divine mandate to rule, based on an understanding that land was divinely inherited. **Confucius** lived toward the end of this dynasty (c. 551 – 479 BCE). His teachings would be the basis for Confucianism, the foundational Chinese philosophy emphasizing harmony and respect for hierarchy.

The Qin dynasty (221 – 206 BCE) was characterized by a centralized administration, expanded infrastructure, standardization in weights and measures, writing, currency, and strict imperial control. The administrative bureaucracy was established by the first emperor, **Qin Shihuangdi**, and it was the foundation of Chinese administration until the twentieth century. In addition, the emperor constructed the **Great Wall of China**; his tomb is guarded by the famous **terracotta figurines**.

Figure 3.4. Great Wall of China

Ancient Greece was composed of small **city-states** like **Athens**, the first known **democracy**, and the military state **Sparta**. Around 460 BCE, Athens became a revolutionary democracy controlled by the poor and working classes. In fact, the term *democracy* comes from the Greek word *demokratia*—"people power." It was participatory rather than representative; officials were chosen by groups rather than elected. Athenian ideals have influenced politics and governance throughout history.

Athens was the strongest of the many small political bodies (in fact, the word *political* comes from the Greek word ***polis*** meaning "city-state" or "community") and much of Greece became unified under Athens following the Peloponnesian war between Athens and Sparta. It was during this period, the **Golden Age** of Greek civilization, that much of the Hellenic art, architecture, and philosophy known today emerged, including the **Parthenon** and other masterpieces of ancient Greek sculpture and architecture. **Socrates** began teaching philosophy, influencing later philosophers like **Plato** and **Aristotle**, establishing the basis for modern Western philosophical and political thought. Mathematical advances included the Pythagorean Theorem, Euclidean geometry, and the calculation of the circumference of the earth. Playwrights like **Sophocles** and **Euripides** emerged; their work influenced later Western literature. The Greeks practiced the Olympic Games to honor their gods, a diverse panoply of deities with a detailed mythology.

DID YOU KNOW?

Despite its status as a democracy, Athens was not fully democratic: women did not have a place in politics, and Athenians practiced slavery.

The Greeks established numerous colonies across the Black Sea, southern Italy, Sicily, and the eastern Mediterranean, spreading Greek culture throughout the Mediterranean world; it was eventually conquered by the rising Mediterranean power, Rome.

Originally a kingdom, Rome became a republic in 509 BCE, and as such, Romans elected lawmakers (senators) to the **Senate**. The Romans developed highly advanced infrastructure, including aqueducts and roads, some still in use today. Economically powerful, Rome began conquering areas around the Mediterranean with its increasingly powerful military, including Greece, expanding westward to North Africa. With conquest of territory and expansion of trade came increased slavery, and working-class Romans were displaced; at the same time, the wealthy ruling class became more powerful and corrupt.

The people, or *Populare*, wanted a more democratic republic. As the Senate weakened due to its own corruption, **Julius Caesar**, a popular military leader widely supported by the *Populare*, emerged. Forcing the corrupt Senate to give him control, Caesar began to transition Rome from a republic to what would become an empire. Caesar was assassinated in 44 BCE; however, in that short time he had been able to consolidate and centralize imperial control. His nephew Octavian eventually gained control of Rome in 27 BCE, taking the name **Augustus Caesar** and becoming the first Roman emperor.

At this time, Rome reached the height of its power, and the Mediterranean region enjoyed a period of stability known as the *Pax Romana*. Rome controlled the entire Mediterranean region, Europe, and much of the Middle East and North Africa. Latin literature flourished, as did art, architecture, philosophy, mathematics, science, and international trade throughout Rome and beyond into Asia and Africa.

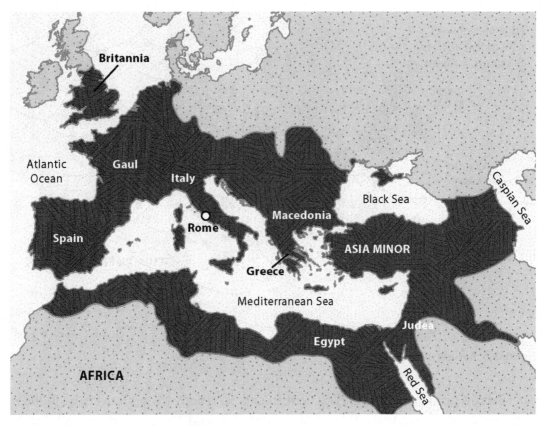

Figure 3.5. Roman Empire (200 AD)

TWENTIETH CENTURY

Elementary-level students should also be aware of major twentieth- and twenty-first-century developments such as the world wars, the Cold War, and globalization.

Instability and tensions in Europe culminated with the assassination of the Austro-Hungarian Archduke Franz Ferdinand in Sarajevo on June 28, 1914, igniting the **system of alliances** that had been in place among European powers.

Austria-Hungary declared war on Serbia, and Russia came to Serbia's aid. As an ally of Austria-Hungary as part of the **Triple Alliance**, Germany declared war on Russia. Russia's ally France prepared for war; as Germany traversed Belgium to invade France, Belgium pleaded for aid from other European countries, and so Britain declared war on Germany.

Germany had been emphasizing military growth since the consolidation and militarization of the empire under Bismarck in the mid-nineteenth century. Now, under **Kaiser Wilhelm II**, who sought expanded territories in Europe and overseas for Germany, Germany was a militarized state and important European power in its own right.

Figure 3.6. Europe during World War I

Britain's imperial power allowed it to call on troops from all over the globe—Indians, Canadians, Australians, South Africans, and New Zealanders all fought in Europe. France, too, imported colonial fighters from North Africa.

In Europe, the 1914 Battle of the Marne between Germany and French and British forces defending France resulted in **trench warfare** that would continue for years, marking the Western Front. At Gallipoli in 1915, Australian and New Zealander troops fought the Ottoman Empire, allies of Germany, near Istanbul. Later that year, a German submarine, or U-boat, sank the Lusitania, a passenger

ship in the Atlantic, killing many American civilians. In 1916, the Battle of Verdun, the longest battle of the war, ended in the failure of the Germans to defeat the French army. On July 1, 1916, the Battle of the Somme became part of an allied effort to repel Germany using artillery to end the stalemate on the Western Front; after four months, however, the front moved only 5 miles.

DID YOU KNOW?

The first international war to use industrialized weaponry, WWI was called "the Great War" because battle on such a scale had never before been seen.

Finally, in 1917, the United States discovered that Germany secretly proposed an alliance with Mexico to attack the US. This finally spurred US intervention in the war; despite Russian withdrawal after the Bolshevik Revolution in October 1917, Germany was forced to surrender in the face of invasion by the US-supported allies.

According to the Schlieffen Plan, Germany had planned to fight a war on two fronts against both Russia and France. However, Russian forces stretched the

German army too thin on the Eastern Front, while it became bogged down in trench warfare on the Western Front against the British, the French, and later the Americans.

Germany lost the war and was punished with the harsh **Treaty of Versailles**, which held it accountable for the entirety of the war. The Treaty brought economic hardship on the country by forcing it to pay **reparations**. German military failure and consequent economic collapse due to the Treaty of Versailles and later worldwide economic depression set the stage for the rise of Adolf Hitler.

The Treaty also created the **League of Nations**, an international organization designed to prevent future outbreaks of international war; however, it was largely toothless, especially because the powerful United States did not join. However, it would be the model for the stronger United Nations.

Instability between the First and Second World Wars resulted from the worldwide **Great Depression**. Growing nationalism in Germany, Italy, and Japan added to political uncertainty.

In Asia, Japan invaded Manchuria, northern China, in 1931. It already controlled Korea, Taiwan, and other Asian territories and began expanding its control farther into Southeast Asia and throughout the Pacific.

In Germany, Hitler's popular platform—to cancel the Treaty of Versailles— allowed him to rise. In 1934 he became the *Führer*, or leader, of Germany, and took total control of the country. He and the Nazis set into motion their agenda of racism and genocide against "non-Aryan" (non-Germanic) or "racially impure" people.

Jewish people were especially targeted. Throughout the 1930s, the Nazis began restricting Jewish rights. In 1938, an organized series of attacks on Jewish businesses, homes, and places of worship called **Kristallnacht** took place, so called because the windows of these places were smashed. In 1939, Jews were forced from their homes into **ghettoes**, isolated and overcrowded urban neighborhoods; in 1941, they were forced to wear **yellow stars** identifying them as Jewish.

Millions of Jewish people were sent to **concentration camps**, where many were murdered through forced labor and systematic gassing. At least six million European Jews were murdered by the Nazis in the **Holocaust**, as were Roma, Slavic people, homosexuals, disabled people, people of color, prisoners of war, communists, and others not considered "Aryan."

> **DID YOU KNOW?**
>
> Killing people based on their ethnicity is called *genocide*.

Meanwhile, Hitler sought to restore Germany's power and expand its reach by annexing and invading various countries. Germany's 1939 invasion of Poland is commonly considered the beginning of the **Second World War**. In 1940, Germany took Paris. The Battle of Britain began in July of that year; however Germany suffered its first defeat and was unable to take Britain.

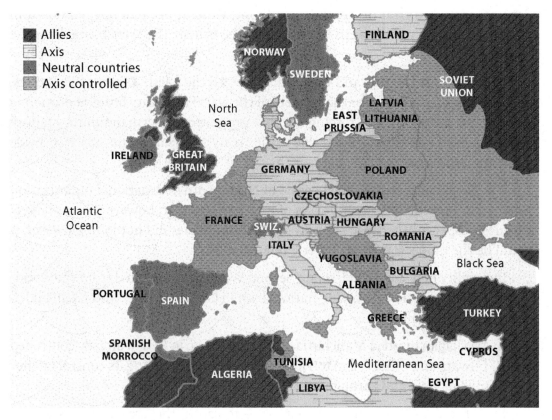

Figure 3.7. Europe during World War II

When Japan joined the **Axis** powers of Germany and Italy, the war officially spread to Asia, which was already in conflict. The **Chinese Civil War** was interrupted when Japan invaded China past Manchuria. In response, the Chinese factions joined forces against Japan; the communists became powerful. In June of 1941, Japan attacked the United States at **Pearl Harbor**. Consequently, the US joined the war in Europe and in the Pacific.

Back in Europe, having broken a promise made to the Soviet Union in 1939, Hitler invaded the USSR; however Germany was defeated at the Battle of Stalingrad, a turning point in the war. In 1944, the Allies invaded France on D-Day. While they liberated Paris in August, the costly Battle of the Bulge extended into 1945. Despite thousands of American casualties, Hitler's forces were pushed back. In the spring of 1945, the US crossed the Rhine while the USSR invaded Berlin; Hitler killed himself, and the Allies accepted German surrender.

The war in the Pacific would continue, however. Strategic battles were fought throughout the islands. **President Truman**, who had succeeded Roosevelt, elected to use the nuclear bomb on Japan to force its surrender rather than invade that country. In 1945, the war ended with Japanese surrender after the US bombed the Japanese cities Hiroshima and Nagasaki. That year in China, the Chinese Civil War recommenced; by 1949 the communists had emerged victorious.

Because of the widespread violence of the war and the millions of soldiers and civilians who died, especially those killed because of genocide, the **United Nations** was formed to prevent another world war. It was based on the League of Nations, and its mission is to champion human rights and uphold international security.

Allied forces took the lead in rebuilding efforts: the US occupied areas in East Asia and Germany, while the Soviet Union remained in Eastern Europe. The Allies had planned to rebuild Europe according to the Marshall Plan; however, the USSR occupied Eastern Europe. The **Cold War** had begun.

The US, Britain, and the USSR had originally agreed to divide Germany and to hold free elections in Eastern Europe, but by 1945, things had changed. The USSR felt betrayed by the US use of the nuclear bomb; likewise, the US and Britain felt betrayed by the Soviet Union, which had occupied Eastern Europe and prevented democratic elections in order to establish a buffer zone following its extraordinarily heavy casualties in WWII—around twenty million. An *iron curtain* had come down across Europe, dividing east from west.

The United States adopted a policy of containment, the idea that communism should be *contained*. Therefore, the United States became involved in the **Korean War** in 1950 and later the controversial **Vietnam War** throughout the 1960s and early 1970s.

Toward the end of the 1960s and into the 1970s, the Cold War began to thaw. The US and USSR signed a series of treaties to limit nuclear weapons. In 1972, President Richard Nixon visited China, establishing relations between the communist government and the United States.

QUICK REVIEW

Name three reasons for the eruption of the Cold War.

However, the climate would change again in the 1970s and 1980s. The **arms race** was underway. President Ronald Reagan pursued a militaristic policy, prioritizing weapons development with the goal of outspending the USSR on weapons technology.

In 1991, the Soviet Union fell thanks in part to reforms like *glasnost* and *perestroika* (or openness and transparency). After a coup overthrowing Premier Mikhail Gorbachev, the Soviet leader, the USSR was dissolved. A Soviet war in Afghanistan and military overspending in an effort to keep up with the United States had weakened the USSR to the point of collapse, and the Cold War ended.

GLOBALIZATION

Globalization is increasing economic, political, and cultural interdependence and interaction throughout the world. At its core, globalization is an economic trend; **multinational corporations (MNCs)** are the primary driving forces of globalization. However, globalization has significant cultural and political impacts as well. For example, the exportation of American fast food restaurants, like McDonald's (one example of an MNC), to other parts of the world reflects the capitalist drive to find new markets. Furthermore, the introduction of this type of food has a significant impact on one of the major distinguishing cultural traits of other countries—their cuisine.

Another example is language; English continues to spread throughout the world as the main language used in business and on the Internet. Spanish, French, Arabic, and Chinese are also widely spoken and used as second or third languages by millions of people in business, in pop culture, and to disseminate news. Looking at causes and events in history is another way to make **cross-cultural comparisons**. For example, students could analyze different holiday traditions from various countries.

In this era of globalization, international markets became increasingly open through free-trade agreements among countries, making doing international business easier. Technological advances like improvements in transportation and the Internet made international trade and communication faster, easier, and cheaper. Political cooperation like the formation of the European Union and other groups all make globalization possible.

The **European Union**, as it is known today, was formed in 1992 after the Cold War. Former communist countries became democratic societies and joined it; as of 2015, twenty-eight countries are members, with more on the path to membership. EU countries cooperate politically; many also share a common currency, the **euro**, and some EU countries even have open borders. In Africa, the **African Union**, similar to the EU, is a forum for African countries to organize and cooperate politically, militarily, and economically. The **G-20**, the world's twenty most important economic and political powers, includes many former colonies and non-European countries.

However, more open borders, reliable international transportation, and faster, easier worldwide communication brought risks, too. In the early twenty-first century, the United States was attacked by terrorists on **September 11, 2001**, resulting in thousands of civilian casualties. Consequently, the US launched a major land war in Afghanistan and another later in Iraq.

SAMPLE QUESTIONS

3) **Which of the following is an example of a cross-cultural comparison?**

   A. A chef studies variations in a recipe depending on the diner's preference for sweets.

   B. A Thai husband learns different holiday traditions from his wife, who is Chinese.

   C. Students compare the prices of groceries in different cities.

   D. A career coach helps clients determine their goals.

Answers:

A.   Incorrect. Personal preferences are not an example of culture.

B.   Correct. Reviewing different holiday celebrations exemplifies studying different cultures.

C.   Incorrect. Studying different prices is economic, not cultural, study.

D.   Incorrect. Determining career goals relates to personal preferences.

4)   **Which of the following happened to Jewish people under the Nazi regime?**

A.   Their homes and businesses were attacked and destroyed.

B.   They were forced to live in ghettoes, overcrowded neighborhoods with poor living conditions.

C.   They were sent to concentration camps and murdered.

D.   all of the above

Answers:

A.   Incorrect. While Jewish people suffered such attacks under the Nazis, they faced other consequences as well.

B.   Incorrect. Jewish people were indeed forced to live in ghettoes; however, they were persecuted in other ways and so there is a better answer choice here.

C.   Incorrect. Millions of Jews were sent to concentration camps, forced into slave labor, and murdered. However, there is a better answer choice here.

D.   Correct. Under the Nazis, Jewish people were forced to live in ghettoes; their businesses and homes were destroyed; and they suffered other persecution. Jews, communists, Roma, homosexuals, and others were also forced into slave labor in concentration camps, and millions were murdered.

UNITED STATES HISTORY

Elementary-level students should be aware of major Native American societies; reasons for colonization; the causes, events, and consequences of the American Revolution and its major figures; important developments like westward expansion, urbanization, and immigration; abolitionism, Southern Secession and reasons, events, and consequences of the Civil War; industrialization, the Great Depression, and the New Deal; the world wars and the Cold War; the Civil Rights Movement; and technology and the US today.

NATIVE AMERICAN SOCIETIES

Prior to European colonization, diverse Native American societies controlled the continent; they would later come into economic and diplomatic contact, and military conflict, with European colonizers and United States forces and settlers.

Major civilizations that would play an important and ongoing role in North American history included the **Iroquois** in the Northeast, known for longhouses and farming in the Three Sisters tradition; they consisted of a confederation of six tribes. The **Algonquin** were another important northeastern civilization; rivals of the Iroquois, the Algonquin were important in the fur trade. Algonquin languages were spoken throughout the Great Lakes region.

> **DID YOU KNOW?**
>
> In the Three Sisters tradition, farmers grow maize, beans, and squash together; these plants naturally complement each other by providing mutual protection from pests and the elements. They also enrich the soil.

Farther west, the **Shawnee** were an Algonquin-speaking people based in the Ohio Valley; however their presence extended as far south and east as the present-day Carolinas and Georgia. While socially organized under a matrilineal system, the Shawnee had male kings and only men could inherit property. Also matrilineal and Algonquin-speaking, the **Lenape** were considered by the Shawnee to be their "grandfathers" and thus accorded respect. Another Algonquin-speaking tribe, the **Kickapoo** were originally from the Great Lakes region and moved west. The Algonquin-speaking **Miami** moved from Wisconsin to the Ohio Valley region, forming settled societies and farming maize. They too took part in the fur trade as it developed during European colonial times. These tribes later formed the Northwest Confederacy to fight US westward expansion.

In the South, major tribes included the **Creek**, **Chickasaw**, and **Choctaw**, the descendants of the **Mississippi Mound Builders** or Mississippian cultures, societies which built mounds from around 2100 to 1800 years ago as burial tombs or the bases for temples. Sharing similar languages, all the tribes would later participate in an alliance—the Muscogee Confederacy—to engage the United States. The Chickasaw and Choctaw were matrilineal; the former also engaged in Three Sisters agriculture like the Iroquois.

Another major southern tribe, the **Cherokee** spoke (and speak) a language of the Iroquoian family. It is thought that they migrated south to their homeland in present-day Georgia sometime long before European contact, where they remained until they were forcibly removed in 1832. Organized into seven clans, the Cherokee were also hunters and farmers like other tribes in the region and would later come into contact—and conflict—with European colonizers and the United States of America.

The nomadic tribes of the Great Plains like the **Sioux**, **Cheyenne**, **Apache**, **Comanche**, and **Arapaho** lived farther west. These tribes depended on the **buffalo**

Figure 3.8. Mississippi Mounds

for food and materials to create clothing, tools, and domestic items; therefore they followed the herds. While widely known for their equestrian skill, horses were introduced by Europeans and so Native American tribes living on the Great Plains did not access them until after European contact. Horseback riding facilitated the hunt; previously, hunters surrounded buffalo or frightened them off of cliffs.

In the Southwest, the **Navajo** controlled territory in present-day Arizona, New Mexico, and Utah. Pastoralists, they had a less hierarchical structure than other Native American societies. The Navajo were descendants of the **Ancestral Pueblo** or **Anasazi** (pictured on the following page), who practiced Three Sisters agriculture and stone construction, building cliff dwellings.

In the Pacific Northwest, Native American peoples depended on fishing, using canoes. Totem poles depicted histories. The **Coast Salish**, whose language was widely spoken throughout the region, dominated the Puget Sound and Olympic Peninsula area. Farther south, the **Chinook** controlled the coast at the Columbia River.

Ultimately, through both violent conflict and political means, Native American civilizations lost control of most of their territories and were forced onto reservations by the United States. Negotiations continue today over rights to land and opportunities and reparations for past injustices.

Figure 3.9. Ancestral Pueblo Cliff Palace at Mesa Verde

THE AMERICAN REVOLUTION

European powers had begun colonizing North America in the sixteenth century to access fur and agricultural resources; by the eighteenth century, Britain controlled most of the east coast of the continent, including the Thirteen Colonies, which became the original United States. France and Britain battled for control of northeastern North America, and following the **French and Indian War**, Great Britain consolidated its control over much of the continent.

Despite British victory in the French and Indian War, it had gone greatly into debt. Furthermore, there were concerns that the colonies required a stronger military presence following Native American attacks and uprisings like **Pontiac's Rebellion** in 1763. Consequently, **King George III** signed the **Proclamation of 1763**, an agreement not to settle land west of the Appalachians, in an effort to make peace; however much settlement continued in practice.

King George III enforced heavy taxes and restrictive acts in the colonies to generate income for the Crown and eventually to punish disobedience. England expanded the **Molasses Act** of 1733, passing the **Sugar Act** in 1764 to raise revenue by taxing sugar and molasses, which were widely consumed in the colonies. In 1765, Britain enforced the **Quartering Act**, forcing colonists to provide shelter to British troops stationed in the region.

The 1765 **Stamp Act**, the first direct tax on the colonists, triggered more tensions. Any document required a costly stamp, the revenue reverting to the British government. Colonists felt the tax violated their rights, given that they did not have direct representation in British Parliament. As a result, they began boycotting British goods and engaging in violent protest. **Samuel Adams** led the **Sons and Daughters of Liberty** in violent acts against tax collectors and stirred up rebellion with his **Committees of Correspondence**, which distributed anti-British propaganda.

Protests against the Quartering Act in Boston led to the **Boston Massacre** in 1770, when British troops fired on a crowd of protestors. By 1773, in a climate of continued unrest driven by the Committees of Correspondence, colonists protested the latest taxes on tea levied by the **Tea Act** in the famous **Boston Tea Party** by dressing as Native Americans and tossing tea off a ship in Boston Harbor. In response, the government passed the **Intolerable Acts**, closing Boston Harbor and bringing Massachusetts back under direct royal control.

In response to the Intolerable Acts, colonial leaders met in Philadelphia at the **First Continental Congress** in 1774 and presented colonial concerns to the king, who ignored them. However, violent conflict began in 1775 at **Lexington and Concord**, when American militiamen (**minutemen**) gathered to resist British efforts to seize weapons and arrest rebels in Concord. On June 17, 1775, the Americans fought the British at the **Battle of Bunker Hill**; despite American losses, the number of casualties the rebels inflicted caused the king to declare that the colonies were in rebellion. Troops were deployed to the colonies; the Siege of Boston began.

DID YOU KNOW?

King George III also hired Hessian mercenaries from Germany to supplement British troops; adding foreign fighters only increased resentment in the colonies and created a stronger sense of independence from Britain.

In May 1775, the **Second Continental Congress** met at Philadelphia to debate the way forward. Debate among leaders like Benjamin Franklin, John Adams, Thomas Jefferson, and James Madison centered between the wisdom of continued efforts at compromise and negotiations, and declaring independence. Again, the king ignored them. By the summer of 1776, the Continental Congress agreed on the need to break from Britain; on July 4, 1776 it declared the independence of the United States of America and issued the **Declaration of Independence**.

When in the Course of human events, it becomes necessary for one people to dissolve the political bands which have connected them with another, and to assume among the powers of the earth, the separate and equal station to which the Laws of Nature and of Nature's God entitle them, a decent respect to the opinions of mankind requires that they should declare the causes which impel them to the separation.

We hold these truths to be self-evident, that all men are created equal, that they are endowed by their Creator with certain unalienable Rights, that among these are Life, Liberty and the pursuit of Happiness. That to secure these rights, Governments are instituted among Men, deriving their just powers from the consent of the governed, that whenever any Form of Government becomes destructive of these ends, it is the Right of the People to alter or to abolish it, and to institute new Government, laying its foundation on such principles and organizing its powers in such form, as to them shall seem most likely to effect their Safety and Happiness. Prudence, indeed, will dictate that Governments long established should not be changed for light and transient causes; and accordingly all experience hath shewn, that mankind are more disposed to suffer, while evils are sufferable, than to right themselves by abolishing the forms to which they are accustomed. But when a long train of abuses and usurpations, pursuing invariably the same Object evinces a design to reduce them under absolute Despotism, it is their right, it is their duty, to throw off such Government, and to provide new Guards for their future security.--Such has been the patient sufferance of these Colonies; and such is now the necessity which constrains them to alter their former Systems of Government. The history of the present King of Great Britain is a history of repeated injuries and usurpations, all having in direct object the establishment of an absolute Tyranny over these States. To prove this, let Facts be submitted to a candid world.

Preamble to the Declaration of Independence

Americans were still divided over independence; **Patriots** favored independence while those still loyal to Britain were known as **Tories**. **George Washington** had been appointed head of the Continental Army and led a largely unpaid and unprofessional army; despite early losses, Washington gained ground due to strong leadership, superior knowledge of the land, and support from France.

Initially, the British seemed to have many advantages in the war, including more resources and troops. Britain won the **Battle of Brooklyn** (Battle of Long Island) in August 1776 and captured New York City. The tide turned in 1777 at **Valley Forge**, when Washington and his army survived the bitterly cold winter and managed to overcome British military forces.

A victory at **Saratoga** led the French to help the rebels in 1778. Now fighting shifted south. Britain captured Georgia and Charleston, South Carolina; however, British forces could not adequately control the country as they proceeded to Yorktown, Virginia in 1781. At the **Battle of Yorktown**, British forces were defeated by the Continental Army with support from France and were forced to surrender.

Meanwhile, the British people did not favor the war and voted the Tories out of Parliament; the incoming Whig party sought to end the war. After troops fought for two more years, the **Treaty of Paris** ended the revolution in September 1783. In 1787, the first draft of the Constitution was written, and George Washington became the first president of the United States two years later. The American Revolution would go on to inspire revolutions around the world.

Manifest Destiny

In the nineteenth century, the idea of **Manifest Destiny**, or the sense that it was the fate of the United States to expand westward and settle the continent, pervaded. In 1803 President Thomas Jefferson oversaw the **Louisiana Purchase**, which nearly doubled the size of the United States. **Meriwether Lewis** and **William Clark** were dispatched to explore the western frontier of the territory: Jefferson hoped to find an all-water route to the Pacific Ocean (via the Missouri River). While this route did not exist, Lewis and Clark returned with a deeper knowledge of the territory the US had come to control.

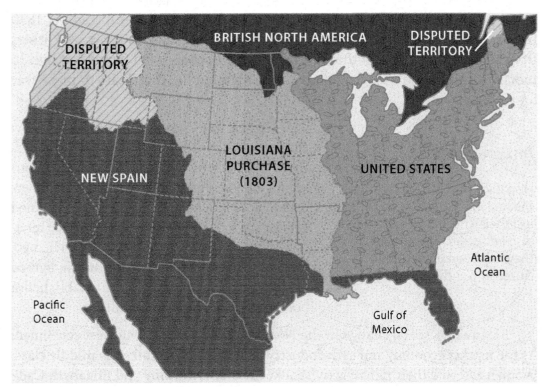

Figure 3.10. Louisiana Purchase

Later, British provocation at sea and in the northwest led to the **War of 1812** between the United States and Britain, which was allied with the Shawnee-led Northwest Confederacy. Growing nationalism in the United States pressured Madison into pushing for war; Congress declared war under President Madison with the intent to defend the United States, end unfair trade practices and poor treatment of Americans on the high seas, and penetrate British Canada. Despite the Confederacy's alliance with Britain, the United States prevailed.

The war resulted in no real gains or losses for either the Americans or the British, yet at the war's end, the United States had successfully defended itself as a country and reaffirmed its independence. Patriotism ran high, strengthening the idea of Manifest Destiny. In 1819, following the Seminole War the United States purchased Florida from Spain in the **Adams-Onis Treaty** (conflict with the Seminole would continue). The **Monroe Doctrine**, President James Monroe's policy that the Western Hemisphere was "closed" to any further European colonization or exploration, asserted US power in the region.

With westward expansion came questions over the expansion of slavery. In 1820, the **Missouri Compromise** allowed Missouri to join the union as a slave state but provided that any other states north of the thirty-sixth parallel (36⁰30') would be free. However, more tension and compromises over the nature of slavery in the West were to come.

With continental expansion came more conflict with Native Americans. Despite legal resistance by the Cherokee, President Andrew Jackson enforced the 1830 **Indian Removal Act**, forcing Cherokee, Creek, Chickasaw, Choctaw, and others from their lands in the Southeast. Thousands of people were forced to travel to Indian Territory (today, Oklahoma) on the infamous **Trail of Tears** to make way for white settlers.

> **DID YOU KNOW?**
>
> Hispanics who had lived in the region under Mexico lost their land and faced discrimination, even though they had been promised US citizenship and equal rights.

The United States continued to grow throughout the nineteenth century. In 1845, the United States annexed Texas, which contributed to the outbreak of the Mexican-American War the next year. As a result, it gained California and the Utah and New Mexico territories in the 1848 Treaty of Guadalupe Hidalgo. In 1846, the United States and Britain agreed on the Oregon Treaty, which established a border at the forty-ninth parallel.

Meanwhile, social change in the Northeast and growing Midwest continued. As the market economy and early industry developed, so did an early **middle class**. Women asserted their rights: activists like **Susan B. Anthony** and **Elizabeth Cady Stanton** worked for women's suffrage, culminating in the 1848 **Seneca Falls Convention**.

The country was increasingly divided over slavery; **sectionalism** grew, strengthening disunity between the North and the South. Reform movements continued to include **abolitionism**, the ending of slavery. The former slave **Frederick Douglass** advocated abolition. An activist leader and writer, Douglass publicized the movement along with the American Anti-Slavery Society and publications like Harriet Beecher Stowe's *Uncle Tom's Cabin*. He and other activists like **Harriet Tubman** helped free slaves using the **Underground Railroad**. An estimated 100,000 slaves escaped the South between 1810 and 1850 through a system of safe houses, even though these actions violated state laws. The radical abolitionist **John Brown** led violent protests against slavery. Abolitionism became a key social and political issue in the mid-nineteenth century; slavery was the main cause of the **Civil War**.

> **DID YOU KNOW?**
>
> *Sectionalism* is when a segment of a group is more loyal to itself than to the rest of the group. It can apply to regions of countries (such as the South of the United States before the Civil War).

Antislavery factions in Congress had attempted to halt the extension of slavery to the new territories obtained from Mexico, but they were unsuccessful; in the

Compromise of 1850, Congress decided that the voters in some new territories would be allowed to decide whether slavery should be legal or determined by popular sovereignty. In 1854, Congress passed the Kansas-Nebraska Act, effectively repealing the Missouri Compromise, allowing those territories to decide slavery by popular sovereignty as well. In response, the new **Republican Party** emerged. One of its members, **Abraham Lincoln**, was elected president in 1860 on an antislavery platform.

CIVIL WAR

Following Lincoln's election, South Carolina immediately seceded, followed by Mississippi, Alabama, Florida, Louisiana, Georgia, and Texas. They formed the Confederate States of America, or the **Confederacy**, on February 1, 1861, under the leadership of **Jefferson Davis**, a senator from Mississippi.

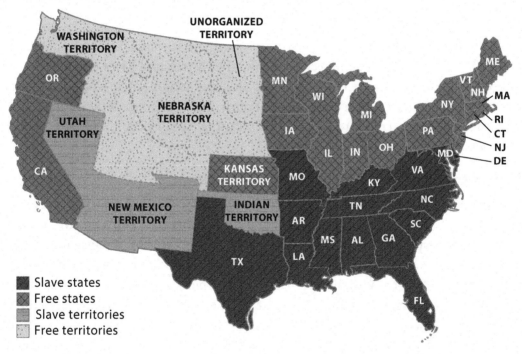

Figure 3.11. Civil War

Shortly after the South's secession, Confederate forces attacked Union troops in Sumter, South Carolina; the **Battle of Fort Sumter** sparked the Civil War. As a result, Virginia, Tennessee, North Carolina, and Arkansas seceded and joined the Confederacy. West Virginia was formed when the western part of Virginia refused to join the Confederacy.

Both sides believed the conflict would be short-lived; however, after the First Battle of Bull Run when the Union failed to route the Confederacy, it became clear that the war would not end quickly. Realizing how difficult it would be to defeat the Confederacy, the Union developed the **Anaconda Plan**, a plan to "squeeze" the Confederacy, including a naval blockade and taking control of the Mississippi River.

Since the South depended on international trade in cotton for much of its income, a naval blockade would have serious economic ramifications for the Confederacy.

However, the Second Battle of Bull Run was a tactical Confederate victory led by General Robert E. Lee and Stonewall Jackson. The Union army remained intact, but the loss was a heavy blow to morale. The Battle of Antietam was the first battle to be fought on Union soil. Union General George B. McClellan halted General Lee's invasion of Maryland but failed to defeat Confederate forces. Undaunted, on January 1, 1863, President Lincoln decreed the end of slavery in the rebel states with the **Emancipation Proclamation**. The Battle of Gettysburg was a major Union victory. It was the bloodiest battle in American history up to this point; the Confederate army would not recover.

DID YOU KNOW?

President Lincoln later delivered the Gettysburg Address onsite, in which he framed the Civil War as a battle for human rights and equality.

Meanwhile, following the Siege of Vicksburg, Mississippi, Union forces led by General Ulysses S. Grant gained control over the Mississippi River, completing the Anaconda Plan. The Battle of Atlanta was the final major battle of the Civil War; victorious, the Union proceeded into the South, and the Confederacy fell. In April 1865, General Lee surrendered to General Grant at Appomattox, Virginia, and the war ended.

RECONSTRUCTION AND INDUSTRIALIZATION

Reconstruction after the war would bring huge changes in the South and redefine how blacks fit into American society. The South was in economic ruins; many Southerners, especially newly freed slaves and other African Americans, sought better economic opportunities by moving to the North. Congress passed the Civil Rights Act in 1866 recognizing the rights of former slaves as US citizens; it also passed the Reconstruction Acts the next year, enforcing military occupation of the South. These acts laid out the process for readmission to the Union: among other requirements, states had to ratify the Thirteenth, Fourteenth, and Fifteenth Amendments. These made slavery illegal, recognized equal rights, and permitted African American males to vote, respectively.

Still, agriculture and infrastructure were ruined, and many were bitter over Northern occupation and involvement. Even though the South was forced to accept the end of slavery, Southern states created 'black codes' which restricted black Americans' rights. African Americans faced ongoing discrimination and violence in the South, including segregation and threats from hate groups.

The end of the Civil War also brought on an increase in **industrialization**. A British phenomenon, industrialization made its way to the United States. Machines replaced hand labor as the main way of manufacturing, exponentially increasing production capacities. Later in the nineteenth century, the US began developing heavy industry.

The **assembly line** developed by Henry Ford enabled **mass production**. Factors that contributed to this boom included the invention of new products (e.g., the automobile, the telephone, and the electric light), improvement of production methods, an abundance of natural resources and infrastructure (railways opened the West further and connected factories and markets to raw materials), and banking (more people wanted to invest in booming businesses, and banks were financing them).

New cities and towns became larger as people started to live and work in urban areas, attracted by employment opportunities. Unfortunately, lack of planning for this phenomenon—**urbanization**—led to inadequate sanitation (which contributed to cholera and typhoid epidemics), pollution, and crime. However, overall, the United States' economy was growing, the middle class was becoming larger, and industry and technology were developing.

> DID YOU KNOW?
>
> Social unrest was a consequence of urbanization; the poor living conditions faced by workers lead to strikes and riots.

WORLD WAR AND COLD WAR

While the United States became increasingly prosperous and stable, Europe was becoming increasingly unstable. Americans were divided over whether the US should intervene in international matters. This debate became more pronounced with the outbreak of **World War I** in Europe.

Inflammatory events like German submarine warfare (*U-boats*) in the Atlantic Ocean, the sinking of the *Lusitania*, which resulted in many American civilian deaths, the embarrassing Zimmerman Telegram (in which Germany promised to help Mexico in an attack on the US), and growing American nationalism, or pride in and identification with one's country, triggered US intervention in the war. On December 7, 1917, the US declared war. With victory in 1918, the US had proven itself a superior military and industrial power. Interventionist President **Woodrow Wilson** played an important role in negotiating the peace; his Fourteen Points laid out an idealistic international vision, including an international security organization.

However, European powers negotiated and won the harsh **Treaty of Versailles**, which placed the blame for the war entirely on Germany and demanded crippling reparations from it, one contributing factor to **World War II** later in the twentieth century. The League of Nations, a collective security organization, was formed, but a divided US Congress refused to ratify the Treaty, so the US did not join it. Consequently the League was weak and largely ineffective.

After the war ended, the US suffered from a slight recession. It wasn't until 1929 that the stock market crashed, which triggered the **Great Depression**. Millions of investors saw their fortunes disappear and consumer spending and investing continued to drop, which led to large unemployment rates. Approximately half the banks closed, and upward of 15 million people were unemployed.

Franklin Delano Roosevelt was elected to the presidency in 1932. FDR offered Americans a **New Deal**: a plan to bring the country out of the Depression. During the **First Hundred Days** of FDR's administration, he stabilized the economy through a series of emergency acts for the immediate repair of the banking system. FDR did not only address economic issues; a number of acts provided long-term relief to the poor and unemployed. The New Deal especially generated jobs through programs that developed infrastructure and provided construction jobs for the unemployed. The economy truly rebounded during the Second World War.

FDR was increasingly concerned about the rise of fascism in Europe, seeing it as a global threat. Thus the United States provided support to Great Britain before entering the war. FDR spoke publicly about the **Four Freedoms**: freedom of speech, freedom of religion, freedom from want, and freedom from fear.

However after the Japanese attack on **Pearl Harbor** on December 7, 1941, the US entered the war. While directly attacked by Japan, which was allied with the fascist Axis powers of Italy and Germany, the United States focused first on the European theater. On June 6, 1944, or **D-Day**, the US led the invasion of Normandy, invading Europe. After months of fighting, following the deadly and drawn-out Battle of the Bulge, the Allies were able to enter Germany and end the war in Europe.

The United States was then able to focus more effectively on the war in the Pacific. President **Harry Truman** had taken power following FDR's death in 1945. Rather than force a US invasion of Japan, which would have resulted in huge numbers of casualties, he authorized the bombing of Hiroshima and Nagasaki in Japan, the only times that **nuclear weapons** have been used in conflict. The war ended with Japanese surrender on September 2, 1945.

DID YOU KNOW?

Japanese Americans faced oppression and discrimination at home simply due to their race and were forced to live in internment camps.

With most of Europe destroyed, the victorious US and the Soviet Union emerged as the two global **superpowers**. Although the Soviet Union and the United States were allies during the war, the relationship between them grew tense as the war ended. When the Soviet Union occupied Eastern European countries, suppressing democracy there, the **Cold War** effectively began.

During the Cold War, the US and the USSR never came into direct conflict; rather, there were alternating periods of tension and relaxed relations, or détente. During the **Cuban Missile Crisis** (1962), Soviet missiles were discovered in Cuba, and military crisis was narrowly averted thanks to the diplomacy of the Soviet leader Nikita Khrushchev and the popular US president John F. Kennedy. The two countries also supported opposing sides in wars throughout the world—the Korean

War, the **Vietnam War**, the Soviet-Afghan War, and many more. Finally, the two superpowers both possessed **nuclear weapons**; thankfully, both sides developed a series of agreements placing limitations on those weapons, and they were never used.

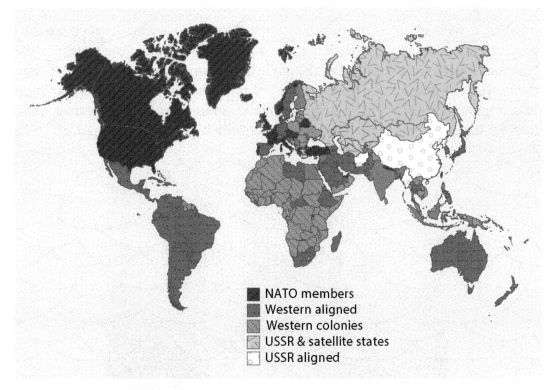

Figure 3.12. The Cold War (1953)

The Cold War extended to **space exploration**, also known as the space race. The Soviets launched the first artificial satellite on October 4, 1957, known as Sputnik. The US launched its own satellite called Explorer 1 the following year. While the US created the National Aeronautics and Space Administration (NASA) to further space exploration, on April 1961 the Soviets launched the first person, Yuri Gargarin, into space. However, the American Neil Armstrong was the first person to set foot on the moon during NASA's Apollo 11 mission on July 20, 1969.

The Cold War ended with the collapse of the Soviet Union in 1991; without two superpowers, the world entered a period of globalization (see the section on world history for details).

Civil Rights

During the 1960s, the US experienced social and political change. The **Civil Rights Movement**, led by activists like the **Rev. Dr. Martin Luther King, Jr.** and **Malcolm X**, fought for African American rights in the South, including the abolition of segregation, and also for better living standards for blacks in northern cities. In Montgomery, Alabama, **Rosa Parks**, an African American woman, was arrested for refusing to give up her seat to a white man on a bus. Buses were segregated at the time, and leaders including Dr. King organized the Montgomery Bus Boycott to challenge segregation; the effort was ultimately successful. Building on their success, civil rights activists led peaceful protests and boycotts to protest segregation at lunch counters, in stores, at public pools, and in other public places.

The movement grew to include voter registration campaigns supported by students and other activists (both black and white) from around the country—the **Freedom Riders**, so-called because they rode buses from around the country to join the movement in the Deep South. Civil rights workers organized the March on Washington in 1963, when Dr. King delivered his famous *I Have a Dream* speech. In 1964, Congress passed the Civil Rights Act, which outlawed segregation.

Figure 3.13. March on Washington

The Civil Rights Movement extended beyond the Deep South. **Cesar Chavez** founded the **United Farm Workers**, which organized Hispanic migrant farm workers in California and the Southwest who faced racial discrimination, poor treatment, and low pay. The UFW used boycotts and nonviolent tactics similar to those used by civil rights activists in the South. The **American Indian Movement (AIM)** brought attention to injustices and discrimination suffered by Native Americans nationwide. **Feminist** activists fought for fairer treatment of women in the workplace and for women's reproductive rights. Finally, activists in New York and San Francisco began openly fighting for the civil rights of gays and lesbians.

THE TWENTY-FIRST CENTURY

By the end of the twentieth century, the United States had established itself as the dominant global economic, military, and political power. It had established military bases and a military presence worldwide, in Europe, Asia, the Pacific, and the Middle East. However, its global power did not prevent conflict. After the terrorist attacks on September 11, 2001, the United States began a war in Afghanistan, and later one in Iraq.

Still, the US dominated global trade: American corporations established themselves globally. American culture was widely popular: since the early twentieth century, American pop culture like music, movies, television shows, and fashion was enjoyed by millions of people around the world. Domestically, society became increasingly liberal. In 2008, the country elected the first African American president, **Barack Obama**. Technology like the **Internet** facilitated national and global communication, media, and business; minority groups like the LGBT community engaged in more advocacy; and environmental issues became more visible. The country continues to evolve.

SAMPLE QUESTIONS

5)   **How did Martin Luther King and other activists achieve civil rights for black Americans?**

    A.   through violent uprisings

    B.   using nonviolence

    C.   with the help of the Soviet Union

    D.   by lobbying Congress only

Answers:

    A.   Incorrect. For the most part, civil rights activists took a nonviolent approach in their work.

    B.   Correct. Nonviolence was a defining characteristic of the mainstream Civil Rights Movement.

    C.   Incorrect. The Civil Rights Movement was a domestic phenomenon.

    D.   Incorrect. Civil rights activists did eventually succeed in getting civil rights legislation passed by working with the government; however, the movement was based in grassroots activism and protest.

6) **Controversy over the Kansas-Nebraska Act of 1854 illustrated which of the following?**

A. immigration

B. Reconstruction

C. westward expansion

D. sectionalism

Answers:

A. Incorrect. The Kansas-Nebraska Act did not address population movements into the country from overseas.

B. Incorrect. Reconstruction happened when the Civil War was over in 1865.

C. Incorrect. The United States had already controlled this territory since the Louisiana Purchase.

D. Correct. The Kansas-Nebraska Act further divided the nation over slavery.

United States Government, Civics, and Democracy

Students should understand and be aware of the purpose of US government and its major principles; the three branches of government; federalism; major speeches and key documents; and the rights and responsibilities of US citizens.

In 1776, colonial leaders including John Adams and Thomas Jefferson began drafting a formal statement of the colonies' intentions for independence from the British government. The Continental Congress adopted the **Declaration of Independence** on the fourth of July of that year, now celebrated as Independence Day in the United States. According to the document, independence from Britain was necessary: it outlined grievances against the British Crown, and it asserted that "all men are created equal; that they are endowed by their Creator with certain unalienable rights; that among these are Life, Liberty and the pursuit of Happiness."

Dominating American political thought since the American Revolution, **republicanism** stresses liberties and rights as central values, opposes corruption, rejects inherited political power, and encourages citizens to be civic minded and independent. It is based on **popular sovereignty**, that is, the concept that the people are the source of political power. These ideas helped to form not only the Declaration of Independence but also the Constitution.

The colonies had broken away from Britain because of what they viewed as an oppressive, overbearing central government. As a result, the first government they created, whose framework was called the **Articles of Confederation**, was an intentionally weak, democratic government. Called a "firm league of friendship," it was designed to create a loose confederation between the colonies (now states) while allowing them to retain much of their individual sovereignty.

As a result, the Articles established a weak government with extremely limited authority: it did not have the power to levy taxes or raise an army. The legislature was intentionally and clearly subordinate to the states. Representatives were selected and paid by state legislatures.

It quickly became clear that this government was too weak to be effective, and by 1787, the new government of the United States was already in crisis. Without the power to levy taxes, the federal government had no way to alleviate its debt burden from the war. In addition, without an organizing authority, states began issuing their own currencies and crafting their own, competing trade agreements with foreign nations, halting trade and sending inflation through the roof. Without a national judicial system, there was no mechanism to solve the inevitable economic disputes. Furthermore, there were uprisings in the country.

A convention of the states was called to address problems in the young United States. At the **Constitutional Convention** in 1787, a decision was made to completely throw out the old Articles and write a new governing document from scratch.

The states did not want a central government that was so strong that it would oppress the states or the people, so they decided to prevent the concentration of power by dividing it. **Separation of powers** limited the powers within the federal government, dividing power among three branches: the executive, the legislative, and the judicial. In addition, each branch was given powers that would limit the power of the other branches in a system called **checks and balances**.

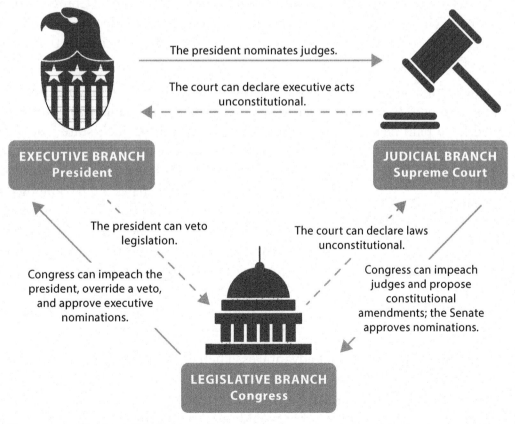

Figure 3.14. Checks and Balances

The executive branch—via the role of president—has the power to veto (reject) laws passed by the legislature. The legislative branch, consisting of Congress, can override the president's veto (with a two-thirds vote) and pass the law anyway. Finally, the judicial branch, consisting of the Supreme Court and other courts, can determine the constitutionality of laws (**judicial review**).

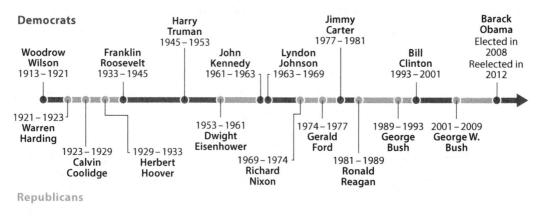

Figure 3.15. Presidential Timeline

At the writing of the Constitution, the branch of the federal government endowed with the most power was the legislative branch, which makes laws. Simply called **Congress**, this branch is composed of a bicameral legislature (two houses). While this structure was not originally adopted under the Articles of Confederation, the framers chose it when reorganizing the government, mainly due to a dispute at the convention over the structure of the legislative body—specifically the voting power of each state.

Small states advocated equal representation, with each state having the same number of representatives, each with one vote. However, the more populous states argued for a plan based on **proportional representation**. Each state would be assigned a number of representatives based on its population (enslaved people deprived of their rights would even be counted among the population, benefiting those states with large slave populations). In the end, the **Great Compromise** was reached. There would be two houses: the **House of Representatives** (the lower house) would have proportional representation, and the **Senate** (the upper house) would have equal representation.

> **DID YOU KNOW?**
>
> According to the Three-Fifths Compromise, enslaved persons were counted as three-fifths of a person in order to determine the population of a state. Slaves could not vote at all.

This system had two other advantages. The House of Representatives would also be directly elected by the people, and the Senate by the state legislatures. This supported the federal structure of the government: one house would serve the needs of the people directly, and the other would serve the needs of the states. Also, it curbed federal power by fragmenting it and slowing down the legislative process. Today, senators are also directly elected by the people.

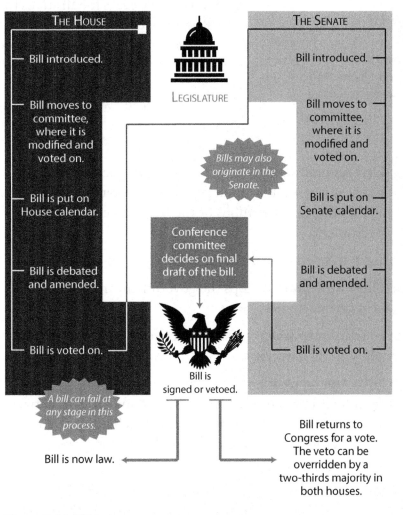

Figure 3.16. Bill to Law

Under the Constitution, the federal government is charged with matters that concern the population at large, such as managing federal lands, coining money, and maintaining an army and navy. It also handles conflicts between the states via the federal judiciary and by regulating interstate trade. Matters of regional or local concern are handled by state or local governments. This relationship is best codified in the Tenth Amendment, which states that any powers not explicitly given to the federal government are reserved for the states. The written Constitution can only be amended by a super majority.

State governments are generally modeled after these three branches, with the executive branch headed by the governor, the legislative branch headed by elected representatives, and the judicial branch headed by the state supreme court. **Local governments** have elected officials and generally follow charters that state constitutions have adopted. As they do with the federal government, the people vote for their state and local government representatives.

It took three years for all states to ratify the Constitution, with Rhode Island being the last to ratify on May 29, 1790. Much of the debate was over the lack of guarantees of basic civil rights in the Constitution. As a solution, James Madison in 1789 introduced twelve amendments to the Constitution. Ten of these twelve are known as the Bill of Rights.

The First Amendment protects **freedom of speech**. Congress may not pass laws that prohibit people from exercising freedom of religion, the press, assembly, or the right to petition against the government.

The Second Amendment allows citizens to bear arms.

The Third Amendment stops the government from quartering troops in private homes.

The Fourth Amendment protects citizens from searches and seizures without a warrant.

The Fifth Amendment ensures that citizens cannot be punished or subject to criminal prosecution without due process. Citizens also have the power of eminent domain, which means that private property cannot be seized for public use without proper compensation.

The Sixth Amendment gives citizens a right to a fair and fast trial by jury, the right to know the crimes for which they are charged, and the right to confront witnesses. Citizens also have the right to legal representation and to gather testimonies from witnesses.

The Seventh Amendment allows civil cases to be tried by jury (in the Articles of Confederation, only criminal trials could be tried by jury).

The Eighth Amendment disallows excessive bail or fines; it also prohibits cruel and unusual punishment.

The Ninth Amendment gives all rights not specifically enumerated in the Constitution to the people; it provides that the list of rights is not exhaustive.

The Tenth Amendment provides that all other powers not provided to the federal government in the Constitution belong to the states.

In the **Gettysburg Address**, Abraham Lincoln referred to the Constitution and the Declaration of Independence, asserting that the Civil War was a test of the survival of the Union as established in 1776. Declaring that the people must ensure that the "government of the people, by the people, for the people, shall not perish from the earth," he claimed that the Declaration of Independence was the ultimate expression of the original democratic intentions for the United States. Using the founding document as a basis for his speech, he pointed out that the Civil War was a "new birth of freedom," bringing equality to US citizens.

With citizenship comes responsibility. Today, US citizens maintain their government by **voting** for public officials at the local, state, and national levels. They also must pay **taxes** in order to provide the revenue the government requires to carry out its functions. The federal, state, and local governments all levy taxes of different kinds: income taxes, sales taxes, property taxes, and others. This money supports everything from installing stop signs to maintaining military aircraft.

US citizens are free to join **civic groups** that lobby government for legislation that works in their interest or that carry out public service in their communities. Some of these groups include the ACLU, which defends individual liberties, the NAACP, which works for African American rights, and the AARP, which supports the interests of the elderly. Citizens can also join groups that carry out **community service** such as the Boy Scouts and the Girl Scouts, or they may do such work through their church, mosque, synagogue, or other place of worship. Some students may already be doing community service themselves.

> **DID YOU KNOW?**
>
> Remind students that if they have purchased items, they have already likely paid taxes themselves.

SAMPLE QUESTIONS

7) **Which of the following is NOT one of the amendments in the Bill of Rights?**

   A. Citizens have the right to bear arms.

   B. The Senate must have equal representation.

   C. Citizens have the power of eminent domain.

   D. The government cannot quarter troops in private homes.

Answers:

   A. Incorrect. According to the Second Amendment, US citizens have the right to bear arms.

   B. **Correct.** The Bill of Rights does not determine representation in Congress.

   C. Incorrect. The Fifth Amendment states that private property cannot be seized for public use without proper compensation.

   D. Incorrect. The Third Amendment prohibits the government from quartering troops in private homes.

8)   **Which of the following is an example of a representative democracy?**

   A.   Citizens vote on legislation.

   B.   Citizens vote on constitutional amendments.

   C.   Citizens can directly vote for policies.

   D.   The House must have proportional representation in order to adequately reflect population size.

Answers:

   A.   Incorrect. In a representative democracy, citizens vote for representatives who vote on legislation.

   B.   Incorrect. Citizens amend a constitution in a direct democracy.

   C.   Incorrect. This is an example of direct democracy, where the people do not elect representatives to vote on policy for them.

   D.   **Correct.** Representatives are elected to the House to represent the people; they vote on legislation on their behalf.

Economics

Elementary-level students should understand the basic concepts of supply and demand, scarcity, opportunity cost, how and why people generate wealth, how technology affects the economy, and the government's role in the economy.

The study of economics is the study of the production and consumption of products as well as how people produce and obtain these goods. It explains how people interact with the market; studying economics usually explains the behavior of people or the government.

One of the most important concepts in economics is **supply and demand**. Supply refers to how much the market can actually offer, and demand is how much desire there is for a product or service. The demand is the relationship between price and quantity, which is how much people are willing to pay for the product. The supply simply means how much product producers are willing to supply at a certain price. This relationship between price and how much product is offered to the market is known as the supply relationship.

Price is used to show the relationship between supply and demand. When the demand is high for a product, the price generally goes up. When the demand is low, price falls. However, if the price is considered too high by the public, there may be excess supply because people will purchase less. Causes of excess supply include other price changes, including the price of alternative goods, and public preferences. Likewise, there might be excess demand if the price is set too low and many people want the product, but there may not be enough supply. This might happen if there is a government ban on the product, the government imposes a price ceiling, or suppliers decide to not raise prices.

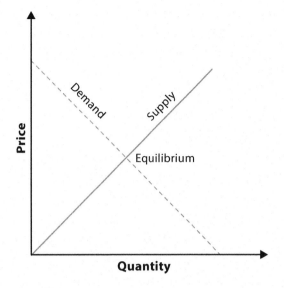

Figure 3.17. Supply and Demand

For example, before Halloween, prices of Halloween candy are high because consumers are willing to pay high prices. They want to purchase enough candy to celebrate the holiday at parties and to distribute to trick-or-treaters, even if it is expensive. However, after Halloween, leftover candy is usually on sale. This is because demand for candy is low: the holiday is over and so people do not need it. That leftover candy represents excess supply. In order to get rid of it, suppliers drop prices to entice consumers with a sweet tooth to buy it even though Halloween is past.

> **DID YOU KNOW?**
>
> An important idea in economics is wants and needs. *Wants* are the goods or services that people desire (like candy or manicures), whereas *needs* are the goods or services required to live and function (like water or medicine).

When supply and demand are equal, the economy is at equilibrium. However, that is not always the case. When there is insufficient supply to meet demand, the result is **scarcity**. People need to choose which want to satisfy. For example, if there is a low supply of chocolate, chocolate prices will be high. Consequently, a consumer must decide whether to spend more money than usual on chocolate or not to buy any at all.

Every choice has a value. **Opportunity cost** is when a consumer makes a choice at the cost of another choice or the value of an opportunity. For example, imagine that someone must choose between eating chocolate cake or apple pie. If that person chose the chocolate cake, he or she gave up the opportunity to eat the apple pie. The opportunity cost is the apple pie. Decisions made by an individual or the government based on opportunity cost are driven by needs, wants, income, and time.

When making economic choices both parts of the value (costs and benefits) should be considered. The ideal choice will have the greatest benefits at the lowest cost. For example, there are two stores that sell chocolate, but the first store sells it at $35 a box and the second store sells it at $40 a box. However, it takes an hour to drive to the first store and it will cost about $10 in gas to get there and back, while it takes 15 minutes and $2.50 in gas to reach the second store. Economically speaking, it is not worthwhile to drive to the first store. Choosing to pay more for the chocolate at the second store is the cost, and the benefit is the time and cost of gas saved by rejecting the first store.

People use resources in order to create **wealth** and enhance their lives. These resources are either goods or services people provide in exchange for money. People provide labor, creating goods and services available for purchase. Labor refers to people who work in almost any job: on farms, in factories, as computer programmers, etc. The goods and services produced enhance people's lives. For example, not everyone owns a farm or can grow a variety of produce, so consumers depend on farmers around the world to grow various agricultural products in order to obtain them. Those farmers use resources such as water and land in order to generate wealth. Likewise, not everyone can fix a computer, so a consumer can bring his or her computer to an expert to be repaired. The owner of a computer repair service would be compensated with cash, and he or she similarly builds wealth by using that cash to invest in the business, buy property, invest in the stock market, or for other purposes.

Technological innovation is also driven by the economy (and vice versa). For example, more efficient transportation has increased trade and the exchange of wealth. Railroads enabled US businesses to transport raw materials to their production facilities, thereby increasing production of goods. These areas then will need more people to provide labor, helping companies and individuals generate more wealth and providing jobs and salaries to workers, who themselves were thus able to generate more wealth in cash. More recently, computers and the Internet have sped up communication and commerce, opening new ways of doing business.

When population increases, people consume more resources, generating more demand for products to meet their needs. In addition, as companies generate more wealth, they can invest in innovation and even more new technology.

The federal government helps to regulate the economy. **Government regulation** falls into either economic regulation or social regulation. Economic regulation controls prices directly or indirectly. The government works to prevent monopolies: the control of a market for a good or service by one company or group. For example, the government may prohibit utility companies from raising their prices beyond a certain point. Antitrust law is another type of economic regulation. It strengthens market forces to protect consumers from businesses and to eliminate or minimize the need for direct regulation. These laws are intended to ensure fair competition in the US economy.

Social regulation encourages businesses to behave responsibly and prohibits harmful behavior. For example, the US Occupational Safety and Health Administration enforces workplace regulations to protect worker safety, and the Environmental Protection Agency regulates industry by upholding environmental standards for emissions and waste.

Finally, the government collects **taxes** not only to cover its expenses but also to help fuel the economy. Federal taxes pay for costs like federal employee salaries and retirement programs, government programs, and the military. Other government programs that are financed through taxes include veterans' benefits and NASA. Payroll taxes help **finance** the Medicare and Social Security programs which provide assistance for the elderly and those with low incomes. Government spending helps to increase the wealth of businesses and individuals. For example, if the government spends money to build bridges and highways, construction businesses generate more income. If an individual is retired or cannot work for health reasons, Social Security will provide assistance.

> **DID YOU KNOW?**
>
> There are currently seven ways the US people pay taxes. They are income, excise, sales, payroll, estate, property, and gift taxes.

SAMPLE QUESTIONS

9) Which of the following terms best describes a situation in which the federal government prevents the only Internet service company in a local community from raising its prices?

   A. economic regulation
   B. social regulation
   C. opportunity cost
   D. scarcity

Answers:

A. **Correct.** In this instance of economic regulation, the government is controlling prices by preventing a monopoly.

B. Incorrect. Social regulation works to ensure ethical business practices. In this example, the government is only concerned with prices.

C. Incorrect. Opportunity cost describes making one choice at the expense of another; it does not apply to this situation.

D. Incorrect. If the supply of a product cannot meet demand for it, the result is scarcity; that concept does not apply in this situation.

10) During Easter, chocolate eggs are sold at three for $3, while caramel eggs are two for $3. A consumer prefers caramel, but is very hungry, so he purchases the chocolate eggs to have one extra egg. Which of the following terms best describes this situation?

A. needs

B. opportunity cost

C. supply

D. demand

Answers:

A. Incorrect. *Needs* refers to goods and services that a consumer requires to live and function. Candy eggs are not necessary for survival; they are *wants*.

B. **Correct.** The customer enjoyed one extra egg at the expense of his preferred flavor, caramel. In this case, the caramel eggs were the opportunity cost: the loss he suffered at the expense of his choice to have an extra chocolate egg at the same price.

C. Incorrect. The question does not provide any information about the supply of either type of egg.

D. Incorrect. The question does not provide any information about the demand for either type of egg.

SOCIAL STUDIES SKILLS AND PROCESSES

Social studies encourages students to investigate questions about people, their values, and the choices they make. In other words, students engage in **inquiry**: they seek information, knowledge, or the truth. Inquiry-based learning in social studies is a process in which students gather information by identifying relevant questions and uncovering sources in order to interpret information and report their findings.

Teachers can help students develop critical thinking skills by encouraging **questioning**. The more questions students ask, the more carefully they evaluate sources and actively research information that helps them to draw conclusions.

Using research and resource materials is a critical component in social studies processes. There are two main types of sources: primary and secondary. **Primary sources** are original records and have information from a person who experienced the event firsthand. Primary sources include original documents like the US Constitution and Declaration of Independence, journals, speeches, physical artifacts, and some first-person accounts in places such as newspapers or historical documents.

Secondary sources are texts created by people who did not personally experience or witness the event. They are based on primary sources. Examples of secondary sources include books, research papers and analyses, and some reports or features in newspapers and magazines written by journalists and other writers.

Using a variety of sources is essential when conducting research. Analyzing the relationship between primary and secondary sources relating to the same subject matter gives students a deeper understanding of the topic being studied. Understanding the advantages and disadvantages of each source also helps students understand and actively engage in **data interpretation**: assessing whether their sources are valid or appropriate.

Using primary sources permits students to draw **conclusions** based on their own interpretations of those sources, rather than relying on secondary interpretations. Primary sources also allow students to more directly address the topic and usually provide information found nowhere else. However, certain primary sources may not have any objective information or accurate facts. Moreover, these types of sources can be difficult to find and analyze.

Secondary sources enrich study by providing different perspectives and expert conclusions. Furthermore, using reputable sources may be more efficient; they may be more accessible or easier to understand. However, secondary sources may focus on issues beyond the topic under study; they may be outdated; or they may be tainted by the author's bias.

Students must think critically when reading or using any source. They should understand how to distinguish between **fact** and **opinion**. Facts are statements that can be proven, and opinions are statements that reflect someone's view; they cannot be proven. Understanding these differences helps students evaluate sources. If students can distinguish between fact and opinion, then they can determine the validity of the source in question.

When interpreting information, students should be aware of variables involved. A **variable** is anything that can take on a different value. For example, age is considered a variable; so is place of origin. There are many kinds of variables, but they mainly fall into dependent and independent variables. Independent variables are manipulated or controlled by the researcher; they are not changed by any other factors. Dependent variables rely on the independent variable; they may be changed by other factors.

Understanding variables helps students interpret information and draw conclusions. For example, a student writing an essay arguing that westward expansion had a positive effect on the US would need to gather sources such as first-hand accounts of people who moved to the West for opportunities, charts demonstrating population growth, and information about the types of jobs available during those times.

DID YOU KNOW?

There are qualitative and quantitative data in variables. Qualitative data is based on human interpretation and quantitative data is based on statistical analysis.

When drawing conclusions, students should demonstrate an ability to address arguments and provide explanations. When constructing their conclusions, they should provide relevant information. They may even offer new perspectives on the research problem. For example, students can find ways to address local community problems. No matter what, they should all demonstrate an understanding of the problem being researched and thoughtful use of the tools available in social studies.

SAMPLE QUESTIONS

11) **Which of the following best describes an independent variable?**

   A. the amount of paint a painter needs to paint a room

   B. the number of errors an student gets on a test

   C. the dosage and timing of an anti-inflammatory drug to test its impact

   D. how much time it will take to drive between Houston and San Antonio

Answers:

   A. Incorrect. The amount of paint required for a room is a dependent variable; it is determined not by the painter but by the room size.

   B. Incorrect. Test scores depend on a number of factors, such as the time the student devoted to studying or the student's confidence level.

   C. Correct. The doctor or scientist who carries out the experiment controls the timing and dose.

   D. Incorrect. While it is possible to estimate how long a trip between the two cities will take, factors like traffic and weather can change and will affect timing. Here, length of time is a dependent variable.

12) **Which of the following are examples of primary sources?**

   A. original photographs, first-hand newspaper reports, textbooks, and interviews

   B. memoirs, original photographs, first-hand newspaper reports, and diary entries

   C. speeches, newspaper reports, essays, and reviews

   D. essays, reviews, textbooks, and analytical papers

Answers:

   A. Incorrect. Textbooks are not primary resources.

   B. Correct. All of these are examples of primary resources.

   C. Incorrect. While speeches are primary sources, only first-hand newspaper reports count as primary resources. If they are reported, then they are considered secondary resources. Essays and reviews are secondary sources.

   D. Incorrect. These are all examples of secondary resources.

TERMS

abolitionism: the ending of slavery

Abraham Lincoln: first Republican president, an abolitionist elected in 1860; his election triggered Southern secession. He led the country through the Civil War, but he was assassinated in 1865 before Reconstruction truly began

absolute location: a location identifiable by specific geographic coordinates

Algonquin: northeastern Native American civilization in the Great Lakes region

ancient Egyptians: emerged as early as 5000 BCE in the Nile Valley; known for their pyramids, art, use of papyrus as paper, and pictorial writing (hieroglyphs); united under one monarch, or pharaoh

anthropology: the study of humans and their cultures

arms race: competitive weapons development between the US and the USSR during the 1980s; the US intended to outspend the USSR, thereby weakening it

Articles of Confederation: the original framework of the US government, designed to create a loose confederation between the colonies (now states) while allowing them to retain much of their individual sovereignty; created an intentionally weak, democratic government

assembly line: a labor-intensive method of production developed by Henry Ford in which workers repetitively execute separate key tasks in production, expediting the product's completion

Assyria: Sumerian-based civilization in the Near East; established military dominance and played an important role in regional trade

Athens: ancient Greek city-state that became a revolutionary democracy controlled by the poor and working classes around 460 BCE; the first known democracy

Augustus Caesar: Julius Caesar's nephew Octavian who gained control of Rome in 27 BCE and became the first Roman emperor

Axis: the alliance of Germany, Italy, and Japan during WWII

Babylonia: Sumerian-based civilization in Mesopotamia; developed courts and an early codified rule of law—the Code of Hammurabi—"an eye for an eye, a tooth for a tooth"

Barack Obama: first African American president, elected in 2008; ended wars in Afghanistan and Iraq; halted the Great Recession; developed programs to provide healthcare to uninsured Americans

Battle of Bunker Hill: took place on June 17, 1775; caused King George III to declare that the colonies were in rebellion

Battle of Fort Sumter: 1861 attack on Union troops in Sumter, South Carolina, by Confederate forces shortly after South Carolina seceded from the Union; this battle sparked the Civil War

Battle of Lexington and Concord: beginning of violent conflict between American rebel militiamen (minutemen) and the British in 1775

Battle of Yorktown: 1781 defeat of British forces by the Continental Army with support from France, ending the Revolutionary War

Bill of Rights: the first ten amendments to the US Constitution; a set of guarantees of certain rights enjoyed by Americans

Boston Massacre: 1770 event in which British troops fired on a crowd of American protestors

Boston Tea Party: 1773 protest of the Tea Act in which American colonial protestors disguised as Native Americans tossed tea off a ship in Boston Harbor

cardinal directions: north, south, east, and west

Cesar Chavez: civil rights activist; led the United Farm Workers, who advocated for Hispanic farm workers who faced racial discrimination, poor treatment, and low pay

checks and balances: each branch of government has certain powers that limit the power of the other branches

Cherokee: Southeastern Native American civilization thought to be descended from the Iroquois; emerged in present-day Georgia; forced during the Trail of Tears to leave their land and migrate to Indian Territory (Oklahoma)

Civil Rights Movement: social and political movement for the rights of African Americans and other disenfranchised people in the 1960s

Cold War: period of ongoing tension and conflict between the US and the USSR, the post-WWII global superpowers; remained "cold" because the two countries never engaged in direct military confrontation

Committees of Correspondence: colonial rebel protest group that distributed anti-British propaganda

concentration camps: forced labor and death camps where the Nazis imprisoned and killed Jews, Roma, Slavic people, homosexuals, disabled people, people of color, prisoners of war, communists, and others as part of the Holocaust

Congress: the branch of the federal government that makes laws (the legislative branch); technically, it has the most power in government

Constitution: the document that provides the framework for the US government

Constitutional Convention: 1787 meeting of the states to resolve problems arising from limitations on federal power. A decision was made to completely throw out the old Articles and write a new governing document from scratch—the Constitution

Creek, Chickasaw, and **Choctaw:** major Muskogean-speaking southeastern Native American civilizations; descendants of the Mississippi Mound Builders

cuneiform: a Sumerian development; the earliest known example of writing using characters to form words (not pictographs)

conflict: the process of disagreement, usually resolved when one of the parties receives either the entirety or a satisfactory amount of the desired goal

cooperation: the process of working together to achieve similar goals; often leads to positive outcomes

D-Day: June 6, 1944, when the US led the invasion of Normandy, invading Europe during WWII

Declaration of Independence: issued on July 4, 1776, this document, written in great part by Thomas Jefferson and signed by the leaders of the Second Continental Congress, asserted US independence from Britain

demand: how much desire there is for a product or service

demokratia: ancient Greek word meaning "people power"

desert: a climate located in the low latitudes north and south of the savannah; the hottest and driest parts of the earth; receives less than 10 inches of rainfall a year

economic regulation: indirect or direct price control by the government

Elizabeth Cady Stanton: women's rights activist; founded the National Woman Suffrage Association and led the 1848 Seneca Falls Convention on women's rights

Emancipation Proclamation: January 1, 1863 declaration by President Lincoln that slavery was abolished in the rebel states

euro: a common currency shared by some European countries

European Union: a forum for European countries to organize and cooperate politically, militarily, and economically; formed after the Cold War to promote European unity

exchange: the process of giving one thing and receiving another (usually with similar value) in return

First Continental Congress: meeting of colonial leaders in Philadelphia in 1774, organized in response to the Intolerable Acts; colonial leaders later presented concerns to the king and were rebuffed

Four Freedoms: in the context of the rise of fascism, FDR defined these as freedom of speech, freedom of religion, freedom from want, and freedom from fear

Franklin Delano Roosevelt: elected to the presidency in 1932; developed the New Deal, rescuing the United States from the Great Depression, and led the country through WWII

genocide: killing people based on their ethnicity

geographic features: physical features of place like continents, bodies of water, plains, plateaus, mountains, and valleys

George Washington: colonial military leader, general of the Continental Army, first US president; his able military leadership helped the colonies eventually secure independence, and his political leadership helped keep the young country united

glasnost: Soviet reform meaning "openness"

government regulation: government involvement in the economy to effect an economic or social outcome

Great Depression: the global economic collapse that resulted in widespread poverty and unemployment in the United States and the world

hieroglyphs: ancient Egyptian writing (unlike cuneiform, pictographs, or pictorial writing)

high latitudes: latitudes from 66.5° north and south to the poles

Holocaust: the dispossession, imprisonment, and murder of at least six million Jews, Roma, Slavic people, homosexuals, disabled people, people of color, prisoners of war, communists, and others by the Nazis

House of Representatives (the lower house of Congress): the body of lawmakers in Congress with proportional representation reflecting the population of each state

human geography: the study of the impact of people on the physical world

humid continental climate: located in the middle latitudes, the agriculturally productive, true four-season climate

humid subtropical climate: located in the middle latitudes, a warm and moist climate on coastal areas north and south of the tropics that receive warm ocean currents and warm winds year round

Indian Removal Act: 1830 law that forced Cherokee, Creek, Chickasaw, Choctaw, and others from their lands in the Southeast to Indian Territory (Oklahoma)

industrialization: the process of manufacturing; the process of an economy transforming from dependence on agricultural to industrial production; replacement of hand labor by machines as the main way of manufacturing, exponentially increasing production capacities

institutions: extensions of core social values created in response to varying individual and group needs; include government, private enterprise, religious institutions, academic institutions, local communities, and the family unit

intermediate directions: the directions between the cardinal directions

Intolerable Acts: 1774 Acts enforced by Britain in response to tensions and violence in the colonies, including closing Boston Harbor and bringing Massachusetts back under direct royal control

iron curtain: a metaphor for the concept of a post-WWII Europe divided between east (with communist governments generally aligned with the USSR) and west (with democratic capitalist governments generally aligned with the US)

Iroquois: northeastern Native American civilization in New York and southern Ontario/Quebec; a confederation of six tribes

John Adams: colonial leader, member of the Continental Congress, federalist, second US president, brother to the radical Samuel Adams; Adams supported a strong federal government and expanded executive power

Julius Caesar: a popular Roman military leader who forced the corrupt Senate to give him control and who began transitioning Rome from a republic to what would become an empire; assassinated in 44 BCE

League of Nations: a largely toothless international organization established after WWI and designed to prevent future outbreaks of international war; the basis for the later United Nations

low latitudes: the region located from the equator to latitudes 23.5° north and south

Louisiana Purchase: 1803 purchase of French-controlled territory in North America by the United States, authorized, controversially, by President Jefferson; nearly doubled the size of the country

Manifest Destiny: the concept that it was the mission and fate of the United States to expand westward and settle the continent

marine climate: the warm and rainy climate located in the middle latitudes in areas that are near or surrounded by water

Martin Luther King, Jr.: civil rights leader who fought for equal rights for African Americans; embraced peaceful protest as a means to achieve legislative and social change to end segregation between black and white Americans

mass production: large-scale production of consumer products (enabled by the assembly line and factories)

Malcolm X: civil rights leader who championed better living standards for blacks in northern cities and the empowerment of African American communities

Mediterranean climate: a climate located in the middle latitudes between latitudes 30° and 40° north and south characterized by wet, mild winters and dry, warm summers

middle latitudes: the region located from latitudes 23.5° to 66.5° north and south

migration: patterns of movement from one place to another, with the intention of settling permanently at the new location

Missouri Compromise: 1820 legislation that allowed Missouri to join the union as a slave state but provided that any other states north of the thirty-sixth parallel (36°30') would be free

monopoly: the control of a market for a good or service by one company or group

multinational corporations (MNCs): companies based in one country with operations in one or more other countries; the primary driving forces of globalization

natural resources: fresh water, arable land, fuel, livestock, and game

Navajo: a pastoral people that controlled territory in present-day Arizona, New Mexico, and Utah; descendants of the Ancestral Pueblo or Anasazi, who built cliff dwellings

New Deal: plan presented by FDR to rescue the United States from the Great Depression; included emergency acts to save the banking system and long-term relief for the poor and unemployed

Nile Valley: the fertile land on the banks of the Nile River conducive to agriculture and irrigation

nuclear weapons: very powerful weapons that can destroy entire cities; possessed by only a few world powers; first developed by the United States and the Soviet Union

opportunity cost: when a consumer makes a choice at the cost of another choice or the value of an opportunity

Pax Romana: a period of stability in the Mediterranean region under the Roman Empire

Pearl Harbor: US military base in Hawaii; on December 7, 1941, Japan attacked Pearl Harbor, causing the US to enter WWII

perestroika: a term meaning "transparency" referring to Soviet reform

pharaoh: ancient Egyptian monarch

physical geography: the study of the natural processes of the earth

Plains tribes: included the Sioux, Cheyenne, Apache, Comanche, and Arapaho who lived in the Great Plains area; nomadic peoples; depended mainly on the buffalo for sustenance

polis: ancient Greek word meaning "city-state" or "community"

political features: towns and cities; county, state, or national borders

president: the head of state and head of the executive branch; has the power to appoint federal officials and judges, sign or veto laws (approve or deny them), and make foreign policy; he or she is also the commander-in-chief of the US armed forces

primary socialization: when a child learns the values, actions, and attitudes that are appropriate for members of his or her particular culture

pyramids: Egyptian burial tombs for pharaohs

Quartering Act: a 1765 law that forced American colonists to provide shelter, even in their homes, to British troops stationed in the region

regions: parts of the world with definable and identifiable characteristics

relative location: where a place is situated in relation to another place or places

reparations: costly financial compensation charged of Germany by the victors of WWI to cover the cost of the war

Samuel Adams: radical colonial American rebel; leader of the Sons and Daughters of Liberty and Committees of Correspondence

savannah: climate located in the low latitudes north and south of the rainforest; dry in the winter and wet in the summer, experiencing an average of 10 to 30 inches of rain

scarcity: insufficient supply to meet demand

Second Continental Congress: meeting of colonial leaders in Philadelphia in 1775 when colonial leaders agreed on declaring independence and forming the United States of America

secondary socialization: occurs when an individual learns the appropriate values, actions, attitudes, and behaviors as a member of a smaller group within a larger society

Senate: the body of lawmakers in Congress with equal representation—two senators are elected to represent each state (the upper house of Congress); governing body of republican ancient Rome as of 509 BCE

separation of powers: limits the powers within the federal government by dividing power among three branches: the executive, the legislative, and the judicial

September 11, 2001: the date that the United States was attacked by terrorists, resulting in thousands of civilian casualties and major land wars in Afghanistan and Iraq

Shawnee: an Algonquin-speaking people based in the Ohio Valley; Shawnee leader Tecumseh led the Northwest Confederacy against the United States in 1812

social regulation: government regulation that encourages businesses to behave responsibly and prohibits harmful behavior

social structures: (as relates to geography) the organization of a society and how social events relate to and affect places, etc.

socialization: a process whereby individuals learn skills, beliefs, values, and behavior patterns of society and how these can influence their own norms and customs

sociology: the study of groups, institutions, and society

Sons and Daughters of Liberty: colonial rebel protest group that carried out violent acts against tax collectors

Sparta: ancient Greek military city-state

spatial relationships: how one place is located in relation to another place

Stamp Act: controversial 1765 tax on all published documentation in the colonies; the first direct tax on the colonists

steppes or prairie: a climate located in the middle latitudes far from the ocean, characterized by flatlands and minimal rainfall

suburbanization: the movement of urban dwellers from cities to live in growing suburbs, semi-rural areas at the outskirts of cities

Sumerians: ancient Near Eastern people who emerged around 2500 BCE; developed irrigation, agriculture, education, math, astronomy, religion, art and literature, city-states, governance, and administration

supply: how much of a product the market can actually offer

Susan B. Anthony: women's rights activist and leader in women's suffrage movement; leader at 1848 Seneca Falls Convention

system of alliances: the complicated diplomatic and military alliances among European powers that led to the outbreak and magnitude of WWI

taiga: a cold climate located in the high latitudes south of the tundra; contains the world's largest forestlands, extreme mineral wealth, and many swamps and marshes

taxes: money paid by the people, organizations, and companies to the government. This money covers government expenses like federal employee salaries and retirement programs, government programs, and the military. It also helps fuel the economy

Tea Act: controversial 1773 tax on colonial tea that triggered the Boston Tea Party

Thomas Jefferson: colonial leader, architect of the Declaration of Independence; third US president; Jefferson was antifederalist and disapproved of a strong US Constitution

Trail of Tears: the forced migration of Cherokee and others from their land in the Southeast to Indian Territory (today, Oklahoma) to make way for white settlers following the Indian Removal Act; the term describes the suffering, poor conditions, and death suffered by many during the migration

Treaty of Versailles: the treaty that ended WWI, held Germany accountable for the entirety of the war, and brought economic hardship to the country by forcing it to pay reparations to the other powers

trench warfare: bloody, long-term fighting in fortified trenches on the Western Front during WWI

tropical rainforests: moist forests exhibiting high biodiversity, located mainly in the equatorial lowlands in Central Africa, Southeast Asia, and the Amazon basin

tundra: a cold climate located in the high latitudes north of the taiga; with extremely cold and long winters, the ground is frozen for most of the year and becomes mushy during the short summer

Underground Railroad: a secret network of safe houses and connections to help Southern slaves escape to the North and to Canada

United Nations: an international organization formed after WWII to prevent another world war, to champion human rights, and to uphold international security

urban planning: managing the development and use of cities

urbanization: the development of cities; became a feature of human development at the advent of the nineteenth-century Industrial Revolution, when unskilled jobs in factories attracted rural workers to cities, offering them higher wages than an agricultural lifestyle did

vice president: fulfills the duties of the president when he or she is unable; becomes president in the event of the president's death; also serves as president of the Senate

War of 1812: conflict between the US, Britain, and the British-allied Northwest Confederacy (led by the Shawnee leader Tecumseh). The US maintained its territorial integrity despite British incursions from Canada; meanwhile, the US gained power in the Northwest (present-day Ohio Valley region), facilitating westward expansion despite resistance from the Shawnee and other tribes allied with the Confederacy

Science

EARTH AND SPACE SCIENCE

ASTRONOMY

Astronomy is the study of space. Our **planet**, Earth, is just one out of a group of planets that orbit the **sun**, which is the star at the center of our **solar system**. Other planets in our solar system include Mercury, Venus, Mars, Jupiter, Saturn, Uranus, and Neptune. Every planet, except Mercury and Venus, has **moons**, or naturally occurring satellites that orbit a planet. Our solar system also includes **asteroids** and **comets**, small rocky or icy objects that orbit the Sun. Many of these are clustered in the asteroid belt, which is located between the orbits of Mars and Jupiter.

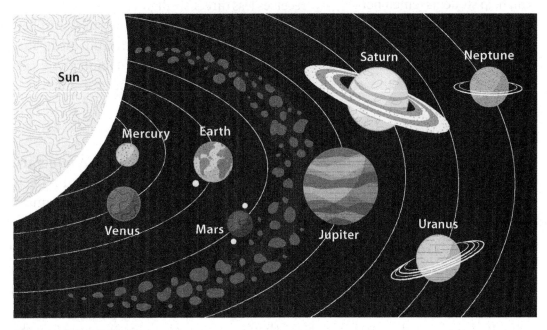

Figure 4.1. Solar System

Our solar system is a small part of a bigger star system called a galaxy. (Our galaxy is called the Milky Way.) **Galaxies** consist of stars, gas, and dust held together by gravity and contain millions of **stars**, which are hot balls of plasma and gasses. The universe includes many types of stars, including supergiant stars, white dwarfs, giant stars, and neutron stars. Stars form in nebulas, which are large clouds of dust and gas. When very large stars collapse, they create **black holes**, which have a gravitational force so strong that light cannot escape.

Earth, the moon, and the sun interact in a number of ways that impact life on our planet. When the positions of the three align, eclipses occur. A **lunar eclipse** occurs when Earth lines up between the moon and the sun; the moon moves into the shadow of Earth and appears dark in color. A **solar eclipse** occurs when the moon lines up between Earth and the sun; the moon covers the sun, blocking sunlight.

The cycle of day and night and the seasonal cycle are determined by the earth's motion. It takes approximately 365 days, or one year, for Earth to revolve around the sun. While Earth is revolving around the sun, it is also rotating on its axis, which takes approximately 24 hours, or one day. As the planet rotates, different areas alternately face toward the sun and away from the sun, creating night and day.

The earth's axis is not directly perpendicular to its orbit, meaning the planet tilts on its axis. The seasons are caused by this tilt. When the Northern Hemisphere is tilted toward the sun, it receives more sunlight and experiences summer. At the same time that the Northern Hemisphere experiences summer, the Southern Hemisphere, which receives less direct sunlight, experiences winter. As the earth revolves, the Northern Hemisphere will tilt away from the sun and move into winter, while the Southern Hemisphere tilts toward the sun and moves into summer.

STUDY TIP

The phrase *My Very Educated Mother Just Served Us Noodles* can help students remember the order of the planets: Mercury – Venus – Earth – Mars – Jupiter – Saturn – Uranus – Neptune.

GEOLOGY

Geology is the study of the minerals and rocks that make up the earth. A **mineral** is a naturally occurring, solid, inorganic substance with a crystalline structure. There are several properties that help identify a mineral, including color, luster, hardness, and density. Examples of minerals include talc, diamonds, and topaz.

Although a **rock** is also a naturally occurring solid, it can be either organic or inorganic and is composed of one or more minerals. Rocks are classified based on their method of formation. The three types of rocks are igneous, sedimentary, and metamorphic. **Igneous** rocks are the result of tectonic processes that bring **magma**, or melted rock, to the earth's surface; they can form either above or below the surface. **Sedimentary** rocks are formed from the compaction of rock fragments that results from weathering and erosion. Lastly, **metamorphic rocks** form when extreme temperature and pressure cause the structure of pre-existing rocks to change.

The rock cycle describes how rocks form and break down. Typically, the cooling and solidification of magma as it rises to the surface creates igneous rocks. These rocks are then subject to **weathering**, the mechanical and/or chemical processes by which rocks break down. During **erosion** the resulting sediment is deposited in a new location. As sediment is deposited, the resulting compaction creates new sedimentary rocks. As new layers are added, rocks and minerals are forced closer to the earth's core where they are subject to heat and pressure, resulting in metamorphic rock. Eventually, they will reach their melting point and return to magma, starting the cycle over again. This process takes place over hundreds of thousands or even millions of years.

> **DID YOU KNOW?**
>
> *Luster* describes how light reflects off the surface of a mineral. Terms to describe luster include dull, metallic, pearly, and waxy.

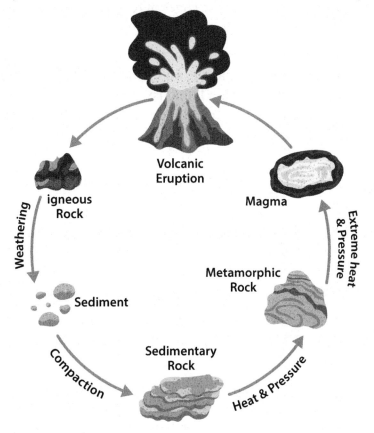

Figure 4.2. The Rock Cycle

Paleontology, the study of the history of life on Earth, is sometimes also considered part of geology. Paleontologists study the **rock record**, which retains biological history through **fossils**, the preserved remains and traces of ancient life. Fossils can be used to learn about the evolution of life on the planet, particularly bacteria, plants, and animals that have gone extinct. Throughout Earth's history, there have been five documented catastrophic events that caused major extinctions. For each mass extinction, there are several theories about the cause but no definitive answers. Theories about what triggered mass extinctions include climate change, ice ages, asteroid and comet impacts, and volcanic activity.

The surface of the earth is made of large plates that float on the less dense layer beneath them. These **tectonic plates** make up the lithosphere, the planet's surface layer. Over 200 million years ago, the continents were joined together in one giant landmass called Pangea. Due to continental drift, or the slow movement of tectonic plates, the continents gradually shifted to their current positions.

The boundaries where plates meet are the locations for many geologic features and events. Mountains are formed when plates collide and push land upward, and trenches form when one plate is pushed beneath another. In addition, the friction created by plates sliding past each other is responsible for most **earthquakes**.

Volcanoes, which are vents in the earth's crust that allow molten rock to reach the surface, frequently occur along the edges of tectonic plates. However, they can also occur at hotspots located far from plate boundaries.

The outermost layer of the earth, which includes tectonic plates, is called the **crust**. Beneath the crust is the **mantle**, and beneath that is the **core**. The core includes two parts: the outer core is a liquid layer, and the inner core is composed of solid iron. It is believed the inner core spins at a rate slightly different than the rest of the planet, which creates the earth's magnetic field.

HYDROLOGY

The earth's surface includes many bodies of water that together form the **hydrosphere**. The largest of these are the bodies of salt water called **oceans**. There are five oceans: the Arctic, Atlantic, Indian, Pacific, and Southern. Together, the oceans account for 71 percent of the earth's surface and 97 percent of the earth's water.

Oceans are subject to cyclic rising and falling water levels at shore lines called **tides**, which are the result of the gravitational pull of the moon and sun. The oceans also experience **waves**, which are caused by the movement of energy through the water.

Other bodies of water include **lakes**, which are usually freshwater, and **seas**, which are usually saltwater. **Rivers** and **streams** are moving bodies of water that flow into lakes, seas, and oceans. The earth also contains **groundwater**, or water that is stored underground in rock formations called aquifers.

Much of the earth's water is stored as ice. The North and South Poles are usually covered in large sheets of ice called **polar ice**. **Glaciers** are large masses of ice and snow that move. Over long periods of time, they scour Earth's surface, creating features such as lakes and valleys. Large chunks of ice that break off from glaciers are called **icebergs**.

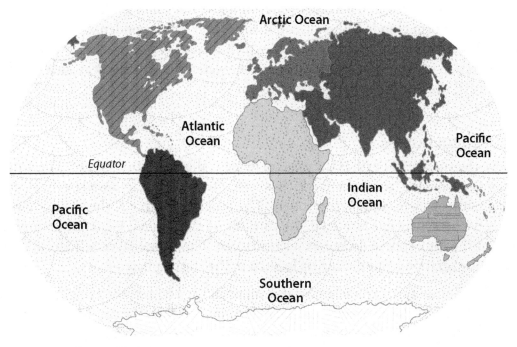

Figure 4.3. The Earth's Oceans

The **water cycle** is the circulation of water throughout the earth's surface, atmosphere, and hydrosphere. Water on the earth's surface **evaporates**, or changes

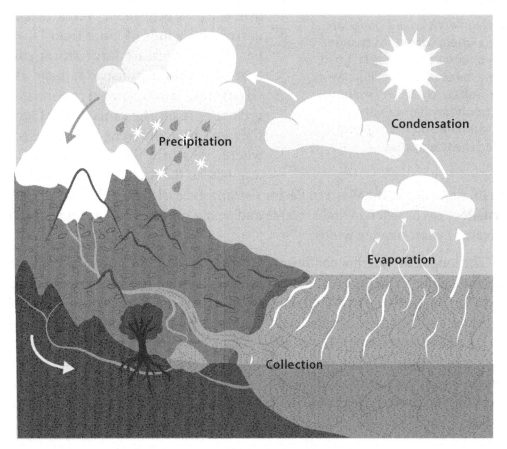

Figure 4.4. The Water Cycle

from a liquid to a gas, and becomes water vapor. Water vapor in the air then comes together to form **clouds**. When it cools, this water vapor condenses into a liquid and falls from the sky as **precipitation**, which includes rain, sleet, snow, and hail. Precipitation replenishes groundwater and the water found in features such as lakes and rivers, thus starting the cycle over again.

METEOROLOGY

Above the surface of Earth is the mass of gasses called the **atmosphere**. The atmosphere includes the troposphere, which is closest to the earth, followed by the stratosphere, mesosphere, and thermosphere. The outermost layer of the atmosphere is the exosphere, which is located 6200 miles above the surface. Generally, temperature in the atmosphere decreases with altitude. The **ozone layer**, which captures harmful radiation from the sun, is located in the stratosphere.

The humidity, or amount of water vapor in the air, and the temperature are two major atmospheric conditions that determine **weather**, the day-to-day changes in atmospheric conditions. A warm front occurs when warm air moves over a cold air mass, causing the air to feel warmer and more humid. A cold front occurs when cold air moves under a warm air mass, causing a drop in temperature.

DID YOU KNOW?

Between each layer, a boundary exists where conditions change. This boundary takes the first part of the name of the previous layer followed by "pause." For example, the boundary between the troposphere and stratosphere is called the tropopause.

Sometimes, weather turns violent. Tropical cyclones, or **hurricanes**, originate over warm ocean water. Hurricanes have destructive winds of more than 74 miles per hour and create large storm surges that can cause extensive damage along coastlines. Hurricanes, typhoons, and cyclones are all the same type of storm; they just have different names based on where the storm is located. Hurricanes originate in the Atlantic or Eastern Pacific Ocean, typhoons in the Western Pacific Ocean, and cyclones in the Indian Ocean. **Tornadoes** occur when unstable warm and cold air masses collide and a rotation is created by fast-moving winds.

The long-term weather conditions in a geographic location are called **climate**. A **climate zone** is a large area that experiences similar average temperature and precipitation. The three major climate zones, based on temperature, are the polar, temperate, and tropical zones. Each climate zone is subdivided into subclimates that have unique characteristics. The tropical climate zone (warm temperatures) can be subdivided into tropical wet, tropical wet and dry, semiarid, and arid. The temperate climate zones (moderate temperatures) include Mediterranean, humid subtropical, marine West Coast, humid continental, and subarctic. The polar climate zones (cold temperatures) include tundra, highlands, nonpermanent ice, and ice cap.

Polar climates are cold and experience prolonged, dark winters due to the tilt of Earth's axis.

1) **What term is used when the moon moves between the earth and the sun?**

   A.   aurora

   B.   lunar eclipse

   C.   black hole

   D.   solar eclipse

   Answers:

   A.   Incorrect. An aurora occurs when particles from the solar wind are trapped in the earth's magnetic field.

   B.   Incorrect. A lunar eclipse is when the earth moves between the moon and the sun, blocking moonlight.

   C.   Incorrect. A black hole is a massive star with a gravitational field so strong that light cannot escape.

   D.   Correct. When the moon moves between the earth and the sun, a solar eclipse occurs, blocking sunlight from the planet.

2) **Which planet does *not* have a moon?**

   A.   Mercury

   B.   Earth

   C.   Jupiter

   D.   Saturn

   Answers:

   A.   Correct. Only the first two planets, Mercury and Venus, lack moons.

   B.   Incorrect. Earth has one moon.

   C.   Incorrect. Jupiter has many moons.

   D.   Incorrect. Saturn has many moons.

LIFE SCIENCE

STRUCTURE AND FUNCTION OF ORGANISMS

Life is made possible by a set of biological molecules that each serve a specific purpose. **Carbohydrates** are the sugars that act as a source of energy for all living things. **Lipids**, or fats, are a way for organisms to store energy, and also help with cell functioning. **Proteins** serve a wide variety of biological functions, and are composed of building blocks called amino acids. Lastly, **nucleic acids**, such as DNA and RNA, store an organism's genetic code, which is all the information needed for the organism to function. Both DNA and RNA are made of small molecules called nucleotides. Within the nucleus, DNA is packed into units called **chromosomes**.

Organisms are living things consisting of at least one **cell**, which is the smallest unit of life that can reproduce on its own. Unicellular organisms, such as amoebas, are made up of only one cell, while multicellular organisms are composed of many cells. In a multicellular organism, the cells are grouped together into **tissues**, and these tissues are grouped into **organs**, which perform a specific function. The heart, for example, is the organ that pumps blood throughout the body. Organs are further grouped into **organ systems**, such as the digestive or respiratory systems.

A cell consists of cytoplasm and genetic material (DNA) held within a **membrane**, or protective covering. Within the cytoplasm of eukaryotic cells are a number of **organelles** which perform specific functions. These include **mitochondria**, which produce energy; **ribosomes**, which produce proteins; and **vacuoles**, which store water and other molecules. Separate from the cytoplasm is the **nucleus**, which is the membrane-bound body that holds the cell's DNA.

Plant cells include a number of structures not found in animal cells. These include the **cell wall**, which provides the cell with a hard outer structure, and chlo-

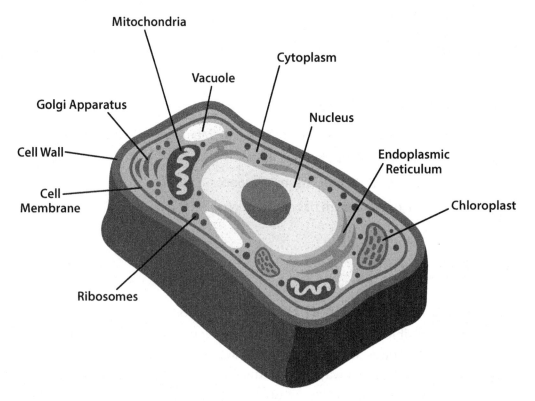

Figure 4.5. Plant Cell

roplasts, where **photosynthesis** occurs. During photosynthesis, plants store energy from sunlight as sugars, which serve as the main source of energy for cell functions.

Cell division, or **mitosis**, is the replication of cells and produces two cells with the same DNA as the original cell. **Meiosis** is the reproduction of sex cells (eggs and sperm). Sex cells are not exact copies of their parent cells and instead have only half the DNA of a somatic (body) cell. When an egg is fertilized by the sperm to form a zygote, half of the new organism's chromosomes come from the egg (mother) and half come from the sperm (father). In humans, sex cells have twenty-three chromosomes, and body cells have forty-six (one set of twenty-three from each parent).

DID YOU KNOW?

Many of the rules of genetics were discovered by Gregor Mendel, a nineteenth-century abbot who used pea plants to show how traits are passed down through generations.

GENETICS AND EVOLUTION

When organisms reproduce, **genetic** information is passed to the next generation through deoxyribonucleic acid, or DNA. Within DNA are blocks of nucleotides called **genes**, each of which contains the code needed to produce a specific protein. Genes are responsible for **traits**, or characteristics, in organisms such as eye color, height, and flower color. During sexual reproduction, the child receives two copies of each gene—one each from the mother and the father. Some of these genes will be dominant, meaning they are expressed, and some will be recessive, meaning they are not expressed. Thus, each child will have a mix of its parents' traits.

When a person's genetic code is damaged, that organism may have a **genetic disorder**. For example, cystic fibrosis, which causes difficulty with basic bodily functions such as breathing and eating, results from damage to the gene which codes for a protein called CFTR. Down Syndrome, which causes developmental delays, occurs when a person has three copies of chromosome twenty-one (meaning they received two copies from a parent as a result of an error in meiosis).

Genes are not static. Over time, **mutations**, or changes in the genetic code, occur that can affect an organism's ability to survive. Harmful mutations will appear less often in a population or be removed entirely because those organisms will be less likely to reproduce (and thus will not pass on that trait). Beneficial mutations may help an organism reproduce, and thus that trait will appear more often. Over time, this process, called **natural selection**, results in the evolution of new species. The theory of evolution was developed by naturalist Charles Darwin when he observed how finches on the Galapagos Islands had a variety of beak shapes and sizes that allowed them to coexist by using different food sources.

CONSIDER THIS

Why might a harmful mutation continue to exist in a population?

CLASSIFICATION OF ORGANISMS

Scientists use the characteristics of organisms to sort them into a variety of **classifications** using a system called taxonomy. The highest level of taxonomic classification is the **kingdom**, and each kingdom is then broken down into smaller categories. The smallest level of classification is a **species**, which includes individuals with similar genetics that are capable of breeding. The entire system is given below:

- ▶ Kingdom
- ▶ Phylum
- ▶ Class
- ▶ Order
- ▶ Family
- ▶ Genus
- ▶ Species

All organisms are sorted into one of five kingdoms: Monera, Protista, Fungi, Plantae, and Animalia. The kingdom **Monera** includes bacteria, which are unicellular organisms that have no nucleus. **Protists** are also unicellular organisms, but they have a nucleus. Both Monera and Protists reproduce asexually by cellular division.

Fungi are a group of unicellular and multicellular organisms that have unique cell walls and reproduction strategies. This kingdom includes common organisms like mushrooms and molds. Fungi can reproduce both asexually by cellular division and sexually through spores. Many species of fungi are decomposers and attain energy by breaking down organic matter in the environment.

Plants are a kingdom of organisms that use the energy from sunlight to make food (the sugar glucose) through the process of photosynthesis. A plant has **roots** that anchor the plant to the ground and absorb water and nutrients from the soil. The **stem** transports nutrients and water from the roots to other parts of the plant, including the **leaves**, where photosynthesis occurs.

Plants can reproduce asexually when a part of the plant (e.g., a cut branch) buds to create a new, identical plant. Plants can also reproduce sexually. Seed plants produce **pollen** (male sex cells) and eggs (female sex cells). When the pollen fertilizes the egg, an embryo is formed. This embryo is protected and nourished by the **seed**. In angiosperms (flowering plants), seeds are contained within fruit. In gymnosperms, such as spruce and pines, seeds are contained within cones.

> STUDY TIP
>
> *LAWN* represents the requirements for plants: Light – Air – Water – Nutrients.

The kingdom Animalia contains multicellular organisms that can move around and must consume other organisms for energy. The kingdom includes several notable classes that divide organisms based on a number of important features. These include whether the organism has a backbone or spine: **vertebrates** do, while **invertebrates** do not. Animals are also classified based on whether they are **exothermic**, meaning their source of body heat comes from the environment, or **endothermic**, meaning their body heat is derived from metabolic processes within the body. Exothermic animals are sometimes known as cold-blooded, and endothermic animals as warm-blooded. Animal classification also looks at animal reproduction: some animals lay eggs, while others give birth to live young.

Amphibians are exothermic vertebrate animals that have gills when they hatch from eggs but develop lungs as adults. Examples of amphibians include frogs, toads, newts, and salamanders. **Reptiles**, such as snakes, lizards, crocodiles, turtles, and tortoises, are cold-blooded vertebrates that have scales and lay eggs on land. **Mammals** are endothermic vertebrate animals that have hair, give live birth, and produce milk for the nourishment of their young.

> **STUDY TIP**
>
> The phrase *King Phillip Came Over From Great Spain* is a way to remember the order of taxonomic classification of organisms: Kingdom – Phylum – Class – Order – Family – Genus – Species.

All organisms have a **life cycle**, the stages of life for that organism. For example, when a frog lays eggs in water, the eggs hatch to become tadpoles with gills. The tadpoles eventually grow legs and develop lungs, and the tail is absorbed into the body. At this point, a tadpole has become an adult frog.

BODY SYSTEMS

Anatomy is the study of the structure of organisms, and **physiology** is the study of how the structures of an organism function. Both disciplines study the systems that allow organisms to perform a number of crucial functions, including the exchange of energy, nutrients, and waste products with the environment. This exchange allows organisms to maintain **homeostasis**, or the stabilization of internal conditions.

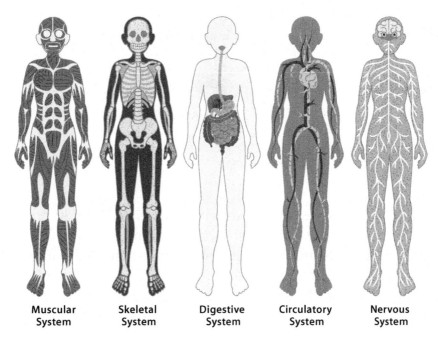

Muscular System   Skeletal System   Digestive System   Circulatory System   Nervous System

Figure 4.6. Body Systems

Humans have a number of body systems that allow us to perform these vital functions, including the digestive, excretory, respiratory, circulatory, skeletal, muscular, immune, nervous, endocrine, and reproductive systems.

The **digestive system** breaks down food into nutrients for use by the body's cells. Food enters through the **mouth** and moves through the **esophagus** to the **stomach**, where it is physically and chemically broken down. The food particles then move into the **small intestine**, where the majority of nutrients are absorbed. Finally, the remaining particles enter the **large intestine**, which mostly absorbs water, and waste exits through the **rectum** and **anus**. This system also includes other organs, including the **liver**, **gallbladder**, and **pancreas**, that manufacture substances needed for digestion.

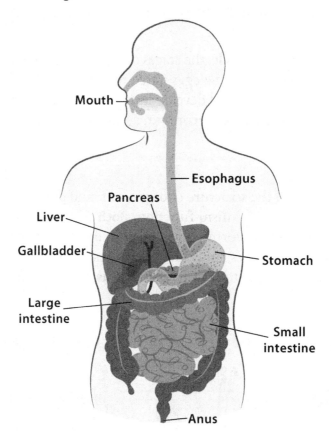

Figure 4.7. Digestive System

The **excretory system** removes waste products from the body. Its organs include the liver, which breaks down harmful substances, and the **kidneys**, which filter waste from the bloodstream. The excretory system also includes the **bladder** and **urinary tract**, which expel the waste filtered by the kidneys; the lungs, which expel the carbon dioxide created by cellular metabolism; and the skin, which secretes salt in the form of perspiration.

The **respiratory system** takes in oxygen (which is needed for cellular functioning) and expels carbon dioxide. Humans take in air primarily through the nose but also through the mouth. This air travels down the **trachea** and **bronchi** into the **lungs**, which are composed of millions of small structures called alveoli that allow for the exchange of gases between the blood and the air.

The circulatory system carries oxygen, nutrients, and waste products in the blood to and from all the cells of the body. The **heart** is a four-chambered muscle that pumps blood throughout the body. Deoxygenated blood (blood from which all the oxygen has been extracted and used) enters the heart in the right side and then is sent by the heart to the lungs, where it collects oxygen. The oxygen-rich blood then returns to the left side of the heart and is pumped out to the rest of the body.

Blood travels through a system of vessels. The largest of these are the **arteries**, which branch directly off the heart. The vessels then branch into smaller and smaller vessels until they become **capillaries**, which are the smallest vessels and the site where gas exchange occurs. Deoxygenated blood travels back to the heart in **veins**.

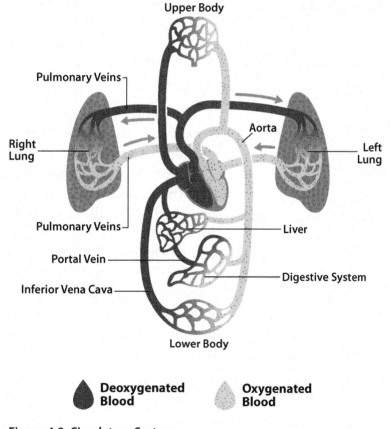

Figure 4.8. Circulatory System

The **skeletal system**, which is composed of the body's **bones** and **joints**, provides support for the body and helps with movement. Bones also store some of the body's nutrients and produce specific types of cells. Humans are born with 237 bones.

However, many of these bones fuse during childhood, and adults will have only 206 bones.

The **muscular system** allows the body to move and also moves blood and other substances through the body. The human body has three types of muscles. Skeletal muscles are voluntary muscles (meaning they can be controlled) that are attached to bones and move the body. Smooth muscles are involuntary muscles (meaning they cannot be controlled) that create movement in parts of the digestive tract, blood vessels, and reproduction system. Finally, cardiac muscle is the involuntary muscle that contracts the heart, allowing it to pump blood throughout the body.

The **immune system** protects the body from infection by foreign particles and organisms. It includes the **skin** and mucous membranes, which act as physical barriers, and a number of specialized cells that destroy foreign substances in the body. The human body has an adaptive immune system, meaning it can recognize and respond to foreign substances once it has been exposed to them. (This is the underlying mechanism behind vaccines.)

The **nervous system** processes external stimuli and sends signals throughout the body. It is made up of two parts. The central nervous system (CNS) includes the brain and spinal cord and is where information is processed and stored. The peripheral nervous system (PNS) includes small cells called neurons that transmit information throughout the body using electrical signals.

DID YOU KNOW?

In science, a **system** is a collection of interconnected parts that make up a complex whole with defined boundaries. Systems may be closed, meaning nothing passes in or out of them, or open, meaning they have inputs and outputs.

The **endocrine system** is a collection of organs that produce **hormones**, which are chemicals that regulate bodily processes. These organs include the pituitary gland, hypothalamus, pineal gland, thyroid gland, parathyroid glands, adrenal glands, testes (in males), ovaries (in females), and the placenta (in pregnant females). Together, the hormones produced by these organs regulate a wide variety of bodily functions, including hunger, sleep, mood, reproduction, and body temperature. Some organs that are part of other systems can also act as endocrine organs, including the pancreas and liver.

The reproductive system includes the organs necessary for sexual reproduction. In males, these include the **testes**, where sperm is produced, and the **urethra**, which carries sperm through the **penis**. In the female reproductive system, eggs are produced in the **ovaries** and released roughly once a month to move through the **fallopian tubes** to the **uterus**. Once fertilized, the new embryo implants in the lining of the uterus and develops over the course of roughly nine months. At the end of **gestation**, the baby exits the uterus through the **vagina**. If the egg is not fertilized, the uterus will shed its lining roughly once a month.

ECOLOGY

Ecology is the study of organisms' interactions with each other and the environment. As with the study of organisms, ecology includes a classification hierarchy. Groups of organisms of the same species living in the same geographic area are called **populations**. These organisms will compete with each other for resources and mates and will display characteristic patterns in growth related to their interactions with the environment. For example, many populations exhibit a **carrying capacity**, which is the highest number of individuals the resources in a given environment can support. Populations that outgrow their carrying capacity are likely to experience increased death rates until the population reaches a stable level again.

Populations of different species living together in the same geographic region are called **communities**. Within a community many different interactions among species occur. **Predators** consume **prey** for food, and some species are in **competition** for the same limited pool of resources. Two species may also have a **parasitic** relationship in which one organism benefits to the detriment of the other, such as ticks feeding off a dog.

> **STUDY TIP**
>
> The five levels of ecology from smallest to largest (Organisms – Populations – Communities – Ecosystems – Biosphere) can be remembered using the phrase *Old People Catch Easy Breaks*.

Within a community, a species exists in a **food web**: every species either consumes or is consumed by another (or others). The lowest trophic level in the web is occupied by **producers**, which include plants and algae that produce energy directly from the sun. The next level are **primary consumers** (herbivores), which consume plant matter. The next trophic level includes **secondary consumers** (carnivores), which consume herbivores. A food web may also contain another level of **tertiary consumers** (carnivores that consume other carnivores). In a real community, these webs can be extremely complex, with species existing on multiple trophic levels. Communities also include **decomposers**, which are organisms that break down dead matter.

The collection of biotic (living) and abiotic (nonliving) features in a geographic area is called an **ecosystem**. For example, in a forest, the ecosystem consists of all the organisms (animals, plants, fungi, bacteria, etc.) in addition to the soil, groundwater, rocks, and other abiotic features.

> **CONSIDER THIS**
>
> What would happen if all of the decomposers disappeared from an ecosystem?

Go on

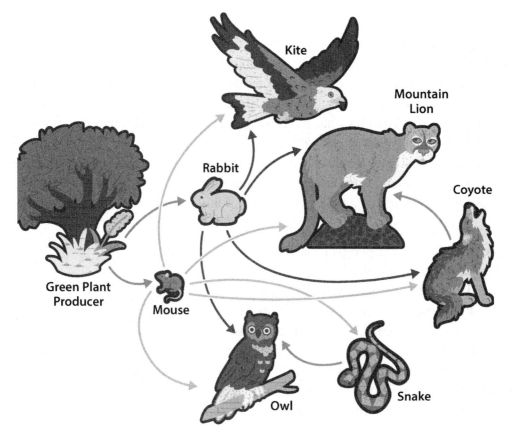

Figure 4.9. Food Web

Biomes are collections of plant and animal communities that exist within specific climates. They are similar to ecosystems, but they do not include abiotic components and can exist within and across continents. For example, the Amazon rainforest is a specific ecosystem, while tropical rainforests in general are considered a biome that includes a set of similar communities across the world. Together, all the living and nonliving parts of the earth are known as the **biosphere**.

Terrestrial biomes are usually defined by distinctive patterns in temperature and rainfall, and aquatic biomes are defined by the type of water and organisms found there. Examples of biomes include:

- ▶ **deserts**: extreme temperatures and very low rainfall with specialized vegetation and small mammals
- ▶ **tropical rainforests**: hot and wet with an extremely high diversity of species
- ▶ **temperate grasslands**: moderate precipitation and distinct seasons with grasses and shrubs dominating
- ▶ **temperate broadleaf forests**: moderate precipitation and temperatures with deciduous trees dominating
- ▶ **tundra**: extremely low temperatures and short growing seasons with little or no tree growth

▶ **coral reefs**: a marine (saltwater) system with high levels of diversity

▶ **lake**: an enclosed body of fresh water

If the delicate balance of an ecosystem is disrupted, the system may not function properly. For example, if all the secondary consumers disappear, the population of primary consumers would increase, causing the primary consumers to overeat the producers and eventually starve. Species called **keystone species** are especially important in a particular community, and removing them decreases the overall diversity of the ecosystem.

> **DID YOU KNOW?**
>
> Deciduous trees lose their leaves in the winter. Evergreen trees keep their leaves year round.

SAMPLE QUESTIONS:

3) **Which organism is a primary consumer?**

   A. mushroom

   B. corn

   C. cow

   D. lion

Answers:

   A. Incorrect. Mushrooms are fungi, which are decomposers.

   B. Incorrect. Corn is a plant, which is a producer.

   C. Correct. Cows eat plants but do not eat other animals; therefore cows are primary consumers.

   D. Incorrect. Lions eat other consumers, which make lions a secondary or tertiary consumer.

4) **Which organism is an amphibian?**

   A. snake

   B. frog

   C. dolphin

   D. pelican

Answers:

   A. Incorrect. Snakes are reptiles.

   B. Correct. Frogs are amphibians; they are born with gills but develop lungs as an adult.

   C. Incorrect. Dolphins are mammals.

   D. Incorrect. Pelicans are birds.

Physical Science

Properties of Matter

The basic unit of all matter is the **atom**. Atoms are composed of three subatomic particles: protons, electrons, and neutrons. **Protons** have a positive charge and are found in the nucleus, or center, of the atom. **Neutrons**, which have no charge, are also located in the nucleus. Negatively charged **electrons** orbit the nucleus. If an atom has the same number of protons and electrons, it will have no net charge. If it has more protons than electrons, it will be positively charged, and if it has more electrons it will be negative. Charged atoms are called **ions**.

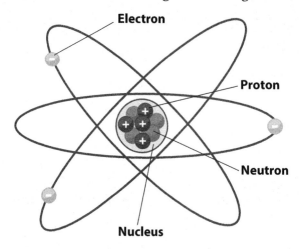

Figure 4.10. Atomic Structure

The mass of an atom is determined by adding the number of protons, neutrons, and electrons. However, electrons have very little mass, so the **atomic mass** is determined by adding just the mass of protons and neutrons.

Elements, such as hydrogen and oxygen, are substances in their simplest form that retain their unique characteristics. Each element has a distinct **atomic number** based on the number of protons in the nucleus. For example, hydrogen has one proton in its nucleus, and oxygen has six. A table of chemical elements arranged by atomic number is called **the periodic table**.

When two or more atoms join together they form a **molecule**. For example, O_3 (ozone) contains three oxygen atoms bound together, and H_2O (water) contains two hydrogen atoms and one oxygen. Water is considered a **compound** because it is made by combining two or more different elements. Atoms can be joined together by different types of bonds. In a **covalent bond**, the atoms share electrons. In an **ionic bond**, two ions with opposite charges are attracted to each other and bind together.

1 H 1.0079																	2 He 4.0026
3 Li 6.9411	4 Be 9.0122											5 B 10.811	6 C 12.011	7 N 14.007	8 O 15.999	9 F 18.998	10 Ne 20.180
11 Na 22.990	12 Mg 24.305											13 Al 26.982	14 Si 28.086	15 P 30.974	16 S 32.065	17 Cl 35.453	18 Ar 39.948
19 K 39.098	20 Ca 40.078	21 Sc 44.956	22 Ti 47.867	23 V 50.942	24 Cr 51.996	25 Mn 54.938	26 Fe 55.845	27 Co 58.933	28 Ni 58.693	29 Cu 63.546	30 Zn 65.39	31 Ga 69.723	32 Ge 72.61	33 As 74.922	34 Se 78.96	35 Br 79.904	36 Kr 83.80
37 Rb 85.468	38 Sr 87.62	39 Y 88.906	40 Zr 91.224	41 Nb 92.906	42 Mo 95.94	43 Tc [98]	44 Ru 101.07	45 Rh 102.91	46 Pd 106.42	47 Ag 107.87	48 Cd 112.41	49 In 114.82	50 Sn 118.71	51 Sb 121.76	52 Te 127.60	53 I 126.90	54 Xe 131.29
55 Cs 132.91	56 Ba 137.33	57-70 *	71 Lu 174.97	72 Hf 178.49	73 Ta 180.95	74 W 183.84	75 Re 186.21	76 Os 190.23	77 Ir 192.22	78 Pt 195.08	79 Au 196.97	80 Hg 200.59	81 Tl 204.38	82 Pb 207.2	83 Bi 208.98	84 Po [209]	85 At [210]	86 Rn [222]
87 Fr [223]	88 Ra [226]	89-102 **	103 Lr [262]	104 Rf [261]	105 Db [262]	106 Sg [266]	107 Bh [264]	108 Hs [269]	109 Mt [268]	110 Uun [271]	111 Uuu [272]	112 Uub [277]		114 Uuq [289]			

* Lanthanide Series	57 La 138.91	58 Ce 140.12	59 Pr 140.91	60 Nd 144.24	61 Pm [145]	62 Sm 150.36	63 Eu 151.96	64 Gd 157.25	65 Tb 158.93	66 Dy 162.50	67 Ho 164.93	68 Er 167.26	69 Tm 168.93	70 Yb 173.04
** Actinide Series	89 Ac [227]	90 Th 232.04	91 Pa 231.04	92 U 238.03	93 Np [237]	94 Pu [244]	95 Am [243]	96 Cm [247]	97 Bk [247]	98 Cf [251]	99 Es [252]	100 Fm [257]	101 Md [258]	102 No [259]

Figure 4.11. Periodic Table

All matter exists in one of four **states**: solid, liquid, gas, or plasma. **Solid** matter has densely packed molecules and does not change volume or shape. **Liquids** have more loosely packed molecules and can change shape but not volume. **Gas** molecules are widely dispersed, and gasses can change both shape and volume. **Plasma** is similar to a gas but contains free moving charged particles (although its overall charge is neutral).

Changes in temperature and pressure can cause matter to change states. Generally, adding energy (in the form of heat) changes a substance to a higher energy state (e.g., solid to liquid). Transitions from a high to lower energy state (e.g., liquid to solid) release energy. Each of these changes has a specific name:

▶ solid to liquid: melting

▶ liquid to solid: freezing

▶ liquid to gas: evaporation

▶ gas to liquid: condensation

▶ solid to gas: sublimation

▶ gas to solid: deposition

Matter changing state is an example of a **physical change**, which is a change in matter that does not alter the chemical composition of a substance. The state of matter changes, but the underlying chemical nature of the substance itself does not change. Other examples of physical changes include cutting, heating, or changing the shape of a substance.

When substances are combined without a chemical reaction to bond them, the resulting substance is called a **mixture**. In a mixture, the components can be unevenly distributed, such as in trail mix or soil. Alternatively, the components can be uniformly distributed, as in salt water. When the distribution is uniform, the mixture is called a **solution**. The substance being dissolved is the **solute**, and the substance being dissolved in is the **solvent**. Physical changes can be used to separate mixtures. For example, heating salt water until the water evaporates, leaving the salt behind, will separate a salt water solution.

DID YOU KNOW?

In both physical and chemical changes, matter is always conserved, meaning it can never be created or destroyed.

In contrast to a physical change, a **chemical change** occurs when bonds between atoms are made or broken, resulting in a new substance or substances. Chemical changes are also called **chemical reactions**. Chemical reactions are either **exothermic**, meaning energy (heat) is released, or **endothermic**, meaning energy is required for the reaction to take place.

Common reactions include:

▶ **oxidation**: a chemical change in which a substance loses electrons, as when iron rusts when exposed to oxygen, forming iron oxide

▶ **combustion**: a chemical reaction that produces heat, carbon dioxide, and water, usually by burning a fuel

▶ **synthesis**: a chemical reaction in which two substances combine to form a single substance

▶ **decomposition**: a chemical reaction in which a single substance is broken down into two or more substances

▶ **neutralization**: a chemical reaction that occurs when an acid and a base react to produce a salt and water

DID YOU KNOW?

A molecule is two or more atoms bound together. A compound is two or more atoms of *different elements* bound together. A compound is always a molecule, but a molecule is not always a compound.

Matter is classified by its **properties**, or characteristics. These properties include mass, weight, density, solubility, conductivity, and pH. **Mass** refers to the amount of matter in an object. Although the terms are often used interchangeably, mass is distinct from **weight**, which is the force of the gravitational pull on an object. Unlike weight, mass stays the same no matter where an object is located. When two objects of the same mass are on the earth and on the moon, the object on the moon will weigh less because the force of gravity on the moon is less than it is on the earth.

Density is the mass of the object divided by its volume, or the amount of space the object occupies. A denser object will contain the same amount of mass in a smaller space than a less dense object. This is why a dense object, such as a bowling ball, will feel heavier than a less dense object, like a soccer ball. The density of an object determines whether an object will sink or float in a fluid. For example, the bowling ball will sink because it is denser than water, while the soccer ball will float.

Solubility refers to the amount of a solute that will dissolve in a solvent. **Conductivity** describes how well a material conducts heat or electricity. Silver, copper, aluminum, and iron are good conductors, while rubber, glass, and wood are poor conductors. Poor conductors are also called **insulators**.

Finally, the pH scale is used to describe the acidity of a substance. **Acids** are compounds that contribute a hydrogen ion (H+) when in solution, and bases are compounds that contribute a hydroxide ion (OH–) in solution. The pH scale goes from 1 – 14, with 7 considered neutral. Acids (such as lemon juice) have a pH lower than 7; bases (such as soap) have a pH greater than 7. Water is neutral with a pH of 7.

FORCE AND MOTION

The motion of objects can be measured using a number of different variables, including speed, velocity, and acceleration. **Speed** describes how quickly something moves, while **velocity** is the rate at which an object changes position. Velocity is different from speed in that it includes a direction. Speed is found by examining how far an object travels; velocity is found by studying how far an object ends up from its starting point. An object that travels a certain distance and then returns to its starting point has a velocity of zero because its final position did not change. Its speed, however, can be found by dividing the total distance it traveled by the time it took to make the trip. **Acceleration** is how quickly an object changes velocity.

A push or pull that causes an object to move or change direction is called a **force**. Forces can arise from a number of different sources. **Gravity** is the attraction of one mass to another mass. For example, the earth's gravitational field pulls objects toward it, and the sun's gravitational field keeps planets in motion around it. Electrically charged objects will also create a field that will cause other charged objects in that field to move. Other forces include **tension**, which is found in ropes pulling or holding up an object; **friction**, which is created by two objects moving against each other; and the **normal force**, which occurs when an object is resting on another object.

> DID YOU KNOW?
>
> The normal force balances out gravity in resting objects. When a book rests on a table, gravity pulls down on it and the normal force pushes up, cancelling each other out and holding the book still.

An object that is at rest or moving with a constant speed has a net force of zero, meaning all the forces acting on it cancel each other out. Such an object is said to be at **equilibrium**. Isaac Newton proposed three **Laws of Motion** that govern forces:

> ▸ **Newton's First Law**: An object at rest stays at rest, and an object in motion stays in motion, unless acted on by a force.

▸ **Newton's Second Law**: Force is equal to the mass of an object multiplied by its acceleration ($F = ma$).

▸ **Newton's Third Law**: For every action, there is an equal and opposite reaction.

The laws of motion have made it possible to build **simple machines**, which take advantage of the rules of motion to make work easier to perform. Simple machines include the inclined plane, wheel and axle, pulley, screw, wedge, and lever.

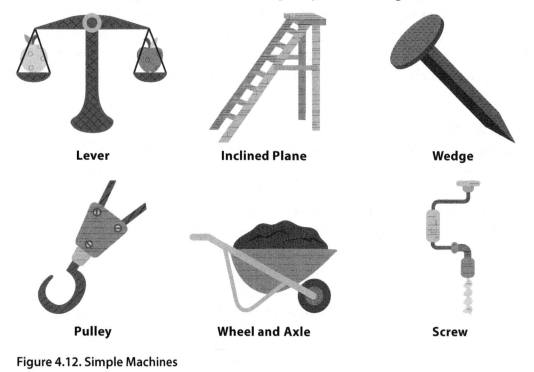

| Lever | Inclined Plane | Wedge |

| Pulley | Wheel and Axle | Screw |

Figure 4.12. Simple Machines

Energy and Matter

Energy is the capacity of an object to do work. In other words, it is the capacity of an object to cause some sort of movement or change. There are two kinds of energy: kinetic and potential. **Kinetic energy** is the energy possessed by objects in motion, and **potential energy** is possessed by objects that have the potential to be in motion due to their position. Potential energy is defined in relation to a specific point. For example, a book held 10 feet off the ground has more potential energy than a book held 5 feet off the ground, because it has the potential to fall farther (i.e., to do more work).

Kinetic energy can be turned into potential energy, and vice versa. In the example above, dropping one of the books turns potential energy into kinetic

> **DID YOU KNOW?**
>
> Like matter, energy is always conserved. It can be changed from one form to another, but never created or destroyed.

energy. Conversely, picking up a book and placing it on a table turns kinetic energy into potential energy.

There are several types of potential energy. The energy stored in a book placed on a table is **gravitational potential energy**; it is derived from the pull of the earth's gravity on the book. **Electric potential energy** is derived from the interaction between positive and negative charges. Because opposite charges attract each other, and like charges repel, energy can be stored when opposite charges are moved apart or when like charges are pushed together. Similarly, compressing a spring stores **elastic potential energy**. Energy is also stored in chemical bonds as **chemical potential energy**.

Temperature is the special name given to the kinetic energy of all the atoms or molecules in a substance. While it might look like a substance is not in motion, in fact, its atoms are constantly spinning and vibrating. The more energy the atoms have, the higher the substance's temperature. **Heat** is the movement of energy from one substance to another. Energy will spontaneously move from high energy (high temperature) substances to low energy (low temperature) substances.

This energy can be transferred by radiation, convection, or conduction. **Radiation** does not need a medium; the sun radiates energy to Earth through the vacuum of space. **Conduction** occurs when two substances are in contact with each other. When a pan is placed on a hot stove, the heat energy is conducted from the stove to the pan and then to the food in the pan. **Convection** transfers energy through circular movement of air or liquids. For example, a convection oven transfers heat through circular movement caused by hot air rising and cold air sinking.

WAVES

Energy can also be transferred through **waves**, which are repeating pulses of energy. Waves that travel through a medium, like ripples on a pond or compressions in a slinky, are called **mechanical waves**. Waves that vibrate up and down (like the ripples on the pond) are **transverse waves**, and those that travel through compression (like the slinky) are **longitudinal waves**. Mechanical waves will travel faster through denser mediums; for example, sound waves will move faster through water than air.

Sound is a special type of longitudinal wave created by vibrations. Our ears are able to interpret these waves as particular sounds. The frequency, or rate, of the vibration determines the sound's **pitch**. **Loudness** depends on the amplitude, or height, of a sound wave.

The **Doppler Effect** is the difference in perceived pitch caused by the motion of the object creating the wave. For example, as an ambulance approaches, the siren's pitch will appear to increase to the observer and then to decrease as the ambulance moves away. This occurs because sound waves are compressed as the ambulance

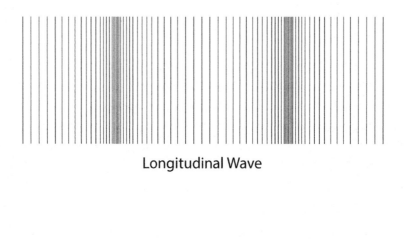

Longitudinal Wave

Transverse Wave

Figure 4.13. Types of Waves

approaches an observer and spread out as the ambulance moves away from the observer.

Electromagnetic waves are composed of oscillating electric and magnetic fields and thus do not require a medium to travel through. The electromagnetic spectrum classifies the types of electromagnetic waves based on their frequency. These include radio waves, microwaves, x-rays, and visible light.

The study of light is called **optics**. Because visible light is a wave, it will display similar properties to other waves. It will **reflect**, or bounce off surfaces, which can be observed by shining a flashlight on a mirror. Light will also **refract**, or bend when it travels between substances. This effect can be seen by placing a pencil in water and observing the apparent bend in the pencil.

Curved pieces of glass called **lenses** can be used to bend light in a way that affects how an image is perceived. Some microscopes, for example, make objects appear larger through the use of specific types of lenses. Eye glasses also use lenses to correct poor vision.

The frequency of a light wave is responsible for its **color**, with red/orange colors having a lower frequency than blue/violet colors. White light is a blend of all the frequencies of visible light. Passing white light through a prism will bend each frequency at a slightly different angle, separating the colors and creating a **rainbow**. Sunlight passing through raindrops can undergo this effect, creating large rainbows in the sky.

ELECTRICITY AND MAGNETISM

Electric charge is created by a difference in the balance of protons and electrons, which creates a positively or negatively charged object. Charged objects create an electric field that spreads outward from the object. Other charged objects in that field will experience a force: objects that have opposite charges will be **attracted** to each other, and objects with the same charge will be **repelled**, or pushed away, from each other.

Because protons cannot leave the nucleus, charge is created by the movement of electrons. Static electricity, or **electrostatic** charge, occurs when a surface has a buildup of charges. For example, if a student rubs a balloon on her head, the friction will cause electrons to move from her hair to the balloon. This creates a negative charge on the balloon and positive charge on her hair; the resulting attraction will cause her hair to move toward the balloon.

Electricity is the movement of electrons through a conductor, and an electric circuit is a closed loop through which electricity moves. Circuits include a **voltage** source, which powers the movement of electrons known as **current**. Sources of voltage include batteries, generators, and wall outlets (which are in turn powered by electric power stations). Other elements, such as lights, computers, and microwaves, can then be connected to the circuit to be powered by its electricity.

Magnets are created by the alignment of spinning electrons within a substance. This alignment will occur naturally in some substances, including iron, nickel, and cobalt, all of which can be used to produce **permanent magnets**. The alignment of electrons creates a **magnetic field** which, like an electric or gravitational field, can act on other objects. Magnetic fields have a north and a south pole which act similar to electric charges: opposite poles will attract, and same poles will repel each other. However, unlike electric charge, which can be either positive or negative, a magnetic field ALWAYS has two poles. If a magnet is cut in half, the result is two magnets, each with a north and south pole.

Electricity and magnetism are closely related. A moving magnet creates an electric field, and a moving charged particle will create a magnetic field. A specific kind of **temporary magnet** known as an electromagnet can be made by coiling a wire around a metal object and running electricity through it. A magnetic field will be created when the wire contains a current but will disappear when the flow of electricity is stopped.

→ Go on

SAMPLE QUESTIONS:

5) **Which type of chemical reaction takes place when kerosene reacts with oxygen to light a lamp?**

   A. oxidation

   B. neutralization

   C. combustion

   D. convection

Answers:

   A. Incorrect. Oxidation is a chemical change in which a substance loses electrons, as happens when iron is exposed to oxygen and rusts.

   B. Incorrect. Neutralization is a chemical reaction that occurs when an acid and a base react to form a salt and water.

   C. **Correct.** Combustion is a chemical reaction that produces carbon dioxide and water. Burning lamp oil (fuel) is combustion.

   D. Incorrect. Convection is the transfer of heat caused by heat rising and cold sinking.

6) **Which substance is a good insulator?**

   A. glass

   B. water

   C. silver

   D. aluminum

Answers:

   A. **Correct.** Glass is a good insulator.

   B. Incorrect. Water is a good conductor.

   C. Incorrect. Silver is a good conductor.

   D. Incorrect. Aluminum is a good conductor.

SCIENCE AND TECHNOLOGY

MEDICAL TECHNOLOGY

Scientists have made great strides in developing **medical technology**, including technology designed to diagnose, prevent, and treat many medical conditions. Diagnostic equipment, which is used to identify medical conditions, includes such technology as **Magnetic Resonance Imaging (MRI)** machines, **x-rays**, and **electrocardiograms (EKGs)**, all of which are used to observe organs and internal structures. Recent developments have also made it possible for doctors to identify some specific genetic disorders by testing a patient's DNA.

Many new or improved treatment options are also available to patients. **Defibrillators**, which reestablish heart rhythms, have become more common and portable. Patients also have reliable options for surgical interventions to treat heart disease, back pain, and damaged joints. Treatments for cancer, including chemotherapy (anticancer drugs) and radiation therapy, continue to improve.

New medicines are being discovered to treat diseases in better ways than ever before. These include **pharmaceuticals** that target conditions like heart disease, mental illness, and seizures as well as bacterial and viral infections. Researchers are also developing new **vaccines** to prevent common infections such as the flu and shingles and also emerging diseases like the Ebola and Zika viruses.

Technology has also changed our relationship with food and nutrition. Processes like pasteurization and refrigeration reduce the risk of food-borne illnesses and allow food to be kept fresh longer. Similarly, water treatment facilities prevent the spread of previously common water-borne bacteria and parasites. Scientists are also constantly revising the **food pyramid**, which is designed to help people understand which types of food make up a healthy diet.

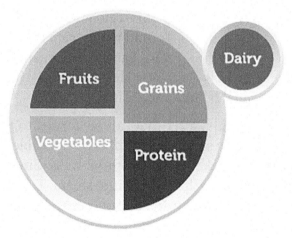

Figure 4.14. USDA Food Recommendations

TECHNOLOGY AND THE ENVIRONMENT

Fossil fuels, such as oil, natural gas, and coal, are nonrenewable resources, meaning the earth contains a finite amount of those substances. These carbon-based fuels were produced over millions of years by the decomposition and compression of organisms that lived long ago. When burned, fossil fuels emit pollutants that damage the environment. Some of these pollutants include greenhouse gases such as carbon dioxide and methane, which when emitted into the atmosphere, trap heat and contribute to **global warming**.

As **nonrenewable resources** become depleted, scientists are working toward advancements in using **renewable resources** as replacements. Other possible sources of energy include nuclear, hydropower, wind, solar, biomass, and geothermal power. These all have less of an impact on the environment than fossil fuels, but many need to be more thoroughly researched and developed before they can supply the energy the world needs.

Nuclear power is created by releasing the energy stored in large atoms by breaking them into smaller atoms. Nuclear power does not release emissions into the atmosphere like burning fossil fuels does, but nuclear power produces dangerous radioactive waste that has the potential to cause other environmental problems.

Through the use of dams, **hydropower** converts the energy in moving water into mechanical energy, which can then be transformed into electricity. Dams do not release harmful emissions like fossil fuels do, but they can be disruptive to natural environments and waterways.

CONSIDER THIS

What would be the pros and cons of using wind, solar, nuclear, and hydropower in your area?

Energy from the **wind** is harnessed using turbines (also called windmills), transforming mechanical energy into electricity. Wind turbines are becoming more common in areas where windy conditions are common, including plains regions and coastlines. **Solar energy** transforms energy from the sun into electricity using solar panels. These panels can be laid out in giant arrays called solar farms in order to provide energy to a large area, but they can also be installed on individual homes or buildings.

Biofuels are biological matter that can be burned to produce heat, steam, or electricity. While biofuels such as ethanol are renewable, they can create many of the same environmental concerns as fossil fuels. Finally, **geothermal** energy converts heat from below Earth's surface into steam. This type of energy has been used since ancient times to heat water and homes and has recently been harnessed to produce electricity.

While commercial agriculture is able to provide food for an extraordinary number of people, many agricultural practices can be damaging to the environment. For example, fertilizers and pesticides may run off fields and pollute nearby lands and waterways. The large swaths of land required for farming can also damage the diversity and stability of ecosystems. Recently, **genetically modified organisms (GMOs)**, which contain genes inserted in their DNA by scientists, have come under scrutiny. While some believe that these GMOs, which include corn, soybean, and potatoes, can create a safer, more plentiful food supply, others question whether the new plants will have detrimental effects on natural environments.

Scientists urge people to protect the environment and Earth's natural resources through **conservation**. One main aspect of conservation is the attempt to limit the number of natural resources that are used to manufacture and dispose of consumer products. By **recycling**, or reusing, common materials like glass, steel, and paper, we limit the resources needed to produce new products. Recycling also reduces the amount of waste put into landfills.

Another important part of conservation is setting aside dedicated tracts of land for protection. National, state, and local parks are important ways to preserve species and ecosystem diversity. Similarly, many **endangered species**, which are at risk for extinction, are protected by national and international governments.

QUICK REVIEW

How can students conserve resources and reduce waste in schools?

SAMPLE QUESTIONS:

7) **Which natural resource is a fossil fuel?**

A. water

B. wind

C. coal

D. sun

Answers:

A. Incorrect. Water is a renewable resource.

B. Incorrect. Wind is a renewable resource.

C. Correct. Coal is a nonrenewable resource that comes from the remains of plants that lived in swamps millions of years ago.

D. Incorrect. Solar power is a renewable resource.

8) **Which medical technology can be used to detect cancerous tumors?**

A. MRI

B. defibrillator

C. EKG

D. patient monitor

Answers:

A. Correct. MRI stands for Magnetic Resonance Imaging and is used to observe organs and internal structures.

B. Incorrect. A defibrillator is used to reestablish heart rhythms.

C. Incorrect. An EKG, or electrocardiogram, is used to observe the rhythms of the heart.

D. Incorrect. A patient monitor measures and records vital signs.

Science Skills and Processes

Scientific Inquiry

Investigation, or **inquiry** science, provides the strongest foundation for scientific thinking. Inquiry science is guided by the scientific method, which provides a framework for observing, measuring, and drawing conclusions about the world.

The first step in the scientific method is **observation**. From these observations, scientists develop questions and do research on current available information about a particular topic. This research helps them formulate a reasonable and testable explanation for their observations, a statement known as a **hypothesis**. Scientists then design and conduct an **experiment** in which they collect data that will demonstrate whether their hypothesis is false or not. It is important to note that a hypothesis can never be proven true—it can be confirmed as false, or enough data can be collected to *infer* that it is true. In order for data to support a hypothesis, it must be consistent and reproducible.

When scientists have repeatedly tested a hypothesis, and that hypothesis has become widely accepted, it becomes known as a **theory**. Theories provide an explanation for a natural phenomenon that is widely accepted by scientists. The theory of evolution, for example, states that natural selection is the mechanism that led to the current diversity of species found on Earth. A scientific **law** is a description of a natural phenomenon. However, unlike a theory, it does not explain how something happens. For example, Newton's law of universal gravitation states the gravitational force between two objects depends on their distance and mass.

> **STUDY TIP**
>
> The phrase *Queen Rachel Hopes Every Coward Gains Courage* can help students remember the scientific method: question – research – hypothesis – experiment – collect data – graph/analyze data – conclusion.

Science, while grounded in observation and data, is not perfect, and scientific knowledge is always growing and changing. Scientists must be able to react to new observations and adjust their hypotheses as needed to address new evidence. By constantly observing, asking questions, and rigorously testing hypotheses, scientists are able to slowly build on the collective pool of scientific knowledge.

Experimental Design

Scientists use a rigorous set of rules to design experiments. The protocols of experimental design are meant to ensure that scientists are actually testing what they set out to test. A well-designed experiment will measure the impact of a single factor on a system, thus allowing the experimenter to draw conclusions about that factor.

Every experiment includes variables, which are the factors or treatments that may impact the outcome of the experiment. **Independent variables** are controlled by the experimenter. They are usually the factors that the experimenter has hypothesized will have an effect on the system. Often, a design will include a treatment group and a **control group** (which does not receive the treatment). The **dependent variables** are factors that are influenced by the independent variable.

For example, in an experiment investigating which type of fertilizer has the greatest effect on plant growth, the independent variable is the type of fertilizer used. The scientist is controlling, or manipulating, the type of fertilizer. The dependent variable is plant growth because the amount of plant growth depends on the type of fertilizer. The type of plant, the amount of water, and the amount of sunlight the plants receive are controls because those variables of the experiment are kept the same for each plant.

When designing an experiment, scientists must identify possible sources of error. These can be **confounding variables**, which are factors that act much like the independent variable and thus can make it appear that the independent variable has a greater effect than it actually does. The design may also include unknown variables that are not controlled by the scientists. Finally, scientists must be aware of human error, particularly in collecting data and making observations, and of possible equipment errors.

CONSIDER THIS

What are the limitations of adhering rigidly to the scientific method?

During the experiment, scientists collect data, which must then be analyzed and presented appropriately. This may mean running a statistical analysis on the data (e.g., finding the mean) or putting the data in graph form. Such an analysis allows scientists to see trends in the data and determine if those trends are statistically significant. From that data, scientists can draw a **conclusion** about the experiment.

Scientists often use **models** in their research. These models are a simplified representation of a system. For example, a mathematical equation that describes fluctuations in a population might be used to test how a certain variable is likely to affect that population. Or, a scientist might use a greenhouse to model a particular ecosystem so she can more closely control the variables in the environment.

FOR REFERENCE

See page 51 – 53 for more information about using charts and graphs.

SAFETY PROCEDURES

When choosing and setting up a lab, teachers need to remember that they are liable for any accidents or hazardous incidents that occur under their supervision. For an elementary classroom, **standard laboratory equipment** includes flat top tables with stools so students can view experiments from several angles. Safety gear, microscopes, beakers, measurement tools, test tubes, eyedroppers, weights, magnets, and timers should be some of the available tools. Measurement tools for length include metric rulers and tape measures. Beakers and graduated cylinders are used to measure volume. Balance scales measure mass.

Standard safety equipment like safety goggles, aprons, protective gloves, and a fire extinguisher must be available. In addition to using standard safety equipment, students should be instructed on wearing appropriate **apparel**. For example, long hair should be tied back and loose clothing and jewelry should be secured. Closed-toed shoes should be worn.

Student **behavior** guidelines are important, but they take on even more significance when students are working in potentially dangerous situations. Adults should model safety practices, such as wearing goggles. Science safety procedures should be outlined for parents and students on a document requiring signatures. Students should be warned about potential dangers in new situations as they arise in each experiment. Students must be diligently supervised; those students who do not meet safety standards should be removed immediately. At the end of an experiment, students must know how to properly clean up equipment and dispose of waste.

Emergency procedures should include proactively monitoring students and equipment and wearing safety gear. Predetermined plans for emergency first aid, electric shock, poisoning, burns, fire, evacuations, spills, and animal bites should be established.

SAMPLE QUESTIONS:

9) **Which tool measures the volume of an object?**

   A. thermometer

   B. graduated cylinder

   C. balance

   D. barometer

   Answers:

   A. Incorrect. A thermometer measures temperature.

   B. Correct. A graduated cylinder measures volume.

   C. Incorrect. A balance measures mass.

   D. Incorrect. A barometer measures atmospheric pressure.

10) **Which step should students take before making a hypothesis in a scientific experiment?**

   A. interpret data

   B. make a graph

   C. research

   D. do the experiment

Answers:

A. Incorrect. Interpreting data comes after an experiment; the hypothesis comes before.

B. Incorrect. Displaying data comes after an experiment; the hypothesis comes before.

C. Correct. Students need to conduct research before making a reasonable and testable hypothesis.

D. Incorrect. The hypothesis comes before an experiment and guides the experimental process.

Go on →

Terms

acceleration: how quickly an object changes velocity

acid: a compound that is able to contribute a hydrogen ion and has a pH lower than 7

adaptations: adjustments to the environment

agrology: the study of the relationship between soil and agriculture

amphibians: a class of cold-blooded vertebrate animals that have gills when they hatch but develop lungs in adulthood

anatomy: the study of the structure of living organisms

asexual: does not require the union of sex cells to reproduce

asteroid: a large rocky body, smaller than a planet, that orbits the sun

atmosphere: the mass of gases that surround Earth

atom: the smallest particle of a chemical element that retains the properties of the element

atomic mass: the mass of an atom calculated by adding the number of protons and neutrons

atomic number: the number of protons in the nucleus of an atom

attraction: a force that draws objects closer

base: a compound that is able to contribute a hydroxide ion and has a pH greater than 7

biomass: plant-based fuel, usually burned, for generating heat, steam, or electricity

biomes: large geographic areas that provide the environmental conditions in which certain organisms live

black holes: a massive star that has collapsed and has a gravitational force so strong that light cannot escape

cell: the smallest living part of an organism

cell division: the separation of a cell into two cells with identical genes

cell membrane: the outer covering of a cell

chemical change: making or breaking chemical bonds between atoms in a chemical reaction

classification: sorting according to characteristics

climate: an area's weather conditions over time

combustion: a chemical reaction that produces carbon dioxide and water, usually from the burning of fuels

comet: a small object made of ice and dust that orbits the sun

communities: interdependent organisms living together in a habitat

compound: a combination of two or more elements

conclusions: inferences based on data collected in an experiment

condensation: the process when water vapor in the air comes in contact with a cold surface and turns into liquid water

conduction: the transfer of heat through physical contact

conductivity: a property that determines how well a material conducts electricity and heat

connections: linking prior knowledge with new information

conservation: protecting the environment and natural resources

controls: the parts of an experiment that stay the same

convection: transfer of heat that occurs in a circular motion caused by heat rising and cold sinking

core: the layer at the center of the earth

covalent bonding: a chemical bond in which electrons are shared

data presentation: an organized display of data

density: a property of matter that can be determined by dividing mass by volume

dependent variable: part of an experiment that responds to, or depends on, the independent variable

deposition: the laying down of sediment in a new location

disciplines: areas of science

DNA: deoxyribonucleic acid (carries genetic information)

Doppler Effect: the change in wavelength when waves are compressed as an object approaches an observer and spread out as the object moves away from the observer

Earth system: the interaction of all physical, chemical, and biological components

earthquake: breaking of rock below the surface that releases energy

eclipse: when Earth, the moon, and the sun align so that light from one object is blocked

ecosystem: a community of organisms and their interaction with each other and the environment

edaphology: the study of how soils affect living things, especially plants

electricity: energy of moving electrons

electron: subatomic particle with a negative charge found outside the nucleus of an atom

elements: substances made of one type of atom

energy conservation: controlling energy consumption

equilibrium: a state of balance

erosion: the movement of sediments from one place to another

evaporation: the process of changing from a liquid to a gas

evolution: the progressive changes of living things throughout Earth's history

experimental design: an experiment that includes an objective, standard protocols, a control group, and independent and dependent variables

experimental error: mistakes made during an experiment caused by limitations of the equipment or external influences

food chain: producers, consumers, predators, and decomposers that live interdependently in an ecosystem

force: any push or pull on an object

fossil fuels: nonrenewable fuels made from organisms that lived millions of years ago

friction: the force of one object resisting another

function: the activity of a part of an organism

geology: the study of Earth

geothermal: converting heat from below the earth's surface to make steam

galaxy: a large system of stars, gas, and dust held together by gravity

generator: a device that transforms mechanical energy into electrical energy

genetic: hereditary

genetic disorder: a hereditary abnormality that creates a health condition

genus: the level of taxonomic classification that ranks above species

glacier: a large mass of slowly moving ice and snow

gravity: the attraction of one mass to another mass

greenhouse gases: gases that trap heat in the atmosphere

groundwater: water that is stored underground in rock layers called aquifers

homeostasis: regulation and stabilization of internal conditions

hurricane: a large, violent storm with winds greater than 74 mph

hydrology: the study of water

hydropower: transforms the energy of moving water into mechanical energy and then electricity

hydrosphere: the water found on and below Earth's surface and in the atmosphere

hypothesis: an educated guess

icebergs: a large chunk of ice that has broken off from a continental glacier and is floating in the ocean

independent variables: part of an experiment that is manipulated to test the effect on the dependent variable

inheritance: a feature passed down from one generation to the next

inquiry: questioning

interdependence: two or more things that rely on each other

ionic bonding: a chemical bond that involves the attraction between two ions with unlike charges

kinetic energy: the energy of motion

kingdom: the highest level of taxonomic classification

laws: descriptions of scientific phenomenon

leaves: the part of a plant where photosynthesis takes place

life cycles: the stages of life in an organism

loudness: the amplitude of a sound wave

mammals: a class of warm-blooded vertebrate animals that have hair, give birth to live young, and produce milk

mantle: the layer of Earth below the crust

mass: the amount of matter in an object

matter: any substance that takes up space and has mass

measurement tools: equipment used to collect data

mechanics: the science of energy and force

medical technology: research and development for improving patient care

medicine: pharmaceuticals used to treat or prevent medical conditions

meteorology: the study of the atmosphere and weather

mixtures: two or more substances combined without a chemical reaction to bond them

models: representations of the real world

molecules: two or more atoms bonded together

moon: a large body that orbits a planet

mutation: a change in genetic information that may be passed on to future generations

natural selection: Darwin's theory that living things that adapt to their environment have a higher survival rate and produce more offspring

neutralization: a chemical reaction that occurs when an acid and a base react to form a salt and water

neutron: subatomic particle with no charge found within the nucleus of an atom

Newton's First Law of Motion: an object at rest stays at rest, and an object in motion stays in motion, unless a force acts on it

Newton's Second Law of Motion: force equals mass multiplied by acceleration; $F = ma$

Newton's Third Law of Motion: for every action, there is an equal and opposite reaction

nonrenewable resources: resources that take millions of years to replenish

nuclear power: energy stored in large atoms that is released when large atoms are broken into smaller atoms

nucleus: the center of a cell that contains DNA

oceanography: the study of oceans

optics: the study of light

organ: a body part that serves an important function in a system

organ systems: groups of organs that work together to perform one or more functions

organism: a living thing

oxidation: a chemical change in which a substance loses electrons

paleontology: the study of the history of life through fossils

parasitism: a relationship between two organisms when one organism benefits to the detriment of the other

pedology: the study of soils in their natural environment

the periodic table: a table of chemical elements listed in order by atomic number

pH scale: a standard measure of acidity or alkalinity where 7 is neutral

photosynthesis: the process by which energy from sunlight is used to make food (glucose) from carbon dioxide and water

physical change: change in a substance that does not change the composition of the substance

physiology: the study of the functions of living organisms

pitch: the frequency of vibrations

planet: a large body in space that orbits a star

plants: a kingdom of organisms that make food using photosynthesis

plate tectonics: a theory that Earth is made of large crustal plates that move over its surface

polar ice: regions at the North and South Poles covered in ice

poles: the ends of a magnet

populations: a group of organisms of the same species

potential energy: the amount of energy of an object due to its position

precipitation: any form of water that falls from the sky

predators: animals that kill other animals for food

prey: an organism that is hunted and killed for food

property: a characteristic

protons: subatomic particle with a positive electric charge found within the nucleus of an atom

radiation: transfer of heat without a medium

reflection: to change the direction of a wave by bouncing the wave off a surface

refraction: the bending of a wave as the wave travels through different media

reliability: the extent to which the results remain the same if an experiment is repeated

renewable resources: resources that replenish quickly

reproduction: the process of making a copy

reptiles: a class of cold-blooded vertebrates that have scales and lay eggs on land

repulsion: a force that pushes objects away

results: outcomes

rock record: a biological history of Earth recorded in rocks

roots: the part of a plant that absorbs water and nutrients from the soil

sexual: requires the union of gametes (sex cells) to reproduce

solar energy: converts energy from the sun into electricity

solar system: a system that includes a star or stars, along with planets, moons, asteroids, meteoroids, and comets, that is held together by gravity

solubility: the amount of a solute that will dissolve in a solvent

solution: the answer to a problem

solutions: a mixture that is evenly distributed and thoroughly dissolved

species: the most specific level of taxonomic classification in which organisms with similar genetics can breed

speed: distance divided by time

stars: large masses of gas

stem: the main stalk of a plant that carries the nutrients and water from the roots to other parts of the plant

structure: the organization of a part of an organism

sun: the star in our solar system

territoriality: animal behavior of defending a specific area

theories: principles explained by science

tides: the movement of large bodies of water caused by the gravitational pull of the moon and the sun

tissue: groups of cells that have a similar function

traits: characteristics

units of measurement: nonstandard, metric, and US customary are systems of measurement; science uses the metric system

velocity: the rate at which an object changes position; change of distance divided by change of time

volcanoes: vents in Earth's crust that allow molten rock to reach the surface

water cycle: the circulation of water throughout Earth's surface, atmosphere, and hydrosphere

wave: a pulse of energy

weather: daily atmospheric conditions

weathering: the mechanical and/or chemical process by which rocks break down

weight: the force of the gravitational pull on an object

wind energy: energy from the wind is transformed into mechanical energy and then electricity

Part II: Practice

Reading and Language Arts Practice

1

A teacher asks, "What word am I trying to say, /p/ /i/ /n/?" and instructs students to say the word. Which strategy is the teacher using to build phoneme awareness?

A.   phoneme blending

B.   phoneme deletion

C.   phoneme segmentation

D.   phoneme substitution

2

Which letter or word part forms the rime in the word *cake*?

A.   c

B.   e

C.   cak

D.   ake

3

An English-language learner who attempts to write simple sentences but uses a very limited vocabulary is functioning at which of the following language proficiency levels?

A.   L1

B.   L2

C.   L3

D.   L4

4

How many phonemes are in the word *chick*?

A.   2

B.   3

C.   4

D.   5

5

The *cl* in the word *clap* is an example of

A.   a syllable.

B.   an onset.

C.   a phoneme.

D.   a rime.

6

A student is able to orally substitute the initial consonant /g/ for /b/ in the word *boat* to make the word *goat*. What concept is the student demonstrating?

A.   phonemic awareness

B.   letter-sound correspondence

C.   phonological awareness

D.   manipulation of onsets and rimes

7

Which of the following letters is most likely to be introduced first in progressive phonics instruction?

A.   a

B.   g

C.   y

D.   m

8

Which of the following best describes reading rate?

A.   using appropriate vocal cues when reading aloud

B.   decoding words correctly when reading aloud

C.   having a significant inventory of known sight words

D.   reading smoothly and steadily when reading aloud

9

Which part of the word *dream* is a phoneme?

A. *ea*

B. *dr*

C. *eam*

D. *re*

10

What is the purpose of sight word instruction?

A. to help students learn letter-sound correspondences to improve accuracy

B. to help students manipulate sounds in words to improve auditory skills

C. to help students recognize words automatically to improve fluency

D. to help students use word parts to improve reading comprehension

Questions 11 – 16 refer to the following text excerpt from *Black Beauty* by Anna Sewell.

> The name of the coachman was John Manly; he had a wife and one little child, and they lived in the coachman's cottage, very near the stables.
>
> The next morning he took me into the yard and gave me a good grooming, and just as I was going into my box, with my coat soft and bright, the squire came in to look at me, and seemed pleased. "John," he said, "I meant to have tried the new horse this morning, but I have other business. You may as well take him around after breakfast; go by the common and the Highwood, and back by the watermill and the river; that will show his paces."
>
> "I will, sir," said John. After breakfast he came and fitted me with a bridle. He was very particular in letting out and taking in the straps, to fit my head comfortably; then he brought a saddle, but it was not broad enough for my back; he saw it in a minute and went for another, which fitted nicely. He rode me first slowly, then a trot, then a canter, and when we were on the common he gave me a light touch with his whip, and we had a splendid gallop.

11

Which inference can the reader make based on the text?

A. John Manly does not like his job.

B. John Manly has respect for horses.

C. John Manly is a coachman with a family.

D. John Manly has bought a new horse.

12

Which point of view is used by the author?

A. first-person

B. second-person

C. third-person objective

D. third-person omniscient

13

Which is the best summary of the excerpt?

A. John Manly is a coachman who lives with his wife and a child in a cottage near a set of stables. He works in the stables grooming horses for the squire.

B. After he has breakfast, John Manly has a splendid gallop by the watermill and along the river with a new horse from the stables.

C. The horse is new to the stables, but the squire does not have time to check his paces, so he asks John Manly to do it, but John has to have breakfast first.

D. The coachman, John Manly, grooms the horse and fits him comfortably with a bridle and saddle. Then, he takes the horse for a ride to test the horse's paces for the squire.

14

Who are the main characters in this excerpt?

A. John Manly, the squire, and the horse

B. John Manly and the horse

C. John Manly and the squire

D. John Manly and his family

15

How can the reader best use the context of the excerpt to understand the meaning of the word *paces*?

A. The reader can find the definition of the word in the paragraph that follows.

B. The reader can figure out the word's meaning by analyzing its root and affix.

C. The reader can use the connotation of the word to determine its meaning.

D. The reader can analyze the setting for a hint to the meaning of the word.

16

What is the tone of the excerpt?

A.   negative and foreboding

B.   cheerful and positive

C.   sad and depressing

D.   elated and ecstatic

Questions 17 – 19 refer to the following text and picture excerpt from *Frederick Francois Chopin: The Story of the Boy Who Made Beautiful Melodies.*

During his boyhood Chopin played much in public, journeying to some of the great cities of Europe, among them Vienna, Berlin, and Munich.

Therefore, when he played in Paris it was as an artist. Here, as at home, he charmed everyone by the beauty of his music and the loveliness of his touch.

He possessed the true piano hand. It was somewhat narrow. The fingers were long and tapering. It seemed at once strong and vigorous, yet delicate and sensitive.

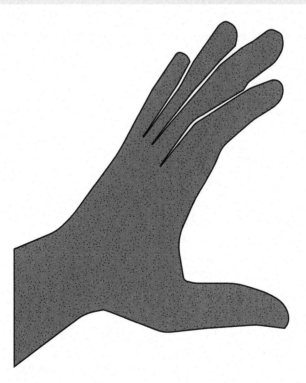

Figure 5.1. The True Piano Hand

17

This excerpt is an example of which type of text?

A. literary

B. informal

C. discipline-specific

D. informational

18

How does the picture of the "true piano hand" help a reader comprehend the excerpt?

A. It helps the reader better understand the tone of the text.

B. It helps the reader feel the beauty of Chopin's music.

C. It helps the reader better understand the word *tapering*.

D. It helps the reader recognize the hands of an artist.

19

Which text feature would best help the reader comprehend where Chopin played?

A. a chart

B. a map

C. a graph

D. a sidebar

20

Which is the root word of *loveliness*?

A. love

B. lovely

C. lov

D. loveli

Questions 21 – 25 refer to the following text excerpt from "King Midas and the Golden Touch" as told by Jean Lang.

The gods had indeed bestowed upon Gordias, the low-born peasant, a surprising gift, but he showed his gratitude by dedicating his wagon to the deity of the oracle and tying it up in its place with the wiliest knot that his simple wisdom knew, pulled as tight as his brawny arms and strong rough hands could pull. Nor could anyone untie the famous Gordian knot, and therefore become, as the oracle promised, lord of all Asia, until centuries had passed, and Alexander the Great came to Phrygia and sliced through the knot with his all-conquering sword.

In time Midas, the son of Gordias, came to inherit the throne and crown of Phrygia. Like many another not born and bred to the purple, his honours sat heavily upon him. From the day that his father's wain had entered the city amidst the acclamations of the people, he had learned the value of power, and therefore, from his boyhood onward, power, always more power, was what he coveted. Also his peasant father had taught him that gold could buy power, and so Midas ever longed for more gold, that could buy him a place in the world that no descendant of a long race of kings should be able to contest. And from Olympus the gods looked down and smiled, and vowed that Midas should have the chance of realising his heart's desire.

21

Which genre does this text excerpt represent?

A. myth

B. fairytale

C. narrative poem

D. drama

22

What can the reader infer about Midas from reading the excerpt?

A. He is physically strong.

B. He is generous.

C. He is insecure.

D. He is angry.

23

Which stage of plot development best describes the excerpt?

A. rising action

B. exposition

C. climax

D. resolution

24

How best can a reader use the excerpt's context to decipher the meaning of the word *coveted*?

A. The reader can use the excerpt's register to determine the word's meaning.

B. The reader can use structural analysis to determine the word's meaning.

C. The reader can use the sentence's syntax to determine the word's meaning.

D. The reader can use the words' connotation to determine the word's meaning.

25

The phrase *born and bred to the purple* is an example of which of the following literary elements?

A.   hyperbole

B.   personification

C.   simile

D.   idiom

26

Which genre features animals and includes an explicit moral lesson?

A.   myth

B.   fable

C.   legend

D.   fairy tale

27

Which best describes the theme of a story?

A.   the way the story is organized

B.   the lesson the author wants to teach

C.   the basic idea the author wants to convey

D.   the point of view of the story

28

How do the two sentences below differ?

The park naturalist visited the class to talk about the migration of Monarch butterflies.

The naturalist visited the class to talk about the migration of Monarch butterflies from the park.

A.   The word *park* acts as an adjective in the first sentence and is part of an adjective phrase in the second sentence.

B.   The word *park* is the subject of the first sentence, and the word *naturalist* is the subject of the second sentence.

C.   The word *park* is the subject of the first sentence and the predicate in the second sentence.

D.   The word *park* acts as an adjective in the first sentence and is part of an adverb phrase in the second.

29

The sentence below is an example of what sentence type?

Despite the fact that the larger dog was ten times its size, the tiny dog continued to bark with ferocity.

A.   simple sentence

B.   compound sentence

C.   complex sentence

D.   compound-complex sentence

30

Which of the answer choice statements about the sentence below is true?

The trail is for advanced hikers because of it's steep incline.

A.   The sentence is written correctly.

B.   There should be a comma before *because*.

C.   The word *it's* should be possessive.

D.   The verb should be past tense.

31

What error has been made in the sentence below?

Lucy thought the first movie was better then the second one.

A.   The verbs are past tense.

B.   *Then* indicates time, not comparison.

C.   *One* is a dangling modifier.

D.   The subject is misplaced.

32

Which of the following strategies is most beneficial for students who are at the beginning stage of writing a story?

A.   revising the story's first paragraph

B.   organizing ideas in a story element chart

C.   drafting the exposition of the story

D.   sharing the story with a classmate

Go on →

Questions 33 – 36 refer to the poem below, "The Moon," from *A Child's Garden of Verses* by Robert Louis Stevenson.

The moon has a face like the clock in the hall;
She shines on thieves on the garden wall;
On streets and fields and harbor quays,
And birdies asleep in the forks of the trees.

The squalling cat and the squeaking mouse,
The howling dog by the door of the house,
The bat that lies in bed at noon,
All love to be out by the light of the moon.

But all of the things that belong to the day
Cuddle to sleep to be out of her way;
And flowers and children close their eyes
Till up in the morning the sun shall rise.

33

Which type of figurative language is used to describe the moon's face?

A. metaphor

B. assonance

C. alliteration

D. simile

34

How does the reader know that the word *quays* is pronounced using /ē/ as opposed to /ā/?

A. from the poet's use of simile

B. from the poet's use of rhyme scheme

C. from the poet's use of personification

D. from the poet's use of point of view

35

Which of the poet's word choices are examples of onomatopoeia?

A. *squalling, squeaking, howling*

B. *garden, streets, fields*

C. *asleep, bed, cuddle*

D. *shines, light, sun*

36

What type of writing does the poem represent?

A.   expository

B.   narrative

C.   descriptive

D.   persuasive

37

Review the following sentence; then review the revision.

Original Sentence:

The scientist looked at the rocks to learn interesting things about the past.

Revision:

The geologist examined the rocks to discover evidence of historical events.

The revised sentence reflects an improvement in which of the following elements of writing?

A.   conventions

B.   organization

C.   sentence fluency

D.   word choice

38

Which best states the purpose of the drafting stage of the writing process?

A.   revising the story's first paragraph

B.   organizing ideas in a story element chart

C.   drafting the exposition of the story

D.   sharing the story with a classmate

39

Which is the primary reason elementary students learn how to paraphrase and cite information from outside sources?

A.   to learn the names of authors

B.   to identify secondary sources

C.   to avoid plagiarism

D.   to condense writing

40

Which is the best writing style for a research paper?

A.   expository

B.   descriptive

C.   narrative

D.   persuasive

41

Which is an example of a secondary source?

A.   a handwritten letter by a former president

B.   a photograph from the turn of the century

C.   an audio recording of a jazz composition

D.   a book that discusses a historical time period

42

Which of the following can be classified as narrative writing?

A.   an opinion piece on a political candidate

B.   an essay on the causes and effects of erosion

C.   a poem that evokes the feeling of a spring thunderstorm

D.   a funny story about an adventure at the zoo

43

Which of the following is considered an unreliable research source?

A.   a self-published report

B.   an edited book of essays

C.   a newspaper article

D.   a university study

44

Which best states the purpose of the rewriting stage of the writing process?

A.   presenting outcomes

B.   organizing ideas

C.   correcting errors

D.   recording thoughts

45

What is the primary purpose of expository writing?

A.   to entertain

B.   to explain

C.   to convince

D.   to describe

46

Which of the following is NOT a positive nonverbal clue in active listening?

A.   smiling at the speaker

B.   leaning forward slightly

C.   looking down at the floor

D.   sitting up straight

47

A student is giving a speech on school start times. The following quote is included in his presentation:

"Elementary school should start at 9:00 a.m. instead of 7:30 a.m. because children do their best thinking when they get enough sleep and have time to eat a healthy breakfast."

Which of the following is the best paraphrase of the speaker's message?

A.   Later school start times are better for learning because children get more rest and eat properly.

B.   School should start at 9:00 a.m. instead of 7:30 a.m. because children do their best thinking when they get enough sleep and have time to eat a healthy breakfast.

C.   Elementary school should start earlier than it does now.

D.   Many students are too tired during the school day to concentrate on learning.

48

Which behaviors best demonstrate focusing on a speaker during active listening?

A.   moving around and eye contact

B.   sitting up straight and interjecting questions

C.   frowning and crossed arms

D.   eye contact and leaning forward

49

Which of the following is Mr. Kahn modeling for students?

Every morning, Mr. Kahn posts a morning message for students that contains errors in Standard English. Students read the message, identify the errors, and make suggestions for corrections.

A.   paraphrasing

B.   editing

C.   decoding

D.   inferring

50

What is finger spelling?

A.   making crayon rubbings of sandpaper letters

B.   using the hands to sign letters

C.   counting letters in words using the fingers

D.   writing letters in trays of colored sand

Answer Key

1)

    A.   **Correct.** The strategy of phoneme blending requires students to combine phonemes to make a word.

    B.   Incorrect. The strategy of phoneme deletion requires students to remove phonemes in words to make new words.

    C.   Incorrect. The strategy of phoneme segmentation requires students to separate the phonemes in a word.

    D.   Incorrect. The strategy of phoneme substitution requires students to replace phonemes in words to make new words.

2)

    A.   Incorrect. The beginning consonant forms the onset of the word *cake*.

    B.   Incorrect. The *e* is silent in the word *cake* and makes the *a* long.

    C.   Incorrect. Dropping the *e* changes the word *cake* into a nonsense word.

    D.   **Correct.** The rime in *cake* is formed by all of the letters that follow the beginning consonant.

3)

    A.   Incorrect. An English-language learner at the L1 level is not yet attempting to write simple sentences.

    B.   **Correct.** An English-language learner at the L2 stage is at the very beginning stages of reading and writing and has a very limited vocabulary.

    C.   Incorrect. An English-language learner at the L3 stage demonstrates an expanded vocabulary and an ability to speak in more complex sentences.

    D.   Incorrect. An English-language learner at the L5 stage can function at the same level as his or her English-speaking peers.

4)

A. Incorrect. The word *chick* is made up of three phonemes, or units of sound. They are the consonant diagraph /ch/, the short vowel /ĭ/, and the consonant diagraph /ck/.

B. **Correct.** The word *chick* is made up of three phonemes, or units of sound: /ch/, /ĭ/, and /ck/.

C. Incorrect. The word *chick* is made up of three phonemes, or units of sound. Both /ch/ and /ck/ are letter combinations that work together to produce one sound.

D. Incorrect. The word *chick* is made up of five letters but only three phonemes, or units of sound. They are the consonant diagraph /ch/, the short vowel /ĭ/, and the consonant diagraph /ck/.

5)

A. Incorrect. The word *clap* is one syllable, and it contains both an onset and a rime.

B. **Correct.** The onset of a syllable is the beginning consonant or consonant blend.

C. Incorrect. The consonant blend *cl* contains two phonemes, /c/ and /l/.

D. Incorrect. The rime of a syllable includes the vowel and remaining consonants, in this case *ap*.

6)

A. **Correct.** Phonemic awareness is an understanding of how phonemes can be orally manipulated to change the meanings of words.

B. Incorrect. When a student connects oral sounds to written letters, he or she is demonstrating an understanding of phonics.

C. Incorrect. Phonemic awareness is only one part of phonological awareness, which also includes creating rhyming words and breaking one-syllable words into onsets and rimes.

D. Incorrect. When students are able to orally manipulate onsets and rimes, they are demonstrating one aspect of phonological awareness.

7)

A. Incorrect. The letter *a* is a vowel with both a short and long sound, which makes it less likely to be introduced during phonics instruction before the less complex consonant *m*.

B. Incorrect. While the letter *g* does contain its hard sound in its name, it also has a soft sound, so it's a more complex letter than *m*, and thus, less likely to be introduced first.

C.   Incorrect. The letter *y* does not contain its sound in its name and can change sounds depending on how it is placed in a word, so it is not likely to be introduced before the letter *m*.

D.   Correct. The letter *m* is most likely to be introduced first because it contains its sound in its name and only forms one sound in words.

8)

A.   Incorrect. Using appropriate vocal expressions when reading aloud demonstrates prosody.

B.   Incorrect. Decoding words correctly when reading aloud demonstrates a reader's accuracy.

C.   Incorrect. Having a significant inventory of known sight words relates to reading accuracy.

D.   Correct. Reading smoothly and steadily when reading aloud is an example of reading rate.

9)

A.   Correct. The diphthong *ea* produces one small unit of sound, /ē/, that cannot be reduced into a smaller unit.

B.   Incorrect. The consonant blend *dr* can be separated into two smaller units of sound, /d/ and /r/, so it is not a phoneme. It is the onset of the word *dream*.

C.   Incorrect. The word part *eam* contains two small units of sound, /ē/ and /m/. It is the rime of the word *dream*.

D.   Incorrect. The word part *re* includes two sounds, /r/ and /ĕ/, and does not represent an appropriate way of breaking the word *dream* into parts.

10)

A.   Incorrect. Phonics instruction is designed to help students learn letter-sound correspondences so they can decode accurately while reading.

B.   Incorrect. Phonemic awareness instruction is designed to help students understand how language is formed by the manipulation of small units of sound.

C.   Correct. Sight word instruction is designed to help students recognize high-frequency words automatically, without decoding, so they can read with fluency.

D.   Incorrect. Word analysis instruction is designed to help students break words into meaningful parts in order to decipher their meanings in text.

11)

A.   Incorrect. Nothing about John Manly's words or actions lead the reader to infer that he does not like his job.

    B.   **Correct.** The way that John Manly takes care to make the horse comfortable before riding leads the reader to infer that he has respect for horses.

    C.   Incorrect. This is information that is directly stated in the text; therefore, it does not need to be inferred.

    D.   Incorrect. The text leads the reader to understand that John Manly is an employee at a horse farm, not the owner of the horse.

12)

    A.   **Correct.** First-person point of view is written from the direct experience of one character—in this case, the horse—as indicated by the pronouns *I* and *my*.

    B.   Incorrect. Second-person point of view is written from the perspective of an external *you*, whether that be the reader or unknown other.

    C.   Incorrect. Third-person objective point of view is written from the perspective of a detached narrator.

    D.   Incorrect. Third-person omniscient point of view is written from the perspective of an all-knowing, detached narrator.

13)

    A.   Incorrect. This is not an adequate summary of the excerpt because all it does is provide details about one of the main characters. It does not address the relationship between John Manly and the narrator.

    B.   Incorrect. This summary leaves out many important details a reader needs to know, such as who John Manly is and why he is riding the new horse.

    C.   Incorrect. This is a confusing summary because it contains irrelevant details and makes it seem as though the squire is one of the main characters instead of focusing on how John Manly interacts with the horse.

    D.   **Correct.** This is the best summary because it provides a brief explanation of the excerpt's main idea and key details. It only includes the most necessary information a reader needs to comprehend the story section.

14)

    A.   Incorrect. The squire is a minor character in this excerpt. His presence simply moves the story along.

    B.   **Correct.** The excerpt is mainly about the interaction between John Manly and the horse. The focus is on the words and actions of both.

    C.   Incorrect. The squire is a minor character in the excerpt, while John Manly is a main character.

    D.   Incorrect. John Manly is one of the main characters, but his family does not play a role in the excerpt. They are mentioned only as a detail of John Manly's life.

15)

A. **Correct.** The author provides a definition of the word *paces* in the next paragraph when he lists them as trot, canter, and gallop.

B. Incorrect. In this instance, the Latin root could be deceptive and thus would not be helpful for determining the meaning of this word. *Pace* means *peace* in Latin; the English word *paces* comes from the Latin *passus* (to step or stretch).

C. Incorrect. The denotation of *paces* is used in this excerpt, so there is no connotation attached.

D. Incorrect. The setting does offer a limited hint as to the meaning of the word *paces*, in that it suggests that a large area is required, but the definition that the author provides within the third paragraph is clearer and more accessible.

16)

A. Incorrect. The horse describes a pleasant afternoon and does not suggest any negative events to come.

B. **Correct.** The horse describes an ordinary scene, expressing enjoyment at his grooming and ride with the attentive John Manly.

C. Incorrect. The horse expresses pleasure, not sadness.

D. Incorrect. The passage is positive, but not overwhelmingly euphoric.

17)

A. Incorrect. This excerpt is an example of informational text, or nonfiction text that provides information on a topic. Literary text is the fictional text of novels, stories, and poetry.

B. Incorrect. This excerpt uses academic language, or the language of school, as opposed to the informal language of conversation.

C. Incorrect. The informational text in this excerpt is accessible to the general public; thus it is not written with terms known specifically to music experts, or discipline specific.

D. **Correct.** This text provides information about the composer Chopin in academic language that is accessible to the general public.

18)

A. Incorrect. The author's word choice, rather than the picture, determines the tone of the excerpt.

B.   Incorrect. The picture does not help the reader feel the beauty of Chopin's music. This would be accomplished with an audio excerpt or more descriptive text.

C.   **Correct.** The picture of the "true piano hand" allows the reader to see that the fingers become thinner at the tips, which is a clue to the meaning of the word *tapering*.

D.   Incorrect. The picture shows a "true piano hand," not a "true artist's hand." Although Chopin is described as an artist, there are many different types of artists who require different types of hands, depending on their expertise.

19)

A.   Incorrect. A chart listing the places Chopin played would just restate the text. It would not add to the reader's understanding.

B.   **Correct.** A map would enable the reader to visualize the locations where Chopin played in relation to each other, thus giving the reader a clearer view of Chopin's area of impact.

C.   Incorrect. A graph is not useful in this instance because there are no numbers to compare.

D.   Incorrect. Places are best visualized on maps or in photographs, so a sidebar with additional text information would not be particularly helpful in this instance.

20)

A.   **Correct.** *Love* is the smallest unit of the word *loveliness* to contain meaning; therefore, it is the root word. Some root words like *love* can stand on their own and are sometimes referred to as base words.

B.   Incorrect. *Lovely* contains both the root word *love* and the suffix *-ly* (meaning "the essence of something").

C.   Incorrect. Lov is a combination of letters with no meaning; thus, it cannot be a root word.

D.   Incorrect. Loveli is the simply word *lovely* with the *y* changed to an *i* before the second suffix (*-ness*, meaning "the state or condition of") is added.

21)

A.   **Correct.** Myths typically include gods and goddesses with abilities that surpass those of humans. Myths describe an earlier version of the world and often attempt to explain how the world came to be as it is.

B.   Incorrect. Fairy tales are make-believe stories that include magic but not gods and goddesses. Fairy tales often include royal characters and standard beginnings and endings such as "once upon a time" and "they lived happily ever after."

C.   Incorrect. Narrative poems are stories told with a poetic structure instead of in prose.

D.   Incorrect. A drama includes stage directions and parts, or dialogue, for different characters; the story is acted out instead of read like a book.

22)

A.   Incorrect. The excerpt describes Midas' father as physically strong, but it does not indicate that Midas is as well.

B.   Incorrect. Midas' thoughts and actions in the excerpt do not suggest generosity. Instead, they reveal his insecurity at not descending from a long line of royalty.

C.   Correct. The excerpt suggests that Midas' yearning for power comes from concern that he is judged negatively by those with a long lineage of royalty; therefore, the reader can conclude that Midas is insecure about his standing as king.

D.   Incorrect. Midas' thoughts and actions in the excerpt do not suggest anger. Instead, they reveal his insecurity at not being from a long line of royalty.

23)

A.   Incorrect. This excerpt includes background information about the character of Midas, but no action, so it has not yet developed beyond the exposition phase of the story.

B.   Correct. This excerpt is introducing background information about the character of Midas, which is a characteristic of the exposition of a story.

C.   Incorrect. This excerpt has not yet developed beyond the exposition phase of the story, so the climax has not yet been revealed.

D.   Incorrect. So far, there is no action in the story, only background information about the character of Midas. Therefore, this excerpt comes from the story's exposition.

24)

A.   Incorrect. The excerpt does have a particular register that includes vocabulary and usage from the Edwardian era, but in this instance, the register does not aid the reader in determining the meaning of the word *coveted*.

B.   Incorrect. Structural analysis is not the optimal choice for determining the meaning of the word *coveted* because it is not a word that has an obvious or common Greek or Latin root.

C.   Correct. The repetition of the word *power* and the use of the words *always* and *more* in an additional phrase emphasize the idea that Midas desires power; thus, the syntax of the sentence, or the way it is constructed, provides significant clues to the meaning of *coveted*.

D. Incorrect. While *coveted* tends to have a negative connotation, this connotation would not be understood apart from the meaning of the word, so in this instance, connotation is not the best choice for helping a reader to comprehend the word's meaning.

25)

A. Incorrect. The expression *born and bred to the purple* does not use the over-exaggeration characteristic of hyperbole.

B. Incorrect. Personification is the attribution of human characteristics to a nonhuman thing or abstract idea; the expression *born and bred to the purple* does not feature personification.

C. Incorrect. A simile is a comparison using *like* or *as*. The expression *born and bred to the purple* does not make such a comparison.

D. Correct. The expression *born and bred to the purple* is an idiom, or an expression that means more than the sum of its parts. An idiom is commonly understood and used by a specific population; its connotations may not be understood beyond that population, even by people who speak the same language. Here, the expression connotes *royalty*.

26)

A. Incorrect. Myths feature gods and goddesses and explain the origins of places, things, circumstances, etc.

B. Correct. Fables feature animals and include explicit moral lessons for readers.

C. Incorrect. Legends are unverified stories from long ago featuring heroes and heroines who overcome overwhelming obstacles.

D. Incorrect. Fairy tales are imaginary, dream-like stories that feature royalty and magical creatures.

27)

A. Incorrect. The way a story is organized may help convey the theme, but it is not the underlying idea that runs through the story.

B. Incorrect. The moral of a story is the lesson the author wants to teach, not the underlying idea that weaves in and out of the text from start to finish.

C. Correct. The theme runs throughout a story from start to finish and is the underlying idea that an author wants to convey.

D. Incorrect. Point of view describes the perspective from which a story is told, not the underlying idea that runs through it from start to finish.

28)

A. **Correct.** The word *park* acts as an adjective describing the noun *naturalist* in the first sentence and is part of an adjective phrase *from the park*, which modifies the noun *migration* in the second sentence.

B. Incorrect. The word *naturalist* is the subject of both sentences. The word *park* acts as an adjective to describe the subject in the first sentence.

C. Incorrect. The word *park* is an adjective that describes the subject in the first sentence and part of an adjective phrase that describes the noun *migration* in the second sentence. The predicate of the second sentence includes the word *park* along with all of the other words following the subject (i.e., "visited the class to talk about the migration of Monarch butterflies from the park").

D. Incorrect. While the word *park* does act as an adjective to describe the noun *naturalist* in the first sentence, "from the park" is an adjective phrase that modifies the noun *migration*, not the verb *visited*.

29)

A. Incorrect. A simple sentence is constructed of only one independent clause.

B. Incorrect. A compound sentence is constructed of two or more independent clauses.

C. **Correct.** The sentence is an example of a complex sentence with one dependent clause and one independent clause.

D. Incorrect. A compound-complex sentence has two or more independent clauses and one or more dependent clauses.

30)

A. Incorrect. The use of the contraction *it's* is incorrect. The possessive *its*, without an apostrophe, should be used instead.

B. Incorrect. No comma is needed before *because* because the dependent clause follows the independent clause.

C. **Correct.** The word *it's* is a contraction meaning *it is*. The possessive form of *its* is written without an apostrophe.

D. Incorrect. The use of a present tense verb is correct because the steepness of the trail is a general truth.

31)

A. Incorrect. The verb tenses are consistent and explain Lucy's thoughts after the movies have been viewed.

B. **Correct.** The word *than*, which is a conjunction used to make comparisons, should be used instead of *then*, which is an adverb that means *at that time*.

C. Incorrect. The word *one* refers back to a countable noun, in this instance, *movie*. It is not a dangling modifier, which is a word, phrase, or clause that modifies a subject misplaced in or missing from the sentence.

D.   Incorrect. The subject of the sentence is *Lucy*, and it is correctly placed at the beginning of the sentence.

32)

A.   Incorrect. Revising part of a story without an organizational framework is less beneficial.

B.   Correct. It is most beneficial for students to use graphic organizers to shape their ideas before writing.

C.   Incorrect. Drafting the beginning of a story without an organizational framework is less beneficial.

D.   Incorrect. Sharing an original story with a classmate should come at the end of the writing process, when the writing has gone through all stages and is ready for an audience.

33)

A.   Incorrect. A metaphor is a direct comparison made without the words *like* or *as*.

B.   Incorrect. Assonance is the use of similar vowel sounds in a line of poetry.

C.   Incorrect. Alliteration is the repetition of closely positioned words that begin with the same sound.

D.   Correct. A simile is a comparison made using the words *like* or *as*.

34)

A.   Incorrect. It is the poet's choice of rhyme scheme that leads the reader to the correct pronunciation of *quays*, not a comparison using *like* or *as*.

B.   Correct. The poet uses an *aabb* rhyme scheme throughout the poem, which lets the reader know that the word *quays* should be pronounced to rhyme with *trees*.

C.   Incorrect. It is the poet's choice of rhyme scheme that leads the reader to the correct pronunciation of *quays*, not the attribution of a human quality.

D.   Incorrect. It is the poet's choice of rhyme scheme that leads the reader to the correct pronunciation of *quays*, not the point of view used to relate the poem.

35)

A.   Correct. Onomatopoeia is the use of words that imitate or resemble sounds.

B.   Incorrect. These words describe the poem's setting.

C.   Incorrect. These words contribute to the calming tone of the poem.

D.   Incorrect. These are sensory words that emphasize illumination.

36)

A.   Incorrect. Expository writing is used to explain or inform a reader about a topic in a formal style.

B.   Incorrect. Narrative writing is used to relate a highly structured fictional story or personal memoir.

C.   Correct. Descriptive writing produces sensory imagery and vivid impressions and is often used in poetry.

D.   Incorrect. Persuasive writing is used to convince a reader of an opinion or point of view.

37)

A.   Incorrect. The conventions remain the same.

B.   Incorrect. The sentences share similar organization.

C.   Incorrect. Both sentences read naturally.

D.   Correct. The revised sentence replaces vague and non-descriptive words with more specific words that provide the reader with a clearer idea of the author's message.

38)

A.   Incorrect. Revising part of a story without an organizational framework is less beneficial.

B.   Correct. It is most beneficial for students to use graphic organizers to shape their ideas before writing.

C.   Incorrect. Drafting the beginning of a story without an organizational framework is less beneficial.

D.   Incorrect. Sharing an original story with a classmate should come at the end of the writing process, when the writing has gone through all stages and is ready for an audience.

39)

A.   Incorrect. Learning the names of authors is secondary to avoiding plagiarism, which is a serious issue in the field of research.

B.   Incorrect. Categorizing source material relies more on content knowledge than paraphrasing and citing information. It is also secondary to avoiding plagiarism, which is a serious issue in the field of research.

C.   Correct. Learning the importance of avoiding plagiarism is a critical component of writing instruction for school and career success.

D.   Incorrect. Learning how to condense writing for maximum impact relies more on content knowledge than paraphrasing and citing information.

40)

    A.   **Correct.** Expository writing is most appropriate for the formal and objective presentation of information required in a research paper.

    B.   Incorrect. A research paper needs to be written with a formal structure and an objective, straightforward tone, so writing that emphasizes imagery is not the best style choice.

    C.   Incorrect. Narrative writing is used to tell a personal or fictional story that entertains a reader, so it is not the best style choice for a research paper.

    D.   Incorrect. Persuasive writing is used to convince the reader of an opinion or point of view, but a research paper needs to be written with an objective tone.

41)

    A.   Incorrect. A handwritten letter by an established historical figure is an example of a primary source because it is significant original, first-hand material.

    B.   Incorrect. A photograph is an example of a primary source because it is original, first-hand material.

    C.   Incorrect. An audio recording is an example of a primary source because it is original, first-hand material.

    D.   **Correct.** A book that discusses a historical time period is an example of a secondary source because it's written by an author who synthesizes and analyzes primary sources to form conclusions.

42)

    A.   Incorrect. An opinion piece is an example of persuasive writing that aims to influence the reader to agree with what is stated and act accordingly.

    B.   Incorrect. A cause-and-effect essay is an example of expository writing that explains and provides information.

    C.   Incorrect. A poem that evokes feeling through imagery is an example of descriptive writing.

    D.   **Correct.** A personal story with a plot arc is an example of narrative writing.

43)

    A.   **Correct.** Self-published materials are considered unreliable sources because expertise has not been established.

    B.   Incorrect. An edited book of essays is considered a reliable research source because expertise is authenticated by the editor selecting the essays.

    C.   Incorrect. A newspaper article is considered a reliable research source because expertise is authenticated by the publisher.

    D.   Incorrect. A university study is considered a reliable research source because expertise is authenticated by the reputation of the institution.

44)

    A.   Incorrect. Presenting outcomes is the purpose of the final stage of the writing process.

    B.   Incorrect. Organizing ideas is the purpose of the first stage of the writing process.

    C.   **Correct.** Correcting errors is the purpose of the rewriting stage of the writing process.

    D.   Incorrect. Recording thoughts is the purpose of the drafting stage of the writing process.

45)

    A.   Incorrect. The primary purpose of narrative writing is to entertain.

    B.   **Correct.** The primary purpose of expository writing to explain.

    C.   Incorrect. The primary purpose of persuasive writing is to convince.

    D.   Incorrect. The primary purpose of descriptive writing is to describe.

46)

    A.   Incorrect. Smiling at the speaker demonstrates active listening because one's focus is on the speaker.

    B.   Incorrect. Leaning forward slightly demonstrates active listening because one's focus is on hearing the speaker's words.

    C.   **Correct.** Looking down at the floor does not demonstrate active listening because one's focus is not on the speaker.

    D.   Incorrect. Sitting up straight demonstrates active listening because it indicates alertness and concentration.

47)

    A.   **Correct.** This sentence paraphrases the original sentence most accurately because it restates the speaker's main idea and reasoning in a revised and concise way.

    B.   Incorrect. This sentence is practically identical to the original statement, so it is not a proper example of paraphrasing.

    C.   Incorrect. This sentence restates the speaker's main idea, but it excludes his reasoning, so it is not a good example of paraphrasing.

    D.   Incorrect. This sentence alters the speaker's message because it excludes the speaker's main idea, which is that school start times should be later.

48)

A.   Incorrect. Moving around demonstrates a lack of focus and is distracting to a speaker.

B.   Incorrect. Interjecting questions does not demonstrate active listening because it interrupts the speaker.

C.   Incorrect. Frowning and crossed arms do not demonstrate active listening because they are nonverbal cues that convey judgment.

D.   Correct. Eye contact and learning forward demonstrate that the listener is actively focusing on the speaker's message.

49)

A.   Incorrect. Students are not restating the message in their own words; they are learning editing skills.

B.   Correct. Mr. Kahn is modeling the editing process and reinforcing concepts related to the conventions of Standard English.

C.   Incorrect. This lesson is designed for students who have advanced beyond the decoding stage of reading instruction.

D.   Incorrect. Mr. Kahn is modeling the editing process, not the comprehension skill of inferencing.

50)

A.   Incorrect. Making crayon rubbings helps students internalize letter shapes, but it is not finger spelling.

B.   Correct. Finger spelling is a form of sign language that uses the hands to represent letters.

C.   Incorrect. Using the fingers to count the number of letters in words develops the concept of print, but it is not finger spelling.

D.   Incorrect. Writing letters in trays of sand helps students practice forming letters, but it is not finger spelling.

Mathematics Practice

1

Which equation demonstrates the associative property of addition?

A. $2 + (1 + 5) = (2 + 1) + 5$

B. $2(1 \times 5) = (2 \times 1)5$

C. $1 \times 3 = 3 \times 1$

D. $2(7 + 4) = 2 \times 7 + 2 \times 4$

2

Using the information in the table, which equation demonstrates the linear relationship between x and y?

x	y
3	3
7	15
10	24

A. $y = 6x - 6$

B. $y = 5x - 6$

C. $y = 4x - 6$

D. $y = 3x - 6$

3

Using the table, which equation demonstrates the linear relationship between x and y?

x	y
3	−18
7	−34
10	−46

A. $y = -6x - 6$

B. $y = -5x - 6$

C. $y = -4x - 6$

D. $y = -3x - 6$

4

Students board a bus at 7:45 a.m. and arrive at school at 8:20 a.m. How long are the students on the bus?

A. 30 minutes

B. 35 minutes

C. 45 minutes

D. 60 minutes

5

Which expression has only prime factors of 3, 5, and 11?

A. 66×108

B. 15×99

C. 42×29

D. 28×350

6

Robbie has a bag of treats that contains 5 pieces of gum, 7 pieces of taffy, and 8 pieces of chocolate. If Robbie reaches into the bag and randomly pulls out a treat, what is the probability that Robbie will get a piece of taffy?

A. 1

B. $\frac{1}{7}$

C. $\frac{5}{8}$

D. $\frac{7}{20}$

7

Which figure is a concave polygon?

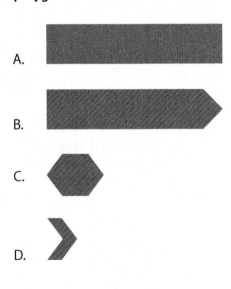

A.

B.

C.

D.

8

Micah invites 23 friends to his house and is having pizza for dinner. Each pizza feeds approximately 4 people. Micah does not want a lot of leftovers. How many pizzas should he order?

A. 4

B. 5

C. 6

D. 7

9

Kim and Chris are writing a book together. Kim writes twice as many pages as Chris. Altogether, there are 240 pages in the book. Which equation shows how many pages Chris writes?

A. $2 + 2p = 240$

B. $p + 2p = 240$

C. $2p - p = 240$

D. $p - 2p = 240$

10

An ice chest contains 24 sodas, some regular and some diet. The ratio of diet soda to regular soda is 1:3. How many regular sodas are there in the ice chest?

A. 1

B. 4

C. 18

D. 24

11

Which inequality is equivalent to $10 \le k - 5$?

A. $k \le 15$

B. $k \ge 15$

C. $k \le 5$

D. $k \le 10$

12

What is $\frac{5}{8}$ as a percent?

A.   0.625%

B.   1.6%

C.   16%

D.   62.5%

13

Simplify $(5^2 - 2)^2 + 3^3$.

A.   25

B.   30

C.   556

D.   538

14

Which statement describes the images?

A.   When the numerator stays the same and the denominator increases, the fraction increases.

B.   When the numerator increases and the denominator stays the same, the fraction increases.

C.   When the numerator and the denominator increase, the fraction decreases.

D.   When the numerator stays the same and the denominator decreases, the fraction decreases.

15

Danny collects coins. The table shows how many of each type of coin Danny collects for 4 days. Which statement is true?

Danny's Coin Collection				
Coin	Day 1	Day 2	Day 3	Day 4
Pennies	1	4	5	1
Nickels	4	3	2	5
Dimes	3	2	2	3
Quarters	0	5	4	1

A.   The mean number of nickels is greater than the mean number of quarters.

B.   The mean number of quarters is greater than the mean number of pennies.

C.   The range of dimes is greater than the range of quarters.

D.   The median number of pennies is 5.

16

Solve for x.

$x = 6(3^0)$

A.   0

B.   18

C.   180

D.   6

17

A table is 150 centimeters long. How many millimeters long is the table?

A.   1.5 mm

B.   15 mm

C.   150 mm

D.   1500 mm

18

Students are asked if they prefer vanilla, chocolate, or strawberry ice cream. The results are tallied on the table below.

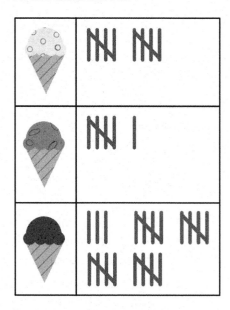

The students display the information from the table in a bar graph. Which student completes the bar graph correctly?

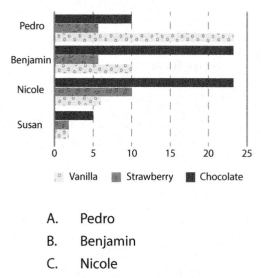

A.   Pedro
B.   Benjamin
C.   Nicole
D.   Susan

19

If the pattern continues, what is the next number?

{2, 5, 14, 41, 122, …}

A.   244
B.   264
C.   422
D.   365

20

What is the value of $3x + 7x$ if $x = 8$?

A.   10
B.   21
C.   31
D.   80

21

What is the value of the digit 4 in the number 654,123?

A.   one thousand
B.   four thousand
C.   ten thousand
D.   forty thousand

22

Which equation is described by the data in the table?

x	y
1	3
2	0
3	−5

A. $y = 4 - x^2$
B. $x^2 + y = 4$
C. $x^2 + y = 2^2$
D.   all of the above

23

The formula for distance is $d = r \times t$. How long will it take a plane to fly 4000 miles from Chicago to London if the plane flies at a constant rate of 500 mph?

A.   20 hours

B.   8 hours

C.   45 hours

D.   3.5 hours

24

Justin has a summer lawn care business. Justin earns $400 per week by taking care of 10 lawns. Justin pays $35/week in business-related expenses. The money Justin saves after x weeks is represented by the expression $x(400 - 35)$. If y represents Justin's total earnings, which expression shows how many dollars Justin earns in a summer?

A. $y = 365x$

B. $35x = 400y$

C. $x + y = 365$

D. $x = 365y$

25

Which expression can be solved using the following steps?

1. Subtract 5 from m.

2. Multiply the result by 2.

3. Cube the result.

A. $[2(m - 5)]^3$

B. $2m^3 - 5$

C. $2m - 5^3$

D. $2(m - 5)^3$

26

Which property is demonstrated by the equivalent expressions?

$7(3 + 5) = 7 \times 3 + 7 \times 5$

A.   distributive

B.   associative

C.   commutative

D.   multiplicative

27

Using the function table, what is the value of $f(20)$?

x	$f(x)$
5	12
10	22
15	32
20	
25	52

A.   20

B.   25

C.   42

D.   50

28

Which number has a prime factorization of 3 odd numbers and 1 even number?

A.   9

B.   21

C.   45

D.   90

29

How much longer is line segment MN than line segment KL?

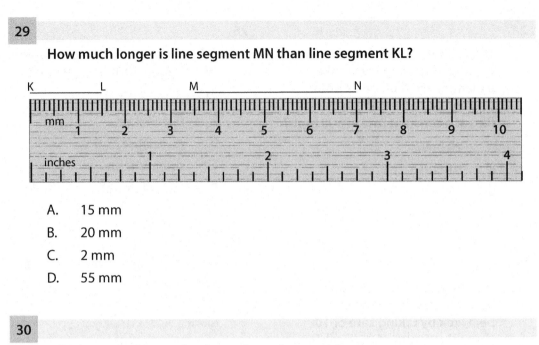

A.   15 mm

B.   20 mm

C.   2 mm

D.   55 mm

30

Which conclusion can be drawn from the graph?

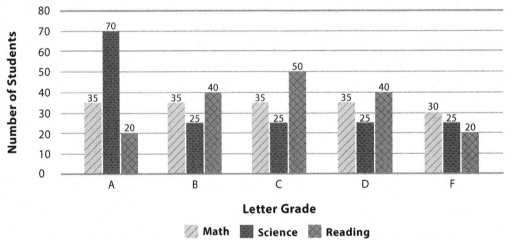

A.   More than twice as many students score an "A" in science than score an "F" in science.

B.   The majority of the students score a "C" in math.

C.   The number of students who score a "B" in reading is equal to the number of students who score a "B" in math.

D.   Next year's students do not need very much science instruction because students already know science.

31

In the fall, 425 students pass the math benchmark. In the spring, 680 students pass the same benchmark. What is the percentage increase in passing scores from fall to spring?

A.   40%

B.   55%

C.   60%

D.   80%

32

Noah and Jennifer have a total of $10.00 to spend on lunch. If each buys his or her own order of french fries and a soda, how many orders of chicken strips can they share?

Menu	
Item	**Price**
Hamburger	$4.00
Chicken Strips	$4.00
Onion Rings	$3.00
French Fries	$2.00
Soda	$1.00
Shake	$1.00

A.   0

B.   1

C.   2

D.   3

33

Lynn has 4 grades in science class. Each grade is worth 100 points. Lynn has an 85% average. If Lynn makes 100% on each of the first 3 grades, what does she earn on her 4th grade?

A.   40%

B.   55%

C.   85%

D.   100%

34

Which expression is equivalent to dividing 300 by 12?

A. $2(150 - 6)$

B. $(300 \div 4) \div 6$

C. $(120 \div 6) + (180 \div 6)$

D. $(120 \div 12) + (180 \div 12)$

35

Aprille has $50 to buy the items on her list. Assuming there is no sales tax, about how much change will Aprille receive after buying all the items on her list?

Aprille's List	
Item	**Price**
Hammer	$13.24
Screwdriver	$11.99
Nails	$4.27
Wrench	$5.60

A. $10

B. $15

C. $35

D. $50

36

Which number has the greatest value?

A. 9299 ones

B. 903 tens

C. 93 hundreds

D. 9 thousands

37

Which number has the least value?

A. 0.305

B. 0.035

C. 0.35

D. 0.3

38

What is the perimeter of the shape?

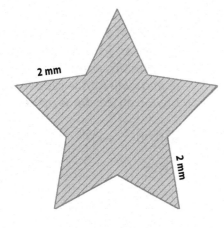

A. 2 mm

B. 4 mm

C. 10 mm

D. 20 mm

39

What is the area of the shape?

A. 64 mm²

B. 16 mm²

C. 128 mm²

D. 6 mm²

40

Which three-dimensional solid has 2 triangular faces and 3 rectangular faces?

A. pyramid

B. cube

C. rectangular prism

D. triangular prism

41

What are the coefficients and the degrees of the terms in the polynomial?

A. coefficients {4, 5}, degrees {3, 2}

B. coefficients {1, 4, 5}, degrees {3, 2}

C. coefficients {3, 2}, degrees {4, 5}

D. coefficients {3, 2}, degrees {1, 4, 5}

42

In which quadrant is the point (−3, −4) located?

A.   I

B.   II

C.   III

D.   IV

43

Which terms can be used to describe the polygon?

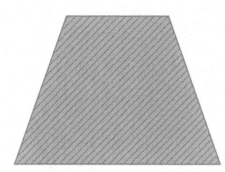

A.   irregular and convex

B.   irregular and concave

C.   regular and convex

D.   regular and concave

44

How many times larger is the digit 3 in the first number compared to the second number?

Number One: 846,307

Number Two: 209,023

A.   2

B.   4

C.   10

D.   100

45

A fruit stand sells apples, bananas, and oranges at a ratio of 3:2:1. If the fruit stand sells 20 bananas, how many total pieces of fruit does the fruit stand sell?

A.   10

B.   30

C.   40

D.   60

46

Which type of number is shown below?

3.65555555…

A.   natural number

B.   whole number

C.   integer

D.   rational number

47

Out of 1560 students at Ward Middle School, 15% want to take French. Which equation can determine how many students want to take French?

A. $x = 1560 \div 15$

B. $x = 15 \div 1560$

C. $x = 1560 \times 0.15$

D. $x = 1560 \div 100$

48

What is the 6th term of the sequence if the pattern is to find the difference between the 2 preceding numbers and then multiply by −3?

{3, 0, −9, −36, ___, _?_ }

A.   −81

B.   −135

C.   135

D.   81

49

Kim drives 75 mph for t hours. If t = time and d = distance, the equation $d = 75t$ describes Kim's drive. Which statement is true?

A.   The dependent variable is t because time depends on the distance Kim travels.

B.   The independent variable is t because the time is being multiplied by the independent rate of 75.

C.   The dependent variable is d because the distance depends on the number of hours Kim drives.

D.   The dependent and independent variables cannot be determined in the equation.

50

Which graph shows the solution to $y = 2x + 1$?

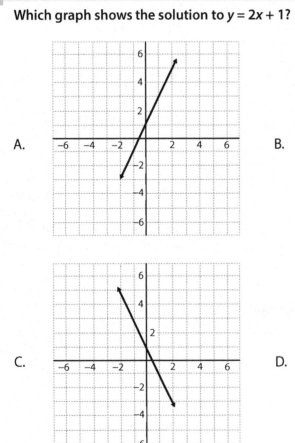

A.

C.

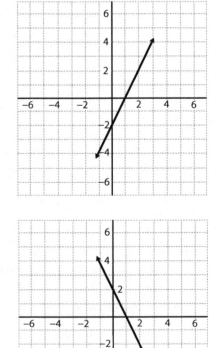

B.

D.

Answer Key

1)

A. **Correct.** $2 + (1 + 5) = (2 + 1) + 5$ is the correct answer. When using the associative property, the answer will remain the same in an addition problem regardless of where the parentheses are placed.

B. Incorrect. $2(1 \times 5) = (2 \times 1)5$ is not the correct answer. This equation demonstrates the associative property of multiplication.

C. Incorrect. $1 \times 3 = 3 \times 1$ is not the correct answer. This equation demonstrates the commutative property of multiplication where the answer in a multiplication problem will remain the same regardless of the order of the numbers.

D. Incorrect. $2(7 + 4) = 2 \times 7 + 2 \times 4$ is not the correct answer. This equation demonstrates the distributive property, which says that multiplication can be distributed over addition.

2)

A. Incorrect. $y = 6x - 6$ is not the correct answer. Solve for y by replacing x with 3.

$y = 6(3) - 6$

$y = 18 - 6$

$y = 12$

The table says that when $x = 3$, $y = 3$, not 12.

B. Incorrect. $y = 5x - 6$ is not the correct answer. Solve for y by replacing x with 3.

$y = 5(3) - 6$

$y = 15 - 6$

$y = 9$

The table says that when $x = 3$, $y = 3$, not 9.

C. Incorrect. $y = 4x - 6$ is not the correct answer. Solve for y by replacing x with 3.

$y = 4(3) - 6$

$y = 12 - 6$

$y = 6$

The table says that when $x = 3$, $y = 3$, not 6.

D. **Correct.** $y = 3x - 6$ is the correct answer. Solve for y by replacing x with 3.

$y = 3(3) - 6$

$y = 9 - 6$

$y = 3$

This is the correct answer because the table says that when $x = 3$, $y = 3$.

3)

A. Incorrect. $y = -6x - 6$ is not the correct answer. Solve for y by replacing x with 3.

$y = -6(3) - 6$

$y = -18 - 6$

$y = -24$

The table says that when $x = 3$, $y = -18$, not -24.

B. Incorrect. $y = -5x - 6$ is not the correct answer. Solve for y by replacing x with 3.

$y = -5(3) - 6$

$y = -15 - 6$

$y = -24$

The table says that when $x = 3$, $y = -18$, not -24.

C. **Correct.** $y = -4x - 6$ is the correct answer. Solve for y by replacing x with 3.

$y = -4(3) - 6$

$y = -12 - 6$

$y = -18$

The table says that when $x = 3$, $y = -18$.

D. Incorrect. $y = -3x - 6$ is not the correct answer. Solve for y by replacing x with 3.

$y = -3(3) - 6$

$y = -9 - 6$

$y = -15$

The table says that when $x = 3$, $y = -18$, not -15.

4)

A. Incorrect. 30 minutes is not correct. There are 15 minutes between 7:45 a.m. and 8:00 a.m. and 20 minutes from 8:00 a.m. until 8:20 a.m.; 15 minutes + 20 minutes = 35 minutes, not 30 minutes.

B. **Correct.** 35 minutes is the correct answer. There are 15 minutes between 7:45 a.m. and 8:00 a.m. and 20 minutes from 8:00 a.m. until 8:20 a.m.; 15 minutes + 20 minutes = 35 minutes.

C.   Incorrect. 45 minutes is not correct. There are 15 minutes between 7:45 a.m. and 8:00 a.m. and 20 minutes from 8:00 a.m. until 8:20 a.m.; 15 minutes + 20 minutes = 35 minutes, not 45 minutes.

D.   Incorrect. 60 minutes is not correct. There are 15 minutes between 7:45 a.m. and 8:00 a.m. and 20 minutes from 8:00 a.m. until 8:20 a.m.; 15 minutes + 20 minutes = 35 minutes, not 60 minutes.

5)

A.   Incorrect. 66 × 108 is not the correct answer. Both numbers are even, so 2 is a factor of both numbers.

B.   Correct. 15 × 99 is the correct answer. The factor trees show the factors for 15 and 99.

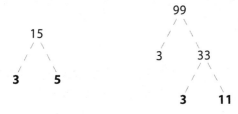

This answer choice has 3, 5, and 11 as the only prime factors.

C.   Incorrect. 42 × 29 is not the correct answer. Forty–two is an even number, so 2 is a factor.

D.   Incorrect. 28 × 350 is not the correct answer. Both numbers are even, so 2 is a factor of both numbers.

6)

A.   Incorrect. 1 is not the correct answer. $7 \div 20 \neq 1$.

B.   Incorrect. $\frac{1}{7}$ is not the correct answer. $7 \div 20 \neq \frac{1}{7}$.

C.   Incorrect. $\frac{5}{8}$ is not the correct answer. $7 \div 20 \neq \frac{5}{8}$.

D.   Correct. 7/20 is the correct answer. Probability is the number of favorable events divided by the number of possible events. In this case, Robbie pulls out 1 treat from a bag that contains 7 pieces of taffy; therefore 7 is the number of favorable events. There are 20 total treats in the bag because $5 + 7 + 8 = 20$. $7 \div 20 = \frac{7}{20}$.

7)

A.   Incorrect. A concave polygon must have an interior angle that measures greater than 180 degrees. A rectangle has four 90 degree angles.

B.   Incorrect. A concave polygon must have an interior angle that measures greater than 180 degrees. The figure depicted is actually a convex polygon.

C.   Incorrect. A concave polygon must have an interior angle that measures greater than 180 degrees. In contrast, the hexagon is a convex polygon.

D.   **Correct.** The interior angle on the left side of the figure is greater than 180 degrees.

8)

A.   Incorrect. 4 is not the correct answer. 23 people ÷ 4 pizzas = 5.75 people/pizza. This would not be enough because each pizza feeds 4 people.

B.   Incorrect. 5 is not the correct answer. 23 people ÷ 5 pizzas = 4.6 people/pizza. This would not be enough because each pizza feeds 4 people.

C.   **Correct.** 6 is the correct answer. 23 people ÷ 6 pizzas = 3.8 people/pizza. There would be some pizza left, but this is the closest Micah will be able to get to 4 people/pizza.

D.   Incorrect. 7 is not the correct answer. 23 people ÷ 7 pizzas = 3.3 people/pizza. Micah would have too much pizza left.

9)

A.   Incorrect. $2 + 2p = 240$ is not the correct answer. If p is the number of pages Chris writes, the equation shows only the pages written by Kim ($2p$) and credits Chris with writing only 2 pages.

B.   **Correct.** $p + 2p = 240$ is the correct answer. If p is the number of pages Chris writes, the equation shows that Kim writes $2p$, or twice as many pages as Chris writes. If the number of pages Chris writes is added to the number of pages Kim writes, the total is 240 pages.

C.   Incorrect. $2p - p = 240$ is not the correct answer. Adding, not subtracting, will find the total number of pages.

D.   Incorrect. $p - 2p = 240$ is not the correct answer. Adding, not subtracting, will find the total number of pages.

10)

A.   Incorrect. 1 is not the correct answer; it represents the number of diet sodas for every 3 regular sodas.

B.   Incorrect. 3 is not the correct answer; it represents the number of regular sodas for every 1 diet soda.

C.   **Correct.** 18 is the correct answer. One way to find the answer is to draw a picture.

Put 24 cans into groups of 4. One out of every 4 cans is diet (light gray) so there is 1 light gray can for every 3 dark gray cans. That leaves 18 dark gray cans (regular soda).

Another way to solve the problem is to use ratios. There is 1 diet soda for every 3 regular sodas, for a total of 4 sodas. Diet = 1, regular = 3, total = 4.

$$\frac{\text{Regular}}{\text{Total}} = \frac{3}{4} = \frac{x}{24}$$

Cross-multiply $4x = 72$ and $x = 18$.

D.   Incorrect. 24 is not the correct answer; it simply represents the total number of sodas.

11)

A.   Incorrect. $k \leq 15$ is not the correct answer. Use the steps to solve the inequality.

$10 \leq k - 5$

$5 + 10 \leq k - 5 + 5$ Add 5 to both sides to isolate the variable.

$15 \leq k$

15 is less than or equal to k. Notice that the answer choice is written as k is less than or equal to 15 ($k \leq 15$), which is backward.

B.   Correct. $k \geq 15$ is the correct answer. The sign is flipped from what is shown in the problem, but k is equal to or greater than 15.

C.   Incorrect. $k \geq 5$ is not the correct answer. Add 5 rather than subtract 5 from both sides of the inequality to isolate the variable.

D.   Incorrect. $k \geq 10$ is not the correct answer. Isolate the variable to solve the problem.

12)

A.   Incorrect. 0.625% is not the correct answer. This answer results from correctly dividing the numerator by the denominator but forgetting to multiply the answer by 100.

B.   Incorrect. 1.6% is not the correct answer. This answer results from confusing the numerator (top number) and the denominator (bottom number) and forgetting to multiply by 100.

C.   Incorrect. 16% is not the correct answer. To change a fraction to a percent, divide the numerator by the denominator and then multiply by 100. This answer results from dividing the denominator by the numerator.

D.   Correct. 62.5% is the correct answer; $5 \div 8 = 0.625$ and $0.625 \times 100 = 62.5\%$.

13)

A.   Incorrect. 25 is not the correct answer. Remember that 5^2 is equal to 5×5.

B.   Incorrect. 30 is not the correct answer. To solve the expression, use the order of operations. Step One: Solve the exponent in parentheses. Step Two: Subtract the numbers in parentheses. Step Three: Solve the exponents. Step Four: Add the numbers.

C.   Correct. 556 is the correct answer. $(5^2 - 2)^2 + 3^3$

$(25 - 2)^2 + 3^3$

$(23)^2 + 3^3$

$529 + 27 = 556$

D.   Incorrect. 538 is not the correct answer. The answer resulted from the mistake of multiplying 3×3 rather than solving 3^3. Remember $3^3 = 3 \times 3 \times 3$.

14)

A.   Incorrect. (A) is not correct because the images show the numerator increasing, not the denominator. If the denominator increases and the numerator remains constant ($\frac{1}{5}, \frac{1}{6}, \frac{1}{7}, \frac{1}{8}$), the fraction decreases.

B.   Correct. The images show the numerator increasing while the denominator stays the same; meanwhile, the fraction is increasing.

C.   Incorrect. When both the numerator and denominator increase, there are inconsistencies in the comparative size of the fraction.

D.   Incorrect. If the numerator stays the same and the denominator decreases, the fraction will increase.

15)

A.   Correct. To calculate the mean, add all the numbers in a set and divide by how many numbers are in the set. The mean number of nickels is $4 + 3 + 2 + 2 = 11$ divided by 4 (because there are 4 numbers in the set) $= 2.75$ nickels. The mean number of quarters is $0 + 5 + 4 + 1 = 10$ divided by $4 = 2.5$ quarters. $2.75 > 2.5$.

B.   Incorrect. The mean of the pennies is $1 + 4 + 5 + 1 = 11$ divided by $4 = 2.75$. The mean number of quarters is $0 + 5 + 4 + 1 = 10$ divided by $4 = 2.5$. The mean number of pennies is equal to the mean number of quarters.

C.   Incorrect. The range is the difference between the highest number and the lowest number in the set. For the dimes, the highest number is 3 and the lowest number is 2, so $3 - 2 = 1$. For the quarters, the highest number is 5 and the lowest number is 0. $5 - 0 = 5$. $1 < 5$.

D.   Incorrect. The mode for the set is 5; the median is a middle number in a set. The set of pennies in numerical order is {1, 1, 4, 5}. In this case, there are two numbers in the middle; therefore, averaging the one and the four will find the median. The median of the set of pennies is 2.5.

16)

A.   Incorrect. 0 is not the correct answer. The answer results from multiplying 3×0. Remember that $3^0 = 1$, not 0.

B.   Incorrect. 18 is not the correct answer. The first step in the equation is to solve the exponent.

C.   Incorrect. 180 is not the correct answer. The problem is not solved by multiplying 6×30.

D.   **Correct.** 6 is the correct answer. Any number with a 0 exponent equals 1. Therefore, $6(3^0) = 6(1) = 6$.

17)

A.   Incorrect. 1.5 mm is not the correct answer. One centimeter = 10 millimeters. The answer results from moving the decimal point two places and in the wrong direction.

B.   Incorrect. 15 mm is incorrect. The answer results from moving the decimal point one place in the wrong direction.

C.   Incorrect. 150 mm is not the correct answer. Millimeters are not equal to centimeters.

D.   **Correct.** 1500 mm is the correct answer. 1 centimeter = 10 millimeters and $150 \times 10 = 1500$.

18)

A.   Incorrect. Pedro's graph is incorrect. He confuses the number of students who prefer vanilla with the number of students who prefer chocolate.

B.   **Correct.** Benjamin completed the graph correctly. His bar graph indicates that 10 students prefer vanilla, 6 students prefer strawberry, and 23 students prefer chocolate ice cream.

C.   Incorrect. Nicole did not complete the graph correctly. She confuses the number of students who like vanilla with the number of students who like strawberry.

D.   Incorrect. Susan's graph is not correct. She did not accurately count the tallies before making her bar graph.

19)

A.   Incorrect. 244 is not the correct answer. The answer results from multiplying the last number in the set by 2. Numbers in the set do not follow the pattern of multiplying by 2 because $2 \times 2 \neq 5$.

B.   Incorrect. 264 is not the correct answer. Numbers in the set are not following a sequence that would match the answer.

C.   Incorrect. 422 is not the correct answer. Numbers in the set are not following a sequence that would match the answer.

D.   **Correct.** 365 is the correct answer. The pattern follows the equation $3n - 1 = x$. n = the last number in the set, and x = the next number in the set. Another pattern is adding by exponents of 3. Remember $3 \times 3 \times 3 \times 3 \times 3 = 3^5 = 243$. The pattern is $2 + 3^1 = 5$, $5 + 3^2 + 14$, $14 + 3^3 = 41$, $41 + 3^4 = 122$, $122 + 3^5 = 365$.

20)

    A.   Incorrect. 10 is not the correct answer because $3(8) + 7(8) = 24 + 56 \neq 10$.

    B.   Incorrect. 21 is not the correct answer because $3(8) + 7(8) = 24 + 56 \neq 21$.

    C.   Incorrect. 31 is not the correct answer because $3(8) + 7(8) = 24 + 56 \neq 31$.

    D.   **Correct.** 80 is the correct answer. $3(8) + 7(8) = 24 + 56 = 80$. Or, put another way, $3x + 7x = 10x$ and $(10)(8) = 80$.

21)

    A.   Incorrect. While 4 is in the thousands place, a 4 in that position is equal to 4000.

    B.   **Correct.** 4000 is the correct answer because $654{,}123 = 600{,}000 + 50{,}000 + 4000 + 100 + 20 + 3$.

    C.   Incorrect. 10,000 is incorrect because 5 is in the ten-thousands place.

    D.   Incorrect. 40,000 is incorrect because 4 is in the thousands place, not the ten-thousands place.

22)

    A.   Incorrect. $y = 4 - x^2$ is a correct answer, but it is not the only correct answer. Substitute 1 for x and 3 for y.

$$3 = 4 - 1^2$$
$$3 = 4 - 1$$
$$3 = 3$$

    B.   Incorrect. $x^2 + y = 4$ is a correct answer, but it is not the only correct answer. Substitute 1 for x and 3 for y.

$$1^2 + 3 = 4$$
$$1 + 3 = 4$$
$$4 = 4$$

    C.   Incorrect. $x^2 + y = 2^2$ is a correct answer, but it is not the only correct answer. Substitute 1 for x and 3 for y.

$$1^2 + 3 = 2^2$$
$$1 + 3 = 4$$
$$4 = 4$$

    D.   **Correct.** All of the above are correct. For each equation, replacing the variables with the numbers in the function table makes a true statement.

23)

    A.   Incorrect. Multiplying the rate by the distance does not find the time, so 20 hours cannot be the correct answer.

    B.   **Correct.** 8 hours is the correct answer. Time is distance divided by rate; 4000 mi/500 mph = 8 hours.

C. Incorrect. 45 hours is not the correct answer. Adding the rate and the distance is not a way to find the time.

D. Incorrect. 5 hours is not the correct answer. Subtracting the rate from the distance is a not a way to find the time.

24)

A. **Correct.** $y = 365x$ is the correct answer. The total savings is equal to the number of weeks Justin works times $365/week profit.

B. Incorrect. $35x = 400y$ is incorrect because the equation says that 400 times the total savings is equal to the business expenses times the number of weeks worked.

C. Incorrect. The weekly profit is not found by adding the number of weeks worked to the total savings.

D. Incorrect. The total number of weeks worked is not equal to the $365/week profit multiplied by the total savings.

25)

A. **Correct.** $[2(m - 5)]^3$ is the correct answer. Using order of operations, the expression is solved using the steps.

B. Incorrect. $2m^3 - 5$ is not the correct answer. In this expression, 5 is subtracted from $2m^3$.

C. Incorrect. $2m - 5^3$ is not the correct answer. In this expression, only 5 is cubed.

D. Incorrect. $2(m - 5)^3$ is not the correct answer. In this expression, only the parentheses are cubed.

26)

A. **Correct.** The equivalent expressions demonstrate the distributive property, which says that multiplication distributes over addition: $a(b + c) = ab + ac$.

B. Incorrect. The associative property states that multiplication or addition problems can be regrouped: $(ab)c = a(bc)$ or $(a + b) + c = a + (b + c)$.

C. Incorrect. The commutative property states that order does not matter when multiplying or adding: $ab = ba$ or $a + b = b + a$.

D. Incorrect. The multiplicative property states that both sides of the equation remain the same if they are multiplied by the same number; on the other hand, the distributive property says that multiplication distributes over addition.

27)

A. Incorrect. 20 is not the correct answer. The relationship between x and $f(x)$ is $\neq$.

B. Incorrect. 25 is not the correct answer. The relationship between *x* and *f(x)* is ≠ +5.

C. **Correct.** 42 is the correct answer. The relationship between *x* and *f(x)* is 2*x* + 2.

D. Incorrect. 50 is not the correct answer. The relationship between *x* and *f(x)* is ≠ 2*x* + 10.

28)

A. Incorrect. 9 is incorrect because the prime factorization of 9 is 3 × 3: there are no even factors.

B. Incorrect. 21 is incorrect because the prime factorization of 21 is 3 × 7: there are no even numbers.

C. Incorrect. 45 is incorrect because the prime factorization of 45 is 3 × 3 × 5: there are no even numbers.

D. **Correct.** 90 is correct because the prime factorization of 90 is 2 × 3 × 3 × 5. Ninety, as the only even number of the answer choices, has an even number (2) as a factor.

29)

A. Incorrect. 15 mm is the length of line segment $\overline{KL}$.

B. **Correct.** Line segment $\overline{MN}$ begins at 35 mm and ends at 70 mm, so 70 − 35 = 35 mm. Line segment $\overline{MN}$ is 35 mm. The length of line segment $\overline{KL}$ is 15 mm. To find out how much longer $\overline{MN}$ is than $\overline{KL}$, subtract, 35 mm − 15 mm = 20 mm.

C. Incorrect. 20 mm = 2 cm, not 2 mm.

D. Incorrect. 55 mm is not the correct answer. 70 mm is where $\overline{MN}$ ends, 15 mm is the length of $\overline{KL}$, and 70 − 15 = 55; however the distance between L and M is ignored.

30)

A. **Correct.** Twenty-five students score an "F" in science, and 70 students score an "A" in science; 2(25) < 70.

B. Incorrect. There are 170 students total with math grades. A majority would be more than half (85). Only 25 students score a "C" in math.

C. Incorrect. Forty students score a "B" in reading and 35 students score a "B" in math.

D. Incorrect. The graph does not include information about next year's students.

31)

A.   Incorrect. 40% is incorrect: $680 - 425 = 255$, $255 \div 425 = .60$, and $.60 \times 100 \neq 40\%$.

B.   Incorrect. 55% is incorrect: $680 - 425 = 255$, $255 \div 425 = .60$, and $.60 \times 100 \neq 55\%$.

C.   **Correct.** 60% is the correct answer. To calculate the percentage increase, find the difference between the ending number and the beginning number ($680 - 425 = 255$). Divide the difference by the beginning number ($255 \div 425 = .60$), and then multiply the decimal by 100 to change to a percentage ($.60 \times 100 = 60\%$).

D.   Incorrect. 80% is incorrect: $680 - 425 = 255$, $255 \div 425 = .60$, and $.60 \times 100 \neq 80\%$.

32)

A.   Incorrect. 0 is not the correct answer because $4.00 can buy 1 order of chicken strips.

B.   **Correct.** 1 is the correct answer. To find out how many orders of chicken strips Jennifer and Noah can buy, use the equation:

$\$10 - 2(\$2.00 + \$1.00) = x$

$\$10 - 2(\$3.00) = x$

$\$10 - \$6.00 = \$4.00$

Four dollars is enough money to buy 1 order of chicken strips to share.

C.   Incorrect. 2 is incorrect because $4.00 is insufficient to buy 2 orders of chicken strips.

D.   Incorrect. 3 is incorrect because $4.00 is not enough money to buy 3 orders of chicken strips.

33)

A.   **Correct.** 40% is the correct answer. To calculate the average, add all of the scores and divide by the total number of scores. Use the variable "x" in place of the missing score. $\quad (100 + 100 + 100 + x) \div 4 = 85$

Isolate the variable. $\quad (300 + x) \div 4 = 85$

Multiply both sides by 4. $\quad (300 + x) = 340$

Subtract 300 from both sides. $\quad x = 40$

B.   Incorrect. If Lynn had scored 55%, her average would be 88.75% because $355 \div 4 = 88.75\%$.

C.   Incorrect. If Lynn had scored 85%, her average would be 96.25% because $385 \div 4 = 96.25\%$.

D.   Incorrect. If Lynn had scored 100%, her average would be 100% because $400 \div 4 = 100\%$.

34)

    A.   Incorrect. $2(150 - 6)$ is not the correct answer.

           $2(150 - 6) \neq 300 \div 12$

           $2(144) \neq 25$

           $288 \neq 25$

    B.   Incorrect. $(300 \div 4) \div 6$ is not the correct answer.

           $(300 \div 4) \div 6 \neq 300 \div 12$

           $75 \div 6 \neq 25$

           $12.5 \neq 25$

    C.   Incorrect. $(120 \div 6) + (180 \div 6)$ is not the correct answer.

           $(120 \div 6) + (180 \div 6) \neq 300 \div 12$

           $20 + 30 \neq 300 \div 12$

           $50 \neq 25$

    D.   **Correct.** $(120 \div 12) + (180 \div 12)$ is the correct answer.

           $(120 \div 12) + (180 \div 12) = 300 \div 12$

           $(10) + (15) = 25$

           $25 = 25$

35)

    A.   Incorrect. $10 is insufficient change.

    B.   **Correct.** To estimate the amount of the change, round the price of each item to the nearest dollar amount and subtract from the total:

           $50 - (\$13 + \$12 + \$4 + \$6)$

           $50 - \$35 = \$15$

           The correct answer is $15.

    C.   Incorrect. $35 is not the correct answer. Adding the price of each item will equal approximately $35. To find out the amount of change, subtract $35 from $50.

    D.   Incorrect. $50 is not the correct answer; it is the amount before any purchases are made.

36)

    A.   Incorrect. 9299 ones is not the correct answer because 9299 ones = 9299.

    B.   Incorrect. 903 tens is not the correct answer because 903 tens = 9030.

    C.   **Correct.** 93 hundreds is the correct answer because 93 hundreds = 9300, and 9300 is greater than the other answer choices.

    D.   Incorrect. 9 thousands is not the correct answer because 9 thousands = 9000.

37)

A. Incorrect. 0.305 is not the correct answer because $0.305 = \frac{305}{1000}$.

B. **Correct.** 0.035 is the correct answer because $0.035 = \frac{35}{1000}$; notice the 0 in the tenths place.

C. Incorrect. 0.35 is not the correct answer because $0.35 = \frac{350}{1000}$.

D. Incorrect. 0.3 is not the correct answer because $0.3 = \frac{300}{1000}$.

38)

A. Incorrect. One side is 2 mm long, but the shape has 10 sides.

B. Incorrect. Each of the 10 sides of this shape must be added to find the perimeter, not just the labeled sides.

C. Incorrect. There are 5 points to a star, but each point has 2 sides. While 5×2 mm = 10 mm, the lengths of all 10 sides must be added to get the perimeter.

D. **Correct.** 20 mm is the correct answer. There are 10 sides and each side is 2 mm in length. To find the perimeter, add the length of each side to find the total. P= 2 + 2 + 2 + 2 + 2 + 2 + 2 + 2 + 2 + 2 = 20 mm.

39)

A. Incorrect. 64 mm^2 is not the correct answer; it is the area of the four small rectangles that protrude on each side.

B. Incorrect. 16 mm^2 is not the correct answer; it is the area of one of the small rectangles that protrude on each side.

C. **Correct.** 128 mm^2 is the correct answer. Find the area of the square as if it did not have cut-outs; each side would be 12 mm long. 12 mm $\times$ 12 mm = 144 mm^2. Next, subtract the area of the cut-outs from the total area of the square. The area of each cut-out is 2 mm $\times$ 2 mm = 4 mm^2. There are cut-outs in each of the 4 corners; therefore, multiply by 4; $4 \times 4 = 16$. Subtract the total area of the four cut-outs from the total area of the square without the cut-outs; $144 - 16 = 128$ mm^2.

D. Incorrect. 6 mm^2 is not the correct answer. Subtracting $8 - 2$ will not find the area of the shape.

40)

A. Incorrect. There are no rectangular faces on a pyramid.

B. Incorrect. There are no triangular faces on a cube.

C. Incorrect. There are no triangular faces on a rectangular prism.

D. **Correct.** A triangle prism has 2 triangular faces and 3 rectangular faces.

41)

A. **Correct.** Coefficients {4, 5}, degrees {3, 2} is the correct answer. The coefficients are the numbers before the exponent in a polynomial. The degrees are the exponents in a polynomial.

B. Incorrect. Coefficients {1, 4, 5}, degrees {3, 2} is not the correct answer. The number 1 is a constant in this polynomial; it is neither a coefficient nor a degree.

C. Incorrect. Coefficients {3, 2}, degrees {4, 5} is not the correct answer. The degrees and coefficients are switched.

D. Incorrect. Coefficients {3, 2}, degrees {1, 4, 5} is not the correct answer. The degrees and coefficients are switched, and 1 is neither a coefficient nor a degree.

42)

A. Incorrect. Points in quadrant I have a positive x and a positive y coordinate.

B. Incorrect. Points in quadrant II have a negative x and a positive y coordinate.

C. **Correct.** Points in quadrant III have a negative x and a negative y coordinate.

D. Incorrect. Points in quadrant IV have a positive x and a negative y coordinate.

43)

A. **Correct.** The polygon is irregular and convex. A polygon is irregular if the sides and angles are not the same. In the trapezoid, the side on top is shorter than the bottom; therefore the trapezoid is irregular. Convex polygons have interior angles that are less than 180 degrees, which is true for this trapezoid.

B. Incorrect. This polygon is irregular, but it is not concave. Concave polygons have interior angles that are greater than 180 degrees. All interior angles in the trapezoid are less than 180 degrees.

C. Incorrect. The polygon is convex, but it is not regular. The trapezoid is not a regular polygon because all sides are not the same length.

D. Incorrect. The polygon is neither regular nor concave. Furthermore, all regular polygons are convex.

44)

A. Incorrect. The 3 has a difference of 2 place values and 2 place values are equal to 100.

B. Incorrect. The number 846,307 is about four times 209,023, but that is not what the question is asking. For this problem, only consider the digit in each number.

C. Incorrect. If there is 1 place value difference between the digits, this would be the correct answer, but there are 2 place value differences between the digits.

D. **Correct.** 100 is the correct answer. In number one, the digit 3 represents 300. In number two, the digit 3 represents 3. $300 \div 3 = 100$.

45)

A. Incorrect. Ten oranges were sold; this number does not account for apples or bananas.

B. Incorrect. Thirty apples were sold; this number does not account for oranges or bananas.

C. Incorrect. Altogether, 40 oranges and apples were sold, but bananas are not accounted for here.

D. **Correct.** 60 is the correct answer:

1. Assign variables: x = apples; y = oranges

2. Write the ratios as fractions.
    apples/bananas $= \frac{3}{2} = \frac{x}{20}$.
    oranges/bananas $= \frac{1}{2} = \frac{y}{20}$.

3. Cross-multiply to solve.
    $60 = 2x$, $x = 30$ apples
    $2y = 20$, $y = 10$ oranges

4. To find the total, add the number of apples, oranges, and bananas together. $30 + 20 + 10 = 60$ pieces of fruit.

46)

A. Incorrect. Natural numbers used when counting. This number contains a repeating decimal.

B. Incorrect. Whole numbers are the set of natural numbers including zero.

C. Incorrect. Integers are positive or negative whole numbers and do not include repeating decimals.

D. **Correct.** This is a rational number. Rational numbers include fractions and repeating decimals.

47)

A. Incorrect. $x = 1560 \div 15$ is not the correct answer. The total is never divided by the percent.

B. Incorrect. $x = 15 \div 1560$ is not the correct answer. The percentage is never divided by the total.

C. **Correct.** $x = 1560 \times 0.15$ is the correct answer. To find a percentage, use a proportion: 15%/100% = x/1560. Cross-multiply: $100x = 1560 \times 15$. Isolate the variable by dividing both sides of the equation by 100: $x = 1560 \times 15/100$. 15/100, expressed as a decimal, is 0.15.

D. Incorrect. $x = 1560 \div 100$ is not the correct answer. This is part of the solution; do not forget to multiply by the percentage.

48)

A. Incorrect. −81 is incorrect; it is the 5th term in the sequence. The question asks for the 6th term.

B. **Correct.** −135 is the correct answer. The difference between −9 and −36 is 27. $27 \times -3 = -81$. This is the 5th term in the set. To find the 6th term, find the difference between −81 and −36 (45). $45 \times -3 = -135$.

C. Incorrect. 135 is incorrect; it is the opposite of the 5th term in the sequence.

D. Incorrect. 81 is incorrect; it is the opposite of the correct answer. Remember that a positive number times a negative number gives a negative answer.

49)

A. Incorrect. t is not the dependent variable because the hours driven do not depend on the distance that is driven.

B. Incorrect. The rate of 75 mph is a constant and is neither a dependent nor an independent variable.

C. **Correct.** (C) is the correct answer. The distance that Kim travels depends on the number of hours Kim drives.

D. Incorrect. Distance is the dependent variable and can be calculated using the constant and the independent variable.

50)

A. **Correct.** Graph A is correct. To solve this problem, use a table to find some coordinates:

x	y
0	1
1	3
2	5

When plotting the coordinates on the graph, graph A is the only graph that has (0,1), (1,3), and (2,5) as points on the line.

B. Incorrect. Graph B is not correct. The point (0,0) is on the line. Substituting into the equation $y = 2x + 1$, if $x = 0$, then $y = 2(0) + 1$ and $y = 1$, so this cannot be the correct answer.

C. Incorrect. (C) is not the correct answer. The line does not contain (0,1), (1,3), or (2,5).

D. Incorrect. Graph D is not the correct answer. The point (0,−5) is on the line. Substituting into the equation $y = 2x + 1$, if $x = 0$, then $y = 1$, and this cannot be the correct answer.

Social Studies Practice

1

Which of the following events contributed to the United States' entry into World War II?

A.   Germany's unrestricted submarine warfare

B.   the attack on Pearl Harbor

C.   the Battle of Britain

D.   the Battle of the Bulge

2

Which of the following factors might contribute to inflation?

A.   high interest rates and a low amount of printed currency

B.   high unemployment rates

C.   a decrease in supply and a low amount of printed currency

D.   a decrease in supply and a large amount of printed currency

3

Luther and Barbara wanted to start a business in the engineering field. They were trying to decide between hiring one staff member and using the leftover money to purchase new inventory, or hiring two staff members to increase their marketing reach. These choices would be an example of

A.   needs.

B.   scarcity.

C.   opportunity cost.

D.   supply and demand.

4

Which of the following continents is located in both the Eastern and Western Hemispheres?

A.   Europe

B.   Africa

C.   North America

D.   A and B

5

Which of the following events is recognized as the beginning of the American Civil War?

A.   the Battle of Paltmito Ranch

B.   the Battle of Fort Sumter

C.   the Missouri Compromise

D.   the Battle of Yorktown

6

Which of the following most contributed to the fall of the ancient Egyptians?

A.   the death of Cleopatra

B.   Alexander the Great conquering their land

C.   severe droughts

D.   Canaanite settlers entering Egypt

7

Which of the following is most likely a lasting influence ancient Romans had on modern society?

A.   the development of direct democracy

B.   the usage of columns in architecture

C.   the development of republican democracy

D.   literacy

8

Which of the following is NOT a true statement about the ancient Greek civilization?

A.   Men and women lived in different parts of a house.

B.   They built aqueducts to carry water to public toilets.

C.   Greek cities had an agora.

D.   Socrates was a famous Greek philosopher.

9

Which of the following terms describes the economic principle of allowing industry to grow without any government intervention?

A.   interdependence

B.   free-market economy

C.   communism

D.   monopoly

10

Which of the following does NOT describe gender roles?

A.   Gender roles feature behaviors considered appropriate for each sex by society, which generally acknowledges only male and female.

B.   There is a consensus that gender roles are socially constructed.

C.   Gender roles center on the ideas of masculinity and femininity.

D.   Prevailing gender roles have been challenged.

11

Which of the following would be the most useful for studying population patterns within the state of Texas over a period of time?

A.   a bar graph detailing population numbers over a period of 30 years

B.   a map with the number of people living in different parts of Texas in the year 2000

C.   a photograph showing how many people were at a state fair

D.   a bar graph detailing population percentages compared with other states

12

Which of the following presidents was responsible for the New Deal?

A.   Herbert Hoover

B.   Rutherford Hayes

C.   Franklin D. Roosevelt

D.   Jimmy Carter

13

Which of the following is NOT a responsibility of the executive branch?

A.   approving laws

B.   making laws

C.   implementing laws

D.   enforcing laws

14

Which of the following describes a significant effect of the depletion of the ozone layer?

A.   people get darker skin

B.   more UV rays enter the earth

C.   increased skin cancer rates, build-up of greenhouse gases, and increased UV levels

D.   increased build-up of greenhouse gases

15

Which of the following constitutional amendments is NOT considered part of the Bill of Rights?

A.   the right to bear arms

B.   the right to address witnesses arranged by the government when on trial

C.   the right to equal protection under the law

D.   freedom of speech

16

Antitrust law strengthens market forces to prevent monopolies. Which of the following terms best describes the implementation of antitrust law?

A.   social regulation

B.   economic regulation

C.   health regulation

D.   social security

17

Which of the following is an example of human geography?

A.   studying climate

B.   studying the spread of Christianity across the world

C.   studying the effect of land features on animals and plants

D.   studying continental movement over a period of time

18

Which of the following is a positive effect of urbanization?

A.   increased tenement housing

B.   sanitary conditions

C.   political machines

D.   increased employment opportunities

19

Asking citizens to be civil minded and independent and making the people as a whole sovereign is characteristic of

A.   republicanism.

B.   government.

C.   economics.

D.   communism.

20

A map of France shows a small box around Nice. Nice is portrayed in greater detail in a box at the bottom. Which of the following terms describes this box?

A.   legend

B.   inset

C.   compass

D.   insert

21

Which of the following did NOT contribute to the outbreak of the American Revolution?

A.   the Boston Tea Party, in which colonists threw 298 chests of tea into the sea

B.   Britain banning further westward expansion with the Proclamation of 1763

C.   General Thomas Gage ordering troops to capture Thomas Jefferson and Samuel Adams

D.   Charles Townshend taxing glass, oil, lead, and paint

22

Which of the following is an event that successfully ended the Cold War?

A.   the August coup

B.   the fall of the Berlin Wall

C.   the Cuban missile crisis

D.   the success of the Sputnik program

23

Which of the following established the concept of judicial review?

A.   the John Peter Zenger trial

B.   *Marbury v. Madison*

C.   the Dred Scott case

D.   the Scopes Monkey trial

24

Which of the following is an example of the separation of powers?

A.   No members of Congress can serve in another branch of government.

B.   The president cannot vote on legislation.

C.   checks and balances

D.   all of the above

25

Which of the following is a significant contribution of ancient China?

A.   Mahjong

B.   toothbrushes

C.   gunpowder

D.   the animal zodiac

26

Which of the following best exemplifies a global marketplace?

A.   A US freelancer goes on vacation in Paris and does remote work for a US client.

B.   A business in the United States orders parts from Taiwan, India, and Mexico then assembles the final product in Germany.

C.   A commercial website purchases inventory from China.

D.   Appliances share a standardized electrical system.

27

Which of the following periods contributed to advancements of mathematics in ancient Greece?

A.   the Classical period (500 – 336 BC)

B.   the Early Bronze Age (2900 – 2000 BC)

C.   the Hellenistic period (336 – 146 BC)

D.   the Archaic period (750 – 500 BC)

28

Which of the following is a responsibility of a citizen of the United States?

A.   to treat others with kindness

B.   to join after-school clubs

C.   to suffer the consequences of breaking a law

D.   to start a business

29

Fred wants to write a paper on Benjamin Franklin and his influence on science. He wants to include Franklin's theories about electricity. Which of the following resources should he use?

A. a chart depicting what devices used electricity after the invention of the lightbulb

B. an essay about the effects of lightning

C. a newspaper report on Franklin's many inventions

D. a draft scientific report Franklin wrote on electricity

30

Which of the following lands was acquired during the Louisiana Purchase?

A. the land roughly bordered by the Rocky Mountains, the Mississippi River, and the Rio Grande River

B. the land roughly bordered by the Rocky Mountains, the Mississippi River, and the northern border of modern-day Texas

C. the land between the Rocky Mountains and the Mississippi River, and modern-day Georgia

D. the land roughly bordered by the Rocky Mountains and the Mississippi River, and including modern-day New Mexico

31

Which of the following major events in US history led to a decline in immigration?

A. the Immigration Act of 1965

B. the Immigration Act of 1924 and the Great Depression

C. World War I, the Great Depression, and the Immigration Act of 1924

D. the Great Depression only

32

Which of the following was NOT a consequence of the scarcity of oil that led to the energy crisis in the 1970s?

A. The president urged US citizens to heat only one room in their homes in the winter.

B. The automotive industry suffered as Japan created more fuel-efficient vehicles.

C. Political leaders asked gas stations to close for one day a week.

D. Oil prices were high for most of the decade.

33

Which of the following is not a responsibility of the president of the United States?

A.   setting foreign policy

B.   writing legislations

C.   delivering the State of the Union address

D.   pardoning felons

34

A sign on the freeway indicates that you are 150 miles from the city of Pittsburgh. This shows your

A.   absolute location.

B.   physical geography.

C.   geographic feature.

D.   relative location.

35

Why did Congress pass the Neutrality Acts?

A.   only to prevent the United States from loaning any money to nations at war

B.   to help the United States have the best chance of winning a foreign war

C.   to prevent the United States from engaging in civil war

D.   to prevent direct and indirect US involvement in foreign conflict

36

Which of the following emerged during World War I?

A.   penicillin

B.   aircraft carriers

C.   radar

D.   nuclear power

37

Which of the following was a method people used to prevent risk of discovery when helping slaves escape through the Underground Railroad?

A.   Escape routes were usually indirect in order to confuse pursuers.

B.   Escape routes were usually direct to get slaves to freedom more quickly.

C.   Children stayed with their mothers.

D.   Information about routes was passed along by small notes.

38

Which of the following historical figures was a major architect of the US Constitution?

A. Thomas Jefferson

B. George Washington

C. James Madison

D. Patrick Henry

39

Which of the following protects freedom of religion in the United States?

A. separation of powers

B. the First Amendment

C. power of eminent domain

D. popular sovereignty

40

Which of the following amendments prevents the government from quartering troops in private homes?

A. the Seventh Amendment

B. the Fourth Amendment

C. the Third Amendment

D. the Ninth Amendment

41

A project in which students research and explore significant contributions made by their community is an example of

A. questioning only

B. collaboration

C. data interpretation only

D. inquiry-based learning

42

A student completes a research project on significant events of the American Revolution. Which of the following is an appropriate method to determine the credibility of the resources he or she has used to conduct research?

A. checking the author and date of research

B. reviewing website design and writing style

C. assuming all online resources are not credible

D. reviewing website design and domain name

43

Which of the following were part of the New England colonies?

A.   New York, Connecticut, and Massachusetts

B.   Connecticut, Massachusetts, and New Hampshire

C.   New Hampshire, Massachusetts, and New Jersey

D.   New York, New Jersey, Pennsylvania, and Delaware

44

Which of the following are considered geographical features on a map?

A.   plains, plateaus, valleys, and mountains

B.   continents, plateaus, cardinal directions, and mountains

C.   bodies of water, plains, plateaus, and countries

D.   plains, plateaus, areas depicting agricultural products, and mountains

45

Which of the following ideas from Thomas Hobbes influenced the US Constitution?

A.   Individual rights should take priority over collective rights.

B.   People should give up some of their rights and form a government to ensure order in society.

C.   Communism is the only way to govern people.

D.   People should create a utopia to avoid the evils of government.

46

Which of the following examples could be used to describe the theme of respect to elementary school students?

A.   defending one's beliefs even when they are unpopular

B.   paying a parking ticket

C.   returning a library book on time

D.   foregoing an opportunity to cut a line

47

Which of the following is considered a negative consequence of the Civil War?

A.   sharecropping in the South

B.   the South was forgiven for leaving the Union

C.   adding amendments to the Constitution to address equal protection for people under the law

D.   the Union helped the South rebuild roads and farms

48

Which of the following statements best describes Reconstruction in the US after the Civil War?

A. Debates over legalizing slavery in the US were ongoing.

B. During its military occupation of the South, the Union developed Black Codes to appease disaffected Southern aristocrats who had lost slaves.

C. Northern troops occupied the South to ensure that laws were being followed and to help reunite the country after the Civil War.

D. President Lincoln led Reconstruction efforts.

49

The framers instituted a system of checks and balances because they were concerned about

A. one branch of government gaining too much power.

B. mob rule.

C. the military taking over the government.

D. the states overpowering the national government.

50

Which of the following is true about the Trail of Tears?

A. The Trail of Tears drove Native Americans to Indian Territory (later, Oklahoma) because white settlers no longer required their assistance in agricultural production.

B. Removal treaties were enacted fairly and peacefully.

C. The Indian Removal Act of 1831 began the forced relocation of Native Americans that year.

D. The Cherokee Nation was forced to give up land east of the Mississippi River during Andrew Jackson's presidency.

Answer Key

1)

A.   Incorrect. Unrestricted submarine warfare occurred in 1917, during World War I.

B.   Correct. On December 7, 1941, Japan bombed Pearl Harbor, hoping to prevent the US from interfering with its intent to invade Southeast Asia and other territories such as Guam and Hong Kong.

C.   Incorrect. The 1940 Battle of Britain was the first major battle of World War II; the US was still technically a neutral party (although it was effectively supporting Britain through the Lend-Lease Act).

D.   Incorrect. The Battle of the Bulge took place after the United States entered World War II.

2)

A.   Incorrect. High interest rates and a low amount of printed currency usually contribute to deflation.

B.   Incorrect. High unemployment rates do not lead to price increases.

C.   Incorrect. A decrease in supply and a low amount of printed currency usually contribute to deflation.

D.   Correct. Inflation occurs when prices increase. Both of these factors contribute to inflation.

3)

A.   Incorrect. This situation describes a choice, not a need, which is something a person absolutely requires.

B.   Incorrect. Scarcity refers to situations when there is not enough supply to meet demand, which does not apply to this situation.

C.   **Correct.** Opportunity cost refers to the cost of the loss of one option when it is rejected for another (in this case, if Luther and Barbara choose to hire one staff member, they lose the marketing potential another employee would make possible, whereas if they choose to hire two, they lose the leftover money).

D.   Incorrect. Supply and demand refers to the number of goods and their demand, which isn't the case here.

4)

A.   Incorrect. The Eastern and Western Hemispheres are divided by the Prime Meridian, which intersects the European countries of the United Kingdom, France, and Spain. Furthermore, Ireland and Portugal are located in the Western Hemisphere, so Europe is indeed in both hemispheres. However, there is a better answer choice.

B.   Incorrect. The Eastern and Western Hemispheres are divided by the Prime Meridian, which intersects the African countries of Algeria, Mali, Burkina Faso, Togo, and Ghana. Furthermore, Morocco, Western Sahara, Mauritania, Senegal, the Gambia, Guinea, Guinea-Bissau, Sierra Leone, Liberia, Côte d'Ivoire, and Cape Verde are located in the Western Hemisphere, so Africa is indeed in both hemispheres. However, there is a better answer choice.

C.   Incorrect. North America is located entirely in the Western Hemisphere, which is divided from the Eastern Hemisphere by the Prime Meridian and the 180th Meridian.

D.   **Correct.** Both Europe and Africa are located in both the Eastern and Western Hemispheres.

5)

A.   Incorrect. The Battle of Palmito Ranch, the final encounter between Union and Confederate forces, is considered the end of the Civil War.

B.   **Correct.** On April 12, 1861, the Confederate army attacked the Union-controlled Fort Sumter in Charleston, South Carolina, triggering the US Civil War.

C.   Incorrect. The Missouri Compromise, also known as the Compromise of 1820, contributed to divisions between the North and the South; however the war did not begin until 1861.

D.   Incorrect. The Battle of Yorktown was the last battle of the American Revolution.

6)

A.   **Correct.** After Cleopatra's death, ancient Egypt became part of the Roman Empire.

B.   Incorrect. The Egyptians welcomed him, and the new administration was based on an Egyptian model.

    C.   Incorrect. Severe droughts started in 2200 BCE.

    D.   Incorrect. The Canaanite settlers accepted Egyptian governance.

7)

    A.   Incorrect. Athenian democracy is the first known example of direct democracy; furthermore, the Romans did not practice this form of government.

    B.   Incorrect. The Greeks developed columns; the Romans adopted them.

    C.   **Correct.** Before it was an empire, Rome was a republic led by senators elected to the Senate.

    D.   Incorrect. The earliest known written language is cuneiform, developed by the Sumerians.

8)

    A.   Incorrect. In ancient Greece, women lived in the back and upstairs part of the house, away from men.

    B.   **Correct.** The ancient Romans, not the ancient Greeks, built aqueducts and developed public toilets.

    C.   Incorrect. An agora was a central marketplace where the ancient Greeks could meet and conduct business.

    D.   Incorrect. Socrates was a Greek philosopher whose thinking was the foundation for later Greek and much modern Western philosophical thought.

9)

    A.   Incorrect. Interdependence describes the circumstances in which economic actors rely on each other to meet their needs.

    B.   **Correct.** In a free-market economy, the prices of goods and services are determined by sellers and consumers.

    C.   Incorrect. Communism is an economic and social system in which resources are collectively owned.

    D.   Incorrect. When one business dominates an entire industry, it holds a monopoly.

10)

    A.   Incorrect. Gender roles are behavioral norms that influence human behavior.

    B.   **Correct.** There is debate over the degree to which gender is defined by physical features, social and cultural expectations, or both.

    C.   Incorrect. Femininity and masculinity are the main concepts of gender.

    D.   Incorrect. Notions of gender roles, gender identity, and inequality continue to be debated in public discourse.

11)

    A.   **Correct.** A bar graph that features the population over a number of years would help researchers analyze population patterns.

    B.   Incorrect. While a population map may help, it only details one year; more information is needed to analyze population patterns.

    C.   Incorrect. This photograph does not indicate the population in the whole of Texas.

    D.   Incorrect. Researchers would use this to compare the population of Texas with that of other states.

12)

    A.   Incorrect. President Hoover was president during the Great Depression.

    B.   Incorrect. Rutherford Hayes served from 1877 to 1881.

    C.   **Correct.** Franklin D. Roosevelt supported laws that helped those unemployed and impoverished due to the Great Depression.

    D.   Incorrect. Jimmy Carter served from 1977 to 1981.

13)

    A.   Incorrect. The executive branch has the power to approve laws—the president signs or vetoes a bill once it has passed through Congress.

    B.   **Correct.** While the executive branch can approve them, only Congress can make laws.

    C.   Incorrect. The executive branch has the power to implement laws.

    D.   Incorrect. The executive branch has the power to enforce laws, and federal law enforcement agencies are part of the executive branch.

14)

    A.   Incorrect. This is not a significant effect.

    B.   Incorrect. More UV rays do enter the earth, but there are more significant effects of ozone layer depletion.

    C.   **Correct.** All of these are consequences of the depletion of the ozone layer.

    D.   Incorrect. An increase in build-up of greenhouse gases is not the only significant effect of ozone layer depletion.

15)

    A.   Incorrect. The Second Amendment guarantees the right to bear arms.

    B.   Incorrect. The Sixth Amendment states that the people have a right to confront witnesses arranged by the government.

    C.   **Correct.** The Bill of Rights is composed of the first ten amendments. The Fourteenth Amendment guarantees equal protection under the law.

D. Incorrect. The First Amendment ensures freedom of speech, religion, and assembly; the right to petition the government; and freedom of the press.

16)

A. Incorrect. Social regulations deal with how businesses behave, such as prohibiting harmful behaviors.

B. Correct. Antitrust law breaks up monopolies to allow fair competition within the economy.

C. Incorrect. Any health regulations would be classified as social regulation.

D. Incorrect. Social security provides direct assistance to individuals; it does not affect the market in that sense.

17)

A. Incorrect. Studying climate only addresses the earth's physical processes.

B. Correct. Human geography studies the relationship between humans and the physical world; studying how Christianity spread worldwide would need to address this relationship.

C. Incorrect. Studying the effect of land features on animals and plants does not address humans and so is physical geography.

D. Incorrect. Studying the movement of continents is an example of physical geography.

18)

A. Incorrect. Tenement housing created poor living conditions due to its unsanitary conditions.

B. Incorrect. Diseases were common because of rapid population increases and poor living conditions.

C. Incorrect. Corrupt politicians would provide services to immigrants only if people voted for them.

D. Correct. Urbanization itself is the development of urban areas due to the arrival of job seekers; employment opportunities are themselves pull factors.

19)

A. Correct. Republicanism also stresses natural rights as central values.

B. Incorrect. There are many forms of government that do not necessarily welcome a civil-minded or independent populace.

C. Incorrect. Economics is the study of the production and consumption of wealth.

D. Incorrect. Communism stresses that all property is owned publicly by a classless society.

20)

    A.   Incorrect. A legend explains the symbols on a map.

    B.   **Correct.** An inset features details that are considered important on a map.

    C.   Incorrect. A compass depicts the cardinal and intermediate directions on a map.

    D.   Incorrect. As insert is not a cartographic feature.

21)

    A.   Incorrect. Colonists were enraged that Britain adjusted the Tea Act to benefit the Crown.

    B.   Incorrect. The Great Proclamation was at odds with colonial desire for expansion.

    C.   **Correct.** While troops were ordered to capture Samuel Adams, they were not asked to capture Thomas Jefferson.

    D.   Incorrect. The chancellor of the exchequer imposed these duties in 1767.

22)

    A.   **Correct.** This 1991 event in which members of the Soviet government attempted to take control from Mikhail Gorbachev contributed to the dissolution of the USSR, effectively ending the Cold War.

    B.   Incorrect. The fall of the Berlin Wall dissolved communism in Germany.

    C.   Incorrect. The Cuban missile crisis was in 1962, at the height of the Cold War.

    D.   Incorrect. This event happened at the height of the Cold War.

23)

    A.   Incorrect. This colonial trial helped to establish freedom of the press in the United States.

    B.   **Correct.** This case established judicial review.

    C.   Incorrect. Dred Scott was a slave who sued for his freedom; the case did not establish judicial review.

    D.   Incorrect. This trial revolved around the question of teaching evolution in schools.

24)

    A.   Incorrect. Members of Congress can only serve in one branch of government during their term; however, all of the options presented are also applicable.

    B.   Incorrect. The president can only sign or veto legislation; he or she cannot vote on it in Congress; the executive branch is separate from the legislative branch. However, this is not the best answer choice.

C.   Incorrect. Checks and balances show the importance of the separation of powers; no one part of the government controls decision making. However, there is a better answer choice here.

D.   Correct. All choices are different examples of the separation of powers.

25)

A.   Incorrect. Although this was an ancient Chinese invention, it was not a significant one.

B.   Incorrect. The toothbrush was invented by the ancient Egyptians.

C.   Correct. Gunpowder is one of the most important inventions of ancient China.

D.   Incorrect. Although the animal zodiac was an ancient Chinese invention, it is not as globally significant as gunpowder.

26)

A.   Incorrect. The freelancer is still a resident of the United States; despite the freelancer's location, he or she is exchanging services within the US market, not internationally.

B.   Correct. A global marketplace involves the exchange of goods and labor around the world.

C.   Incorrect. It is unclear where the commercial website is based, so it is unclear whether the purchase is international.

D.   Incorrect. This is an opinion, not necessarily a fact about the global marketplace (although it could facilitate global trade).

27)

A.   Incorrect. The Classical period is most known for its development of the principles of democracy.

B.   Incorrect. The early Bronze Age is most known for its invention of bronze.

C.   Correct. This period in time saw advancements such as the Pythagorean Theorem and the calculation of the circumference of the earth.

D.   Incorrect. The Archaic period is most known for its development in pottery and sculpture.

28)

A.   Incorrect. While being kind is likely to help a citizen strengthen personal relationships, it is not his or her responsibility.

B.   Incorrect. Joining after-school clubs is voluntary.

C.   Correct. Citizens have a responsibility to understand laws and pay the consequences if they break them.

D.   Incorrect. Starting a business can help a citizen generate wealth, but it is voluntary.

29)

A.   Incorrect. This example does not address Franklin's thoughts on electricity.

B.   Incorrect. An essay about the effects of lightning does not address Franklin's thoughts on electricity unless he wrote it himself, and it is not clear from this example that he did.

C.   Incorrect. A newspaper report on Franklin's inventions is a secondary resource that only talks about Franklin's inventions, not his thoughts on electricity.

D.   Correct. This is a primary resource that delves into the thought process behind Franklin's theories on electricity.

30)

A.   Incorrect. The Louisiana Purchase did not include land as far south as the Rio Grande; this territory (mainly Texas) belonged to Spain.

B.   Correct. Napoleon sold this section of land in 1803 to finance his European wars.

C.   Incorrect. Georgia was not included in the Louisiana Purchase; it was one of the original colonies and first states.

D.   Incorrect. New Mexico was not part of the Louisiana Purchase; the Southwest was controlled by Spain at the time.

31)

A.   Incorrect. The Immigration Act of 1965 encouraged more immigration in order to attract skilled labor and reunite families.

B.   Correct. Both the Immigration Act of 1924 and the Great Depression discouraged immigration to the United States.

C.   Incorrect. World War I did not contribute to declining immigration.

D.   Incorrect. This was only one contributing factor to declining immigration; furthermore, it was a global event not isolated to the United States. There is a better answer choice.

32)

A.   Correct. The British prime minister recommended limiting heat usage in winter; the US president did not.

B.   Incorrect. The US automotive industry slowed down because it produced larger cars that required more fuel.

  C. Incorrect. In an effort to limit overwhelming lines at gas pumps and to conserve gasoline, political leaders asked that gas stations close for one day a week.

  D. Incorrect. Scarcity (in this case, oil scarcity) results in higher demand and thus higher prices.

33)

  A. Incorrect. The president has the Senate's consent to carry out foreign policy.

  B. **Correct.** The president is responsible for enforcing law, not creating it.

  C. Incorrect. The president periodically reports on the state of the nation, in what has become known as the annual State of the Union address.

  D. Incorrect. Presidents can pardon felons convicted of federal crimes.

34)

  A. Incorrect. Absolute location refers to a specific location based on geographic coordinates.

  B. Incorrect. Physical geography is the study of the earth's natural processes, not location.

  C. Incorrect. A geographical feature refers to a location's physical features.

  D. **Correct.** Relative location refers to the location of a place relative to another, in this case Pittsburgh.

35)

  A. Incorrect. This stipulation was only part of the Neutrality Acts.

  B. Incorrect. The Neutrality Acts were meant to prevent US involvement in foreign wars.

  C. Incorrect. The Neutrality Acts were meant to keep the United States out of foreign wars.

  D. **Correct.** The purpose of the Neutrality Acts was to prevent direct and indirect US interference in armed conflict overseas.

36)

  A. Incorrect. Penicillin was discovered and used during World War II.

  B. **Correct.** The first time an airplane flew from a ship was in 1912.

  C. Incorrect. Radar was developed and used during World War II.

  D. Incorrect. Nuclear power was developed, weaponized, and used during the Second World War.

37)

    A. **Correct.** Routes were indirect to thwart pursuers chasing escapees and their allies.

    B. Incorrect. Direct routes posed too great a risk; pursuers could more easily catch fugitives.

    C. Incorrect. Sometimes children were separated because they were unable to keep up with their groups; furthermore, women were rarely able to escape the plantation unnoticed.

    D. Incorrect. Information was transmitted verbally in an effort to maintain confidentiality.

38)

    A. Incorrect. Jefferson drafted the Declaration of Independence.

    B. Incorrect. Washington was the commander-in-chief of the Continental Army during the American Revolution and later became the first president of the United States.

    C. **Correct.** Madison not only advocated the ratification of the Constitution; he had also helped to write the Federalist Papers.

    D. Incorrect. Henry was an anti-Federalist who opposed the ratification of the Constitution.

39)

    A. Incorrect. Separation of powers is meant to prevent any one branch—executive, legislative, or judicial—from dominating government.

    B. **Correct.** The First Amendment protects freedom of religion as well as freedom of speech, assembly, the press, and the right of the people to petition the government.

    C. Incorrect. Eminent domain refers to the government's ability to seize private property for public use in certain situations. According to the Fifth Amendment, private property cannot be taken for public use without proper compensation.

    D. Incorrect. Popular sovereignty is the concept that government is a social contract, legitimized only by the consent of the people.

40)

    A. Incorrect. The Seventh Amendment states that civil cases may be tried by a jury.

    B. Incorrect. The Fourth Amendment protects citizens from searches and seizures without a warrant.

    C. **Correct.** The Third Amendment forbids the government from quartering troops in homes, an abuse suffered by Americans under British rule.

D.   Incorrect. The Ninth Amendment states that citizens may enjoy rights other than those outlined in the Constitution and that the Constitution does not override those rights.

41)

A.   Incorrect. Questioning is only one aspect of inquiry-based learning. This project asks students to draw conclusions as well.

B.   Incorrect. The description of this project does not specify whether the students work in groups.

C.   Incorrect. This project involves data interpretation, but it requires other steps as well.

D.   Correct. In inquiry-based learning, students gather relevant sources and interpret them in order to develop their own conclusions.

42)

A.   Correct. Checking the author and date of research helps to determine if the information is credible and up-to-date.

B.   Incorrect. Website design and writing style may provide indications as to the credibility of a source, but they alone do not determine legitimacy.

C.   Incorrect. There are many credible online resources.

D.   Incorrect. A domain name can indicate the legitimacy of a source, but website design is not always indicative of a credible source.

43)

A.   Incorrect. New York was not part of the New England colonies.

B.   Correct. All three were part of the New England colonies.

C.   Incorrect. New Jersey was not part of the New England colonies.

D.   Incorrect. These were all part of the Middle Colonies.

44)

A.   Correct. Geographical features depict the physical aspects of a place on a map.

B.   Incorrect. Cardinal directions are not considered geographical features.

C.   Incorrect. Countries are considered political features.

D.   Incorrect. Agricultural products are not considered a geographical feature.

45)

A.   Incorrect. Hobbes believed in collective rights; otherwise, he believed, individuals would only address their own needs, to the detriment of others.

B. **Correct.** Hobbes advocated governments creating and ensuring social order.

C. Incorrect. Hobbes believed that a monarchy was the best way to govern people.

D. Incorrect. Hobbes believed that people were naturally negative and that a utopia would be impossible to construct.

46)

A. Incorrect. Defying unpopularity exhibits courage, a theme of citizenship.

B. Incorrect. Paying a parking ticket is a responsibility, an element of citizenship.

C. Incorrect. It is responsible to return a library book on time; responsibility applies to citizenship.

D. **Correct.** Respect, another aspect of citizenship, involves taking into consideration the feelings of others.

47)

A. **Correct.** Sharecropping enabled landowners in the South to maintain control of former slaves.

B. Incorrect. Forgiving the South for their actions helped to unite the nation as a whole.

C. Incorrect. Equal protection as addressed in the Fourteenth Amendment was a positive outcome of the Civil War.

D. Incorrect. Rebuilding the South benefitted the country as a whole.

48)

A. Incorrect. Slavery was illegal according to the Thirteenth Amendment of the United States Constitution, of which ratification was a requirement for readmission into the Union.

B. Incorrect. Southern governments developed Black Codes in an effort to continue oppression of freed black Americans.

C. **Correct.** During Reconstruction, there were efforts to rebuild the devastated South, which was under Union military occupation following the Civil War.

D. Incorrect. While Lincoln did make some plans for Reconstruction, he died before he had a chance to implement them.

49)

A.   **Correct.** The purpose of checks and balances was to prevent tyranny in any branch of the government.

B.   Incorrect. While there was some concern among the founders about the dangers of a pure democracy, checks and balances do not address the relationship between the government and the people.

C.   Incorrect. Separation of powers kept the military in check. Also, with a civilian commander in chief, the military remains accountable to civilian authority.

D.   Incorrect. Checks and balances do not refer to the relationship between the state and national governments.

50)

A.   Incorrect. White settlers wanted to grow cotton on Native American land themselves; they never employed Native American workers.

B.   Incorrect. President Jackson and the government frequently ignored the legal rights of Native Americans.

C.   Incorrect. The Indian Removal Act was passed in 1831, but the forced migration of the Cherokee and other tribes did not occur that year.

D.   **Correct.** This series of incidents happened in 1838 and 1839.

Science Practice

1

Which of these is a biome?

A.   a desert

B.   a cornfield

C.   a herd of bison

D.   a beehive

2

What is the name of the phenomenon when a star suddenly increases in brightness and then disappears from view?

A.   aurora

B.   galaxy

C.   black hole

D.   supernova

3

What term describes the resistance to motion caused by one object rubbing against another object?

A.   inertia

B.   friction

C.   velocity

D.   gravity

4

Which planet orbits closest to Earth?

A.   Mercury

B.   Venus

C.   Jupiter

D.   Saturn

5

Which tool is used to measure the mass of an object?

A.   a thermometer

B.   a graduated cylinder

C.   a balance

D.   an abacus

6

Which organism has cells that contain mitochondria?

A.   whale

B.   mushroom

C.   tulip

D.   all of the above

7

Which condition can be diagnosed by an electrocardiogram (EKG)?

A.   diabetes

B.   torn ligaments

C.   cancer

D.   tachycardia

8

Which action is an example of mechanical weathering?

A.   Calcium carbonate reacts with water to form a cave.

B.   An iron gate rusts.

C.   Tree roots grow under the foundation of a house and cause cracks.

D.   Bananas turn brown after they are peeled.

9

What are the negatively charged particles inside an atom?

A.   protons

B.   neutrons

C.   electrons

D.   ions

10

Organisms in the same class are also in the same_____.

A.   phylum

B.   order

C.   genus

D.   species

11

Which type of rock forms when lava cools and solidifies?

A.   igneous

B.   sedimentary

C.   metamorphic

D.   sandstone

12

Which unit measures pressure?

A.   kilometers

B.   grams

C.   grams per second

D.   pounds per square foot

13

Which organism regulates its body temperature externally?

A.   lobster

B.   dolphin

C.   whale

D.   pelican

14

Which organism is a decomposer?

A.   apple trees

B.   mushrooms

C.   goats

D.   lions

15

Which pH level is classified as a base?

A.   2

B.   4

C.   6

D.   8

16

Which body system is responsible for the release of growth hormones?

A.   digestive system

B.   endocrine system

C.   nervous system

D.   circulatory system

17

Which example illustrates a physical change?

A.   Water becomes ice.

B.   Batter is baked into a cake.

C.   An iron fence rusts.

D.   A firecracker explodes.

18

Which energy source is nonrenewable?

A.   water

B.   wind

C.   coal

D.   sunlight

19

How long does it take the earth to rotate on its axis?

A.   one hour

B.   one day

C.   one month

D.   one year

20

Which organism is a reptile?

A.   crocodile

B.   frog

C.   salamander

D.   salmon

21

By what process do producers make sugars and release oxygen?

A.   digestion

B.   chloroplast

C.   decomposition

D.   photosynthesis

22

Which type of wave is a longitudinal wave?

A.   surface wave

B.   light wave

C.   sound wave

D.   electromagnetic wave

23

Which example demonstrates refraction?

A.   rainbow

B.   echo

C.   mirror

D.   radio

24

Which factor is an abiotic part of an ecosystem?

A. producers

B. consumers

C. water

D. decomposers

25

What term describes a relationship between two organisms where one organism benefits to the detriment of the other organism?

A. mutualism

B. parasitism

C. commensalism

D. predation

26

Which organelle makes proteins?

A. mitochondria

B. cytoplasm

C. vacuole

D. ribosomes

27

Which statement is true?

A. Earth is much closer to the sun than it is to other stars.

B. The moon is closer to Venus than it is to Earth.

C. At certain times of the year, Jupiter is closer to the sun than Earth is.

D. Mercury is the closest planet to Earth.

28

Which metal attracts magnets?

A. iron

B. copper

C. silver

D. gold

29

Which example demonstrates electrostatic attraction?

A. Items in a car continue to move forward when the car stops suddenly.

B. Tides are affected by the moon.

C. The moon revolves around Earth.

D. Plastic wrap sticks to a person's hand.

30

In which part of a plant does photosynthesis take place?

A. the roots

B. the stem

C. the leaves

D. the flower

31

Which example has the least amount of kinetic energy?

A. a plane flying through the sky

B. a plane sitting on the runway

C. a ladybug flying toward a flower

D. a meteorite falling to Earth

32

Which of the following is caused by geothermal heat?

A. geysers

B. glaciers

C. tsunamis

D. tornadoes

33

Which term describes space weather?

A. supernova

B. black hole

C. volcanic lightning

D. solar flares

34

Which gas is found in large quantities in Earth's atmosphere?

A.   carbon monoxide

B.   bromine

C.   nitrogen

D.   fluorine

35

Which term describes an element?

A.   atom

B.   molecule

C.   proton

D.   ion

36

Which statement is true?

A.   Mass and weight are the same thing.

B.   Mass is affected by gravitational pull.

C.   Weight is affected by the gravitational pull.

D.   Mass is related to the surface area of an object.

37

When Earth moves between the moon and the sun, it is called a

A.   solar eclipse.

B.   lunar eclipse.

C.   black hole.

D.   supernova.

38

Which element is most common in the universe?

A.   carbon

B.   lithium

C.   potassium

D.   titanium

39

Which storm is least likely to form over ocean water?

A.   hurricane

B.   typhoon

C.   cyclone

D.   tornado

40

Which substance can be used to neutralize an acid spill?

A.   sodium bicarbonate

B.   citric acid

C.   cat litter

D.   water

41

Which gas is produced by burning fossil fuels?

A.   helium

B.   oxygen

C.   nitrogen

D.   carbon dioxide

42

A warm air mass moving into a cold air mass is called a

A.   warm front.

B.   cold front.

C.   isobar.

D.   tornado.

43

Which of the following is NOT a cause of extinction?

A.   poor reproduction

B.   climate change

C.   habitat conservation

D.   overexploitation by humans

44

Which term describes the top layer of the earth's surface?

A.   stratosphere

B.   lithosphere

C.   atmosphere

D.   biosphere

45

What term describes the speed and direction of a moving soccer ball?

A.   velocity

B.   momentum

C.   mass

D.   energy

46

Which substance is a good thermal conductor?

A.   plastic

B.   rubber

C.   porcelain

D.   aluminum

47

Which example demonstrates body systems working together to maintain homeostasis?

A.   Jessica's tracheotomy opened a breathing obstruction.

B.   Max's muscles, tendons, and ligaments allow his joints to bend.

C.   Kevin's bones thicken from an excessive production of growth hormones.

D.   Stacy shivers from the cold.

48

What is the primary role of amino acids in cells?

A.   break down carbohydrates

B.   break down fats

C.   build proteins

D.   filter waste

49

What part of the atom flows through a circuit to power a lightbulb?

A. protons

B. neutrons

C. electrons

D. nucleus

50

Which simple machine is shown in the following picture?

Figure 9.1. Simple Machine

A. inclined plane

B. pulley

C. screw

D. wedge

Answer Key

1)

A. **Correct.** A biome is a large ecological community that includes specific plants and animals. Other biomes include rainforests and grasslands.

B. Incorrect. A cornfield is a part of a prairie biome.

C. Incorrect. Animals are part of a biome.

D. Incorrect. A beehive is part of a biome.

2)

A. Incorrect. Aurora is the phenomenon of colored lights that appear in the sky near the North and South Poles.

B. Incorrect. The galaxy is a large group of stars held together by gravity.

C. Incorrect. Black holes are collapsed stars whose gravitational pull is so strong that light cannot escape.

D. **Correct.** Before a star collapses, the star burns brighter for a period of time and then fades from view. This is a supernova.

3)

A. Incorrect. Inertia is an object's tendency not to change position or direction unless an outside force acts upon it.

B. **Correct.** Friction occurs when motion is impeded because one object is rubbing against another object.

C. Incorrect. Velocity is the rate at which an object is displaced from its original position.

D. Incorrect. Gravity is a force that attracts objects to one another.

4)

    A.   Incorrect. Mercury is the planet closest to the sun. Venus orbits between Mercury and Earth.

    B.   **Correct.** Venus's orbit is closest to Earth. Venus is the second planet from the sun and Earth is the third planet from the sun.

    C.   Incorrect. Jupiter is the fifth planet from the sun.

    D.   Incorrect. Saturn is the sixth planet from the sun.

5)

    A.   Incorrect. A thermometer measures temperature.

    B.   Incorrect. A graduated cylinder measures volume.

    C.   **Correct.** A balance measures mass.

    D.   Incorrect. An abacus is a tool used to calculate numbers.

6)

    A.   Incorrect. Mitochondria are found in animal cells.

    B.   Incorrect. Mitochondria are found in fungi cells.

    C.   Incorrect. Mitochondria are found in plant cells.

    D.   **Correct.** Plant, animal, and fungi cells have mitochondria.

7)

    A.   Incorrect. Blood tests are used to diagnose diabetes.

    B.   Incorrect. Magnetic Resonance Imaging (MRI) is used to see soft tissue damage, such as torn ligaments.

    C.   Incorrect. There are a variety of tests that diagnose cancer, such as blood tests, Magnetic Resonance Imaging (MRI), and ultrasounds.

    D.   **Correct.** Tachycardia is an abnormally fast heartrate, and electrocardiograms show the electrical activity of the heart.

8)

    A.   Incorrect. Cave formation is an example of chemical weathering. Chemical weathering involves a chemical change.

    B.   Incorrect. Rusting is an example of chemical weathering.

    C.   **Correct.** Mechanical weathering involves breaking a substance down without changing the composition of the substance.

    D.   Incorrect. Bananas turning brown is an example of a chemical change.

9)

A.   Incorrect. Protons are positively charged particles in the nucleus.

B.   Incorrect. Neutrons are particles in the nucleus that have no charge.

C.   Correct. Electrons are negatively charged particles in an atom; electrons orbit the nucleus.

D.   Incorrect. Ions are atoms that have lost or gained electrons and have a charge.

10)

A.   Correct. A kingdom is the largest group of living things. A kingdom is then subdivided into progressively smaller groups in the following order: kingdom, phylum, class, order, family, genus, and species. The order can be remembered using the mnemonic device: *Keep Pots Clean or Family Gets Sick.*

B.   Incorrect. An order is a smaller group than a class.

C.   Incorrect. A genus is a smaller group than a class.

D.   Incorrect. A species is a smaller group than a class.

11)

A.   Correct. Igneous rocks form when liquid rock cools and solidifies.

B.   Incorrect. Sedimentary rocks form when sediments are cemented together.

C.   Incorrect. Metamorphic rocks form when igneous or sedimentary rocks are exposed to extreme temperature and/or pressure to the point that the rocks are changed physically or chemically.

D.   Incorrect. Sandstone is a type of sedimentary rock.

12)

A.   Incorrect. Length is measured in kilometers.

B.   Incorrect. Mass is measured in grams.

C.   Incorrect. Mass flow rate is measured in grams per second.

D.   Correct. Pressure is measured in pounds per square foot.

13)

A.   Correct. The metabolic rate of crustaceans is too low to regulate their temperature. Crustaceans use behavioral techniques, such as moving to shallow water, to maintain body temperature.

B.   Incorrect. Dolphins are mammals. Mammals are endothermic, meaning they have a mechanism to regulate body temperature internally.

C.   Incorrect. Whales are mammals.

D.   Incorrect. Birds are endothermic.

14)

A.   Incorrect. Plants produce their own food through photosynthesis, making them producers.

B.   Correct. Mushrooms are fungi. Fungi break down organic material left by dead animals and plants, making them decomposers.

C.   Incorrect. Goats eat producers, such as grass, making them primary consumers.

D.   Incorrect. Lions are carnivorous animals that feed on primary consumers and secondary consumers, making them secondary or tertiary consumers.

15)

A.   Incorrect. Acids have a pH between 0 and 7.

B.   Incorrect. Acids have a pH between 0 and 7.

C.   Incorrect. Acids have a pH between 0 and 7.

D.   Correct. Bases have a pH between 7 and 14.

16)

A.   Incorrect. The digestive system turns food into energy.

B.   Correct. The endocrine system releases hormones, including growth hormones.

C.   Incorrect. The nervous system is a network of communication cells.

D.   Incorrect. The circulatory system delivers nutrients to cells and removes wastes from the body.

17)

A.   Correct. When water changes form, it does not change the chemical composition of the substance. Once water becomes ice, the ice can easily turn back into water.

B.   Incorrect. The chemical composition of the substance changes and cannot be reversed. Baking a cake is an example of a chemical change.

C.   Incorrect. Rusting is an example of a chemical change.

D.   Incorrect. Setting off fireworks causes a chemical change.

18)

A.   Incorrect. Water can generate hydropower, which is a renewable energy source.

B.   Incorrect. Wind is a renewable energy source.

C.   Correct. Coal is nonrenewable because once coal is burned, it cannot be quickly replaced.

D.   Incorrect. Solar energy is a renewable energy source.

19)

A.   Incorrect. One hour is 1/24 of the time it takes for the earth to rotate on its axis.

B.   Correct. Earth takes approximately 24 hours to rotate on its axis.

C.   Incorrect. The moon takes approximately one month to revolve around the earth.

D.   Incorrect. The earth takes approximately one year to revolve around the sun.

20)

A.   Correct. Reptiles like crocodiles have scaly skin, are hatched from eggs on land, and are cold-blooded.

B.   Incorrect. Amphibians like frogs are hatched from eggs in water, have gills but develop lungs, and become land animals as they mature.

C.   Incorrect. Salamanders are amphibians.

D.   Incorrect. Fish like salmon live in water; they also have a backbone, gills, scales, and fins.

21)

A.   Incorrect. Digestion is the process whereby large food particles are broken down into small particles.

B.   Incorrect. A chloroplast is the part of the cell where photosynthesis takes place.

C.   Incorrect. Decomposition is the process where substances are broken down into smaller parts.

D.   Correct. Photosynthesis describes the process by which plants convert the energy of the sun into stored chemical energy (glucose).

22)

A.   Incorrect. Waves on the surface of the ocean are transverse waves.

B.   Incorrect. Light waves are transverse waves.

C.   Correct. Sound waves are longitudinal waves because the vibrations travel in the same direction as the energy.

D.   Incorrect. Electromagnetic waves are transverse waves.

23)

A.   Correct. The light of the sun hits rain droplets and bends into a band of colors. The bending of waves is refraction.

B.   Incorrect. Echo is an example of sound reflection.

C.   Incorrect. A mirror is used to show light reflection.

D.   Incorrect. A radio is an example of sound waves reflecting off layers in Earth's atmosphere.

24)

A.   Incorrect. Producers are living things, which are biotic factors.

B.   Incorrect. Consumers are biotic factors because they are alive.

C.   Correct. Nonliving things in an ecosystem, like air and water, are abiotic factors.

D.   Incorrect. Living things are biotic factors.

25)

A.   Incorrect. In mutualism, both organisms benefit.

B.   Correct. Parasitism describes a relationship in which one organism benefits from another organism, to the detriment of the host organism.

C.   Incorrect. Commensalism is when one organism benefits from another without causing harm to the host organism.

D.   Incorrect. Predation is killing and consuming other organisms for food.

26)

A.   Incorrect. Mitochondria release chemical energy from glucose to be used by the cell.

B.   Incorrect. Cytoplasm provides support to the cell.

C.   Incorrect. Vacuoles store water.

D.   Correct. Ribosomes are responsible for production of proteins.

27)

A.   Correct. The sun is the only star in our solar system. The sun is about ninety-three million miles from Earth; the next closest star is about twenty-five trillion miles away.

B.   Incorrect. The moon orbits Earth.

C.   Incorrect. Even when Jupiter is closest to the sun and Earth is farthest from the sun, Earth is always closer to the sun than Jupiter is.

D.   Incorrect. Mercury is the closest planet to the sun, and Venus is closer to Earth.

28)

A.   Correct. Magnets readily attract iron.

B.   Incorrect. Not all metals are attracted to magnets; copper is not.

C. Incorrect. Magnets do not attract all metals; for example, they do not attract silver.

D. Incorrect. Gold is not attracted to magnets.

29)

A. Incorrect. Newton's First Law is that *objects in motion stay in motion*.

B. Incorrect. Tides are affected by the gravitational pull of the moon. Gravitational force is the attraction between two masses.

C. Incorrect. The moon revolves around Earth because of the gravitational pull between the two masses.

D. Correct. Electrostatic force is an attraction between charged surfaces.

30)

A. Incorrect. Roots extract water and minerals from the soil.

B. Incorrect. The stem transports nutrients to other parts of the plant.

C. Correct. Through photosynthesis, leaves use the sun's energy to convert carbon dioxide into glucose (food).

D. Incorrect. The flower is the reproductive part of a plant.

31)

A. Incorrect. A plane flying through the sky would have kinetic energy because of its mass and velocity.

B. Correct. Something that is not moving has zero velocity; therefore it has no kinetic energy.

C. Incorrect. Even though it has a low mass and a low velocity, a ladybug does have a small amount of kinetic energy.

D. Incorrect. A meteorite falling toward Earth would have a large amount of kinetic energy because of its mass and velocity.

32)

A. Correct. Geysers are caused by geothermal heating of water underground.

B. Incorrect. Glaciers are formed when snow and ice do not melt before new layers of snow and ice are added.

C. Incorrect. Tsunamis are caused by earthquakes on the ocean floor.

D. Incorrect. Tornadoes are caused by instability of warm, humid air in the lower atmosphere mixing with cool air in the upper atmosphere.

Go on

33)

A.   Incorrect. A supernova is a huge explosion of the core of a star that marks the end of the life cycle of the star. Since supernovas occur outside our solar system, they are not considered space weather.

B.   Incorrect. Black holes occur outside our solar system, so they are not considered space weather.

C.   Incorrect. Volcanic lightning is a lightning storm that occurs during a volcanic eruption when positively charged lava is launched into the negatively charged atmosphere. This does not occur in space; therefore, volcanic lightning is not considered space weather.

D.   Correct. Solar flares are huge explosions on the sun. Space weather refers to conditions in the solar system that could potentially affect the work of astronauts in space and cause auroras on Earth.

34)

A.   Incorrect. Carbon monoxide is a rare gas.

B.   Incorrect. Bromine is a rare gas.

C.   Correct. Nitrogen makes up 78 percent of Earth's atmosphere.

D.   Incorrect. Fluorine is a rare gas.

35)

A.   Correct. An atom is the smallest unit of an element.

B.   Incorrect. A molecule is the simplest form of a compound, consisting of two or more atoms.

C.   Incorrect. A proton is a positively charged particle in the nucleus of an atom. A proton by itself will not make an element.

D.   Incorrect. An ion is an electrically charged atom or group of atoms.

36)

A.   Incorrect. Mass is the amount of matter in an object. Weight is a measure of the gravitational pull on an object. Weight changes in space, but mass does not.

B.   Incorrect. Weight is affected by gravitational pull, not mass.

C.   Correct. Weight is affected by gravitational pull.

D.   Incorrect. The surface area or size of an object does not indicate the mass of that object.

37)

A. Incorrect. A solar eclipse is when the moon moves between the sun and Earth.

B. Correct. A lunar eclipse is when Earth moves between the moon and the sun.

C. Incorrect. A black hole is a collapsed star with tremendous gravitational pull.

D. Incorrect. A supernova is an explosion of the core of a star.

38)

A. Correct. Carbon is a common element found in every organic compound and in the atmosphere of some planets.

B. Incorrect. Lithium is highly reactive and is found in small amounts in igneous rocks.

C. Incorrect. Potassium is found in Earth's crust and is essential to plant growth.

D. Incorrect. Titanium makes up less than 1 percent of Earth's surface.

39)

A. Incorrect. Hurricanes form over warm ocean water. Depending upon where a hurricane forms, it can also be called a typhoon or a cyclone.

B. Incorrect. A hurricane that forms in the western Pacific Ocean is called a typhoon.

C. Incorrect. A hurricane that forms in the Indian Ocean is called a cyclone.

D. Correct. Tornadoes occur when warm air masses collide with cold air masses over land.

40)

A. Correct. Sodium bicarbonate, which is a base, will neutralize an acid.

B. Incorrect. Citric acid neutralizes a base spill.

C. Incorrect. Once the spill is neutralized, cat litter may be used to absorb it.

D. Incorrect. An acid spill needs to be neutralized before water is used.

41)

A. Incorrect. Helium is found in large quantities on the sun. It is an inert, colorless, tasteless gas.

B. Incorrect. Oxygen makes up about 20 percent of Earth's atmosphere.

C. Incorrect. Seventy-eight percent of Earth's atmosphere is made of nitrogen, and nitrogen is essential for all living organisms.

D. Correct. Carbon dioxide is formed when fossil fuels containing carbon are burned. Excess carbon dioxide is responsible for global warming.

42)

A. **Correct.** A warm front is when a warm air mass moves into a cold air mass.

B. Incorrect. A cold front is when a cold air mass moves into a warm air mass.

C. Incorrect. An isobar is a contour line indicating locations of equal barometric pressures.

D. Incorrect. A tornado is caused by unstable air.

43)

A. Incorrect. Poor reproduction is one of the identified causes of extinction. If a species is not able to reproduce, it will eventually die out.

B. Incorrect. Climate changes, such as the Ice Age and global warming, are responsible for the extinction of a species.

C. **Correct.** Habitat conservation restores the natural habitat of organisms, protecting a species.

D. Incorrect. Overexploitation by humans through hunting for sport, animal testing, and illegal trapping has caused the endangerment of many species.

44)

A. Incorrect. The stratosphere is a layer of the earth's atmosphere.

B. **Correct.** The lithosphere is the top layer of the earth's surface.

C. Incorrect. The atmosphere refers to the layer of gases that surrounds the earth.

D. Incorrect. The biosphere is the part of Earth where life exists; the biosphere includes the atmosphere, the oceans, and the life-supporting areas above and below Earth's surface.

45)

A. **Correct.** Velocity is the speed of an object in a certain direction.

B. Incorrect. Momentum is calculated by multiplying the velocity of an object by its mass.

C. Incorrect. Mass refers to the amount of matter in an object.

D. Incorrect. Energy describes the capacity to do work.

46)

A. Incorrect. Plastic is an insulator. Insulators block the flow of heat from one object to another.

B. Incorrect. Rubber is an insulator.

C. Incorrect. Porcelain is an insulator.

D. **Correct.** Aluminum is a good thermal conductor because heat energy can move easily through it.

47)

A. Incorrect. A tracheotomy is not a body system reaction; it is a medical intervention.

B. Incorrect. Max's muscles, tendons, and ligaments are part of the muscular system. The bending of joints is a normal function, not a way to maintain homeostasis.

C. Incorrect. Excessive production of growth hormones is an example of disease.

D. Correct. Homeostasis refers to body systems working together to ensure that temperature, pH, and oxygen levels are optimal for survival. Sensors in Stacy's nervous system trigger her muscular system to shiver in an attempt to warm her body.

48)

A. Incorrect. Amino acids do not break down carbohydrates.

B. Incorrect. Fats (lipids) are insoluble in cells.

C. Correct. Ribosomes make proteins by building amino acid chains.

D. Incorrect. Lysosomes in the cytoplasm filter waste from a cell.

49)

A. Incorrect. Protons remain in the nucleus of an atom.

B. Incorrect. Neutrons remain in the nucleus of an atom.

C. Correct. Electrons are negatively charged subatomic particles that exist outside the nucleus of an atom. A power source forces moving electrons through a circuit.

D. Incorrect. The nucleus is the part of an atom that contains protons and neutrons.

50)

A. Correct. An inclined plane is a flat surface raised to an angle so that loads can be easily lifted.

B. Incorrect. A pulley is a wheel with ropes that change the direction of the force in order to lift an object.

C. Incorrect. A screw is a rod-shaped object with a spiral groove.

D. Incorrect. A wedge is a type of inclined plane, such as an axe, that has both a wide and a thin end.

10-3-16

CPSIA information can be obtained
at www.ICGtesting.com
Printed in the USA
LVOW03s1757140916
504606LV00014B/198/P